Creativity in Young Children

Other Redleaf Press Books by Thomas Rendon

Saving Play: Addressing Standards through Play-Based Learning in Preschool and Kindergarten, coauthored with Gaye Gronlund

Creativity in Young Children

What Science Tells Us and Our Hearts Know

Thomas Rendon and Zachary Stier, EdD

Redleaf Press®
www.redleafpress.org
800-423-8309

Published by Redleaf Press
10 Yorkton Court
St. Paul, MN 55117
www.redleafpress.org

First edition 2025
Cover design by Louise OFarrell
Cover photographs by iStock.com/FatCamera and Adobe stock/akkash
Interior design by Louise OFarrell
Interior photographs by Adobe stock/Rawpixel.com and Adobe stock/LanaSham
Typeset in FreightText Pro
Printed in the United States of America

32 31 30 29 28 27 26 25   1 2 3 4 5 6 7 8

Excerpts from the Developmentally Appropriate Practice Position Statement copyright © 2020 NAEYC®. Reprinted with permission. Full text of this Position Statement is available at www.naeyc.org/resources/position-statements/dap/contents.

Excerpts from the Equity Position Statement copyright © 2019 NAEYC®. Reprinted with permission. Full text of this Position Statement is available at www.naeyc.org/resources/position-statements/equity.

Library of Congress Cataloging-in-Publication Data
Names: Rendon, Thomas, author. | Stier, Zachary, author.
Title: Creativity in young children : what science tells us and our hearts
  know / by Thomas Rendon and Zachary Stier, EdD.
Description: First edition. | St. Paul, MN : Redleaf Press, [2025] |
  Includes bibliographical references and index. | Summary: "Young
  children are first and foremost creative beings. Creativity in Young
  Children deepens understanding of the what of creativity, its
  connections to child development, and how it shapes and is shaped by the
  people, communities, and world around us"— Provided by publisher.
Identifiers: LCCN 2024044382 (print) | LCCN 2024044383 (ebook) | ISBN
  9781605548111 (paperback) | ISBN 9781605548128 (ebook)
Subjects: LCSH: Creative ability in children. | Child psychology.
Classification: LCC BF723.C7 R46 2025 (print) | LCC BF723.C7 (ebook) |
  DDC 155.4/135--dc23/eng/20241104
LC record available at https://lccn.loc.gov/2024044382
LC ebook record available at https://lccn.loc.gov/2024044383

Printed on acid-free paper

I DEDICATE THIS BOOK to my family for their unfailing love, to my coauthor, Tom Rendon, for his friendship and mentorship, to the children and families who have called me their neighborhood librarian, and to Fred Rogers, who modeled the most important traits that demonstrate what it means to be human.

—*Zach*

I DEDICATE THIS BOOK to my wife, Julia, who endured endless interruptions while I asked her all manner of questions, from grammatical to metaphorical. She provided practical and down-to-earth advice for a topic that generally encourages a person to fly. She is both an excellent writer and an inspiring model of creativity, making amazing fabric creations (for example, a clutch purse out of cigar ribbons) for the sheer fun of it. Her companionship is invaluable. I also dedicate this book to my father and mother. My father passed away during the writing of this book and never learned about its existence, but his ambition inspired me to take the risk to write it. My mother, as you will learn in these pages, also paved the way for my creative path through example and whimsy. Thanks, of course, to Zach Stier, who became a close friend in the writing of this book and shared deeply and generously from his life and passion for learning.

—*Tom*

Contents

Foreword by Ryan Rydzewski   ix

Acknowledgments   xiii

Introduction   1

Part One ▶ What Is Creativity?   5

Chapter One   Creativity and the Creative Process   7

Chapter Two   Creativity and Child Development   23

Chapter Three   Creativity in Context   43

Part Two ▶ Seven Big Ideas about Creativity   51

Chapter Four   Big Idea 1: Creativity as a Life-Force   53

Chapter Five   Big Idea 2: The Neuroscience of Creativity   65

Chapter Six   Big Idea 3: Creativity and Neurodiversity   79

Chapter Seven   Big Idea 4: Creativity as Curriculum   95

Chapter Eight   Big Idea 5: Creativity in Formal and Informal Settings   115

Chapter Nine   Big Idea 6: Creativity and Diversity, Equity, and Inclusion   131

Chapter Ten   Big Idea 7: Creativity and Trauma   149

Part Three ▶ Creativity for Real   161

Chapter Eleven   Creativity in Action   163

Chapter Twelve   Creativity Now!   185

References   195

Index   209

Foreword

There's an old story about Mister Rogers—one I read while researching *When You Wonder, You're Learning*.

Fred Rogers and his camera crew had come to New York to film a scene for *Mister Rogers' Neighborhood*. He stood with the architect Maya Lin in Penn Station, where Lin's glass-and-metal clock graced the terminal's ceiling. Called "Eclipsed Time," Lin's sculpture was, by many accounts, a creative triumph: over the course of each day, a gigantic metal disk slid slowly across a light, marking the time in fifteen-minute intervals. At noon, the station's light was brightest; at midnight, commuters saw an "eclipse" when the disk blocked most of the light.

"It's very conceptual," Lin told the *New York Times*. "Maybe it will let people slow down a little and not worry so much."

Not everyone took to the concept. "If Mister [expletive] Rogers can tell me how to read that [expletive] clock, I'll watch his show every day for a [expletive] *year*—that's what someone in the crowd said while watching Mister Rogers and Maya Lin," wrote Tom Junod, a journalist who'd tagged along to profile Fred for *Esquire*.

Junod continued:

> . . . but it didn't even matter whether Mister Rogers could read the clock or not, because every time he looked at it, with the television cameras on him, he leaned back from his waist and opened his mouth wide with astonishment, like someone trying to catch a peanut he had tossed into the air, until it became clear that Mister Rogers could show that he was astonished all *day* if he had to, or even forever, because Mister Rogers lives in a *state* of astonishment . . .

I love this story. And I know this state well, because my two-year-old lives in it, too. Fire trucks, basketballs, garbage crews, rocks . . . the list of things that *astonish* my son could fill the rest of this book. But at the top of his list are trains—"choo choos," in his vernacular—and so, on a beautiful blue morning in Pittsburgh, we, too, stand in a train station, waiting to board the city's light rail.

The thing you should know about Pittsburgh's "T" is that no one rides it for fun. We Pittsburghers are glad it's there, but it's really just a commuter train—not an attraction in and of itself. Its stations don't include world-class clocks, nor are they marvels of architecture. (The alluringly titled "Palm Garden Station," for example, includes neither palms nor gardens and isn't much more than a bench.) When we talk about the T, it's because it made us late, or because its cars were cramped, or because it didn't show up at all. No one in Pittsburgh, ever, has said, "I had a great time on the T today."

None of this matters to my son. As the trolley pulls into the station and the conductor waves hello, Russell looks how I imagine Fred Rogers looked: awestruck, agape, utterly rapt. The enchantment continues onboard the "choo choo," with Russell delighting at every tunnel, every bridge, every car and bus that waits for the trolley to pass. He's ecstatic. To my surprise, so am I.

We wind through wooded hillsides, watching the trees turn golden-orange. Time slows to a Maya Linean crawl. The world, for one fall morning, feels limitless, like a collection of wonders curated just for my son, wonders I hope will never cease to *astonish*.

But I know the statistics. I know that many children will, by the time they hit fourth grade, start to lose interest in the creative world around them. I know that Russell's future—and your future, too—hinges on his *not* losing interest, on his becoming a person who builds better trains or sculpts beautiful clocks or simply reminds us that the world is, despite the rush, worth riding around in.

I admit the pressure can weigh on me. Sometimes, I fear I'm falling short. I know that whether Russell nurtures his creative self or neglects it depends, in large part, on me. (Me! A guy with a job to get to and laundry to fold and . . .)

And then I read this book.

From its very first pages, *Creativity in Young Children* felt like a triumph—one that, like Maya Lin's clock, let me slow down and not worry so much. With its generous mix of research and practical advice, it's a guidebook for what Fred Rogers called "our job in life": encouraging young children to discover, and express, the things that make them *them*.

That's the job that put us on the T. I've begun, thanks to this book, to encourage discovery however I can—to regard Russell's creative potential as "a sacred life force that is animating everything a child does and is and will become," as Thomas Rendon and Zachary Stier so beautifully write. I've become a more encouraging builder of toy railroads. I've become (a little) more patient when Russ digs dirt from our houseplants and dumps it onto the floor. I've become, I think, more alive to his world, and more alert to the gifts that our young children give us.

If you let it, this book will do the same for you. Or rather, as its subtitle suggests, it will remind you what you already know—because you were a child once, too. It will help you get back to that child, so that you and the children you care for might stand in awe of clocks and commuter trains. It will help you get back to being *astonished*.

The funny thing about writing a book is that after a while, you see your subject everywhere. Fortunately for me, my subject is Fred Rogers. And so I glimpse him again and again: in my son, Russell; in train conductors who wave to young kids; in Thomas Rendon and Zachary Stier; and in these pages that have found their way to you.

> —Ryan Rydzewski, coauthor of *When You Wonder, You're Learning:*
> *Mister Rogers' Enduring Lessons for Raising Creative, Curious, Caring Kids*
> Pittsburgh, Pennsylvania
> October 2024

Acknowledgments

Thanks to all those who taught us about creativity, including Roger Beaty, Baroness Susan Greenfield, Scott Barry Kaufman, Mark Runco, and Keith Sawyer. Each gave generously of their time and expertise, and their ideas are borrowed throughout this book. We are also indebted to the hosts of the sites we visited, including Rebecca Wilson (Van Meter Community Schools), Phyllis Peter (Newton Public Library), Daina McKeever (MATURA Head Start, Winterset), Dawn Johnson (Kids World Daycare and Preschool, Centerville), Katie Dreyer (Pella Public Library), and Mary Minard (Moore Elementary School, Des Moines). We also thank Melissa York at Redleaf for her patient and scrupulous editing. She made this book much better.

Introduction

We frame this book about creativity as a journey of discovery. It began with curiosity, which is a driver of creativity. We asked questions that led us to new ideas. Our learning increased. Often a single interview or book or article struck a responsive chord. So we stopped, dug in deeply, and reported back to each other about what we learned. It's all recorded here. We wanted to share what we learned and reflect on it with readers who share our interest in creativity and our passion for early childhood education.

We two authors come to this book with different backgrounds in education. Tom has had a long career in early childhood, including as a trainer, curriculum developer, and program administrator. Zach is a librarian, and he has a strong educational background in early childhood education. Tom approaches this as a formal educator, Zach as an informal educator. These two perspectives allow us to bridge the gap between formal and informal learning and take a broad view of the topic—realizing that formally or informally we all are learning all the time.

This is not the definitive or most authoritative book on creativity and young children. We wrote a book we think is interesting and hope will be helpful. We consulted other books about creativity for young children. Many were very good and helpful. But they were not saying the things we thought needed to be said. We decided we wanted to start not with children, but with creativity itself. What is it? How does it work? What are people saying about it? We had read widely in the field of child development, but not so much in the field of creativity. When we read some of that literature, we entered a new world filled with lots of fascinating ideas. But something was missing. Few were talking about young children. We decided to write about what we discovered about creativity, using the lens of early childhood education. What were these new ideas we were discovering, and how might they be useful for educators, caregivers, and anyone nurturing the development of young children?

We followed our curiosity. We allowed what we knew about child development and what we were learning about creativity to smelt in our heads. We watched

to see what exotic metals could be produced in the crucible of our brains. What would happen? We wanted to be surprised. We latched onto all the new and original ideas that emerged. And then we sought to put those ideas to practical consideration as tools for parents and caregivers in the raising and educating of young children. This *new*-plus-*useful* formula will become important when you read chapter 1. In short, we took a creative approach to writing a book about creativity. Creativity is self-justifying. It drives all our thoughts and reconciles all our passions. And it drove the most important creation of our lives over the past three years: this book.

The book is divided into three parts. The first gets right to the meat of things, discussing the *what* of creativity (chapter 1), its connections to child development (chapter 2), and how it shapes and is shaped by the people, communities, and world around us (chapter 3). The second part is our seven Big Ideas (chapters 4 through 10). These are the big takeaways from our research. We started with five Big Ideas, but that grew to seven as the implications of creativity's power became apparent. The final part of the book is a turn toward creativity in action, including case studies in chapter 11 and our personal stories and calls to action in the final chapter.

By having the courage to write a book about a subject we were far from experts in, we embraced an important lesson about creativity. Creativity is for us to notice and ride like a wave just to see how far we go and where it will take us. It is *cumulative* and *consummatory*, as John Dewey would say. That is, it builds over time and leads to some final, often unexpected place. There would be no such thing as hands-on learning if we weren't all creative to some extent. Creativity allows us to engage in the activity and learn something from the process. So it was in writing this book.

Along with courage, we cultivated a sense of openness. We avoided second-guessing or assuming we already knew something. We decided not to worry about where the research would lead or what might come of it. Maybe not being experts helped us. Maybe that's why it took three years. We wanted to be open to whatever awaited us and wherever it took us. Openness to experience, as we discuss in chapter 5, is a personality trait strongly associated with creativity. It is a predisposition not to shy away from the new and unfamiliar. It was another way in which writing this book was an exploration of creativity.

Writing this book was a journey of discovery. We hope reading it will be the same for you. But more importantly, we hope it inspires you to take your own journey of discovery, not just learning about the world or gaining skills in teaching or caregiving, but discovering who you are.

Part One
What Is Creativity?

The first part of this book takes a big-picture look at creativity, describing what we know and what we are not sure of regarding creativity, considering how it might play a role in the ways children grow and learn, and exploring the context within which young children's creativity takes place.

Chapter 1 surveys the many and varied definitions of creativity, plumbs its myths and meanings, and considers what should be included in the creative process. Since the whole book is about what happens when we look at creativity from the perspective of child development, we make direct and intentional connections between the two in chapter 2. We include a short but deep dive into the work of John Dewey, Maria Montessori, Jean Piaget, Lev Vygotsky, and Erik Erikson to reveal what their pioneering ideas contribute to our understanding of creativity. Thinking about child development pioneers, chapter 3 borrows heavily from the work of Urie Bronfenbrenner and his famous bioecological model. It turns out that exploring the environment in which we live opens our eyes to its influences on children. But the model also stresses that children influence their environment. By describing the micro-, meso-, and exo-systems around us, we discover new ways to guide creativity's uses and purposes in a positive and life-affirming direction.

Chapter One   # Creativity and the Creative Process

How to think about the creativity of children

When we talked to people about this book, they would ask, "What's it about?" Our best response was a single word: *creativity*. That engaged them. They had questions and ideas. The very word conjures up thoughts of mystery and the esoteric. It evokes curiosity and wonder. It literally got their creative juices flowing.

That's one thing about creativity. No one talks about it without some kind of metaphor, and what are metaphors but a kind of creative thinking and expression? You can't even talk about creativity without being creative.

Both its evocative nature and the idea that everyone seems to have some personal experience with it are key to understanding creativity. If everyone has creative experiences, then everyone is creative. And if everyone is creative, young children are creative too. That is the central fact that drives this book—not because anyone is surprised by the fact that children, even the youngest children, are creative, but because we do not seem to treat children as if they are first and foremost creative beings. This book makes the point that they are, and that it matters, and that it should change the way we raise, nurture, and teach our children.

We need to treat children as if they are creative. We need to know how to recognize the inner Marie Curie or Michelangelo in every child and make that the beginning of how we understand them, connect with them, nurture their development, and engage with them in exploring and making sense of the world around them and the world inside their brains. We want to encourage you, as a reader, to help children discover their own creative beings. What we have learned in our work with children and from the large reservoir of creativity research is that creativity is so critical to the way humans grow, learn, and make sense of and shape their world that it should be at the center and not the periphery of early childhood education.

We have come to believe that if you nurture creativity in children and fan the sparks of original ideas, you are providing children with everything they need for cognitive and social-emotional learning. That orientation changes everything.

Our first question as educators and parents/guardians is not "What do we teach children?" but "What is already going on inside of children that needs attention and focus?" Educating children is about their learning and their development. It is not about what we do. We like to remind people that the root word in *education* is *educe*, which means to draw or bring out, to elicit. That means there is something inside of children already—ideas, motivations, feelings. Our role, it seems to us, is to see children as they are, take their hands, and walk with them to the next step. So if children are not empty vessels, what is going on inside of them? In a word, *creativity*.

To tackle this important—and confusing—topic, we must ask two key questions:

- What is creativity?

- How do children experience creativity or act in a creative way?

What Is Creativity?

In the course of researching this book, we found many definitions. We even found an article about how hard it is to define creativity. Here are some definitions we ran into:

- "Any human act that gives rise to something new is referred to as a creative act."—Lev Vygotsky (2004, 7)

- "Intelligence is the ability to apprehend and perceive what is. Imagination is the ability to perceive what could be. Creativity is the combination of both intelligence and imagination."—Scott Barry Kaufman (Harris 2020)

- "Creative activity is a type of learning process where the teacher and pupil are located in the same individual."—Arthur Koestler (1968, 235)

- "Creativity [is] using our imagination to come up with ideas or make something new."—Annie Reneau (2017)

- "A creative idea is one that is both novel and useful in a particular social setting."—Laurel Fogarty, Nicole Creanza, and Marcus Feldman (2015, 736)

- "To see a World in a Grain of Sand / And Heaven in a Wild Flower / Hold Infinity in the palm of your hand / And Eternity in an hour."—William Blake, "Auguries of Innocence" (We owe this elegant and evocative definition of creativity to Nancy Andreasen [2015, 13:19], a creativity researcher from the University of Iowa.)

- "Creativity is intelligence having fun."—As seen by author Tom on a banner outside the Iowa Science Center

Can all these definitions be true? If so, how can this thing we call *creativity* be so many things? If not, which would you reject as untrue? We prefer to hold them all together and continue to look at how each one is true every day in the life of a single child. Mystery should make us curious, not confused. As scholar E. Paul Torrance (1988, 43) wrote,

> Creativity defies precise definition. This conclusion does not bother me at all. In fact, I am quite happy with it. Creativity is almost infinite. It involves every sense—sight, smell, hearing, feeling, taste and even perhaps the extrasensory. Much of it is unseen, nonverbal and unconscious. Therefore, even if we had a precise concept of creativity, I am certain we would have difficulty putting it into words.

Originality + Utility

But to write a book, we had to start narrowing down what exactly we were talking about. We eventually arrived at a working equation: **Creativity = Originality + Utility**. This definition is similar to one by Mark Runco and Garrett Jaeger (2012, 22): "Creativity requires both originality and effectiveness." Ronald Beghetto, James Kaufman, and John Baer (2015, 21) came up with a slightly different creativity formula or equation: **C = [O x A]context** where creativity (C) is defined by multiplying originality (O) and appropriateness (A) in contexts. The key change here is the use of a multiplication sign rather than an addition sign, so creativity is instantly reduced to zero if either O or A is zero. In other words, even if something is superappropriate or superuseful, it is not creative if there is no O, or originality. Likewise, something can be off-the-charts original and unique, but if it fails to have any utility, forget it. Furthermore, the context has a profound moderating effect on the O × A results. It is so important that we dedicate chapter 3 to discussing it.

But first, let's unpack the other two variables: originality and appropriateness (or what we call *utility*).

Originality

Originality means that whatever is generated in thought or action is new, innovative, different, unusual, or one of a kind. That sense of freshness or novelty is part of what captures our attention when we see something creative.

Something seems original not just because of its new and unexpected qualities, but because it comes from another person's unique characteristics and life experiences. No two people and no two lives are identical. Who we are, our unique selves, is shaped by genetic and experiential factors and the interaction of the two. So a chief contributor to creativity is our life experiences because they make our contributions different from anyone else's.

Sometimes an idea is so new that our minds reject it because it violates some expectation we have about how things are supposed to appear or act or follow. As we go through our lives, we develop rules and habits for looking at the world so we can make sense of it based on what we observe, and then we make predictions based on patterns we've seen. So if something appears illogical, we reject it because it doesn't fit predictable patterns. If something is rude or offensive, we may reject it because it violates our sense of what is proper and acceptable. If something is utterly confusing, we reject it as incomprehensible. This entire process—perceiving the world, trying to make it fit into our preconceptions, and then coming to an understanding or making decisions based on how we have constructed the world—is how we define learning. This is what Swiss psychologist Jean Piaget taught us about how children learn: by constructing an understanding of the world. And that construction is never what the world is actually like; it's only a reflection, a subjective shadow on a cave wall, as Plato explained. As we learn, our construction of the world changes; it gets more complicated, sophisticated, and multifaceted.

In this way, creativity and learning are not only connected but are perhaps even part of the same thing. It is these new, surprising, and unique thoughts, feelings, and objects that provoke our understanding of the world. "How can the world be the way I imagine it to be," we ask ourselves, "if it also includes this new idea or this object or this phenomenon?" As we incorporate these new ideas, our understanding of the world grows and changes. That is really a definition of education. Unless creativity is new or different or challenging to what we previously thought, it is not creativity. We need newness in our lives to keep us growing and changing.

Utility

By *utility*, we mean usefulness or purpose, even if that purpose is simply delight or joy or aesthetic pleasure. Some may want to push back on this and think about creative products that serve no purpose. We would argue that a new idea that served absolutely no purpose would never stick in one's mind long enough to be meaningful. It is the purpose or the meaning we ascribe to an act of creativity that gives it a reason to be.

As creativity researcher James C. Kaufman (2016, 5) put it, "It isn't enough to just be different—creativity must also be appropriate to the task at hand." This makes sense to us when you think about creative problem solving. Say you are hungry, to use an example from Kaufman's book. I could heat up some canned soup—not a very creative solution. Or I could serve you "steamed nuts" (by which Kaufman meant steel nuts!). Very original, but not very relevant to the problem at hand. One of the researchers we interviewed for this book, Baroness Susan Greenfield, told us that creativity had to be broad enough to have meaning for others. For some, a work of art may be utterly meaningless and therefore not very useful or terribly creative. For others, it generates an "aha moment," changing paradigms in the brain and making the world different. Who is right? It may not matter for our purposes. We can subjectively disagree about whether something is useful or what its true purpose is, just as we can disagree about what makes something creative or not. What we are saying here is that the creative act or product must be useful for someone in order for it to be creative for them.

Our originality + utility definition is also helpful, because as we begin to observe children being creative, we can plumb the depths of their thinking and behavior by asking what is new and what is its purpose. That helps us know how best to nurture the inventive spark.

Power + Memory

Another source for making sense of creativity might be the Greek idea of the Muses. The Greeks were masters at explaining mysterious phenomena like lighting, thunder, the starry sky, or a sunrise. They explained the interior dramas around sex and pride by creating myths and gods to tell stories about what was happening in the world and inside the mind. The Greeks believed that creativity was the work of the Muses. The Muses were the daughters of Zeus (the father of the gods) and Mnemosyne (the goddess of memory). Creativity is therefore the product of power (personified in Zeus) and memory (personified by Mnemosyne). The nine Muses of Greek mythology support an array of creative endeavors: epic poetry (Calliope), history (Clio), love poetry (Erato), lyric poetry (Euterpe), tragedy (Melpomene), hymns (Polyhymnia), choral song and dance (Terpsichore), comedy (Thalia), and astronomy (Urania). What this teaches us about creativity is that our power and potential, combined with memory and ideas about our origins, bring forth inspirational forces (the Muses).

The idea of the Muses also suggests that creativity, even our own creativity, is not something under our control. We must wait for a Muse to visit us and grace our imaginations with new ideas or inspirations. The Muses were independent agents who acted on their own. They were goddesses and thus represented feminine characteristics like fertility, generativity, and life. These ideas from the Greeks also teach us that creativity is not just in the arts but in the sciences and humanities as well.

Thinking beyond a strict dictionary definition opens the imagination to make new connections and new understanding about a complicated subject. It gives us permission to think outside the constraints of logic and sequential reasoning. This idea will become very important as we ask ourselves how and why we should be promoting creativity in young children.

What Creativity Is Not

Before leaving the question "What is creativity?" let's ask ourselves what it is *not*. Several common myths or misconceptions around creativity persist, and to move forward we need a clear picture of what is not true.

Mathias Benedek and his colleagues (2021) published an article about what myths people believe about creativity. They surveyed 1,417 people from six countries about fifteen creativity myths, dividing them into four categories: myths around definition, myths about the creative process, myths surrounding the creative individual, and myths about what stimulates creativity. Here they are along with our ideas about why they are not true.

Definition myths

- *Creativity cannot be measured.* If originality and utility are key ingredients of creativity, we can determine if both are present and to what degree. Furthermore, there are many tests for creativity that have been shown to be valid and reliable (for example, the Torrance Test for Creative Thinking [Torrance 1998]).

- *Creativity is essentially the same as art.* Creativity can be any original and useful idea, act, or object. We do not want our work nurturing creativity in young children to begin and end with painting pictures.

- *Creative ideas are naturally a good thing.* It is natural for people to be creative, but they can use their creativity for mischief and evil. Further, what makes a good thing is often socially and culturally determined.

Creative-process myths

- *Creative accomplishments are usually the result of sudden inspiration.* If creativity means originality plus utility, any way we get original ideas that have a purpose is a creative accomplishment, whether that is a sudden inspiration or the result of a lot of trial and error.

- *Creative thinking mostly happens in the right hemisphere of the brain.* Numerous neuroscience studies have disproved this claim. Creative thinking activates different parts of the brain at different times in both hemispheres.

- *Creativity tends to be a solitary activity.* It can be solitary, but creativity is also present in social groups. Your collection of creatives convened in a learning environment provides a perfect setting for collaborative creativity. Other people like parents, caregivers, educators, and librarians are an important part of the context variable in the creativity equation discussed above (**C = [O × A]context**). Being creative together is probably more common for more people.

Creative-person myths

- *Creativity is a rare gift.* If creativity is a natural and inevitable part of the human experience, it is anything but a rare gift. It is universal. We all are creative.

- *People have a certain amount of creativity and cannot do much to change it.* Neuroscience makes clear that creativity is a form of cognition and consciousness. And if we can do anything to change how we think or become aware of things, we can change our creativity. We can train our minds to have thought patterns or habits directed toward creative thinking and expression.

- *Children are more creative than adults.* Creativity is universal and has latent potential in every single person. But children do have some advantages. It has to do with those brain networks that are more likely to be engaged in creative thinking. We will discuss this in great detail in chapter 5, but suffice it to say that children often and perhaps more easily slip into a default state where the mind is idle. They can be more spontaneous. But they also lack the experience and knowledge that are the fuel of creativity.

- *Mental health disorders usually accompany exceptional creativity.* This is not true, because mental health disorders often interfere with cognitive processing. Like everyone, people with mental health disorders are also creative, and their specific disabilities may or may not contribute to creativity. But people who experience a variety of neurodiverse thought patterns (for example, those on the autism spectrum) may generate a greater number of original ideas because their brains function differently than the brains of neurotypical people. In chapter 6, we show how neurodiversity helps some people make important contributions to their creativity. In chapter 10, we talk about how trauma both interferes with creativity and can be transformed into creative expression.

Creative-stimulation myths

- *People get more creative ideas under the influence of alcohol or marijuana.* Changing or interfering with cognitive processes does not mean more creative ideas; it may mean fewer. Changing how your brain thinks can open you up to new awareness or different types of thinking, perhaps leading to more original thoughts. But alcohol or drugs affect each person differently, so their use is no guarantee that one will produce more creative ideas. Plus the utility requirement requires one to be tethered closely to reality.

- *Long-term schooling harms the creativity of children.* Ken Robinson is famous for his diatribes against rote education and the mechanized learning process (Robinson 2006; 2010). He is largely correct in his critique, but it is not "long-term school" that is at fault but rather poorly designed teaching that fails to recognize and draw from students' innate creativity. How to do that, at least for early childhood education, is a key point of this book.

- *Brainstorming in a group generates more ideas than if people were thinking by themselves.* This is the flip side of the myth above that creativity is mainly a solitary activity. You can generate a lot of creative ideas in a well-facilitated brainstorming process, but creativity also occurs within a single person. The myth here is that it generates "more" ideas. It certainly can, but what matters is how the brainstorming occurs. The fact is that creativity is both a solitary and a group activity, and both can result in the development of creative ideas.

- *One is most creative with total freedom in one's actions.* There is good evidence that adding constraints can increase one's creativity. One famous example is Dr. Seuss's writing of *Green Eggs and Ham*: his publisher challenged him to write a story using just fifty common sight words, and this classic book was the result.

These last points suggest that a number of these myths are not total lies but rather oversimplifications that can lead us to wrong conclusions about what creativity is and how it can be nurtured in young children. Pigeonholing our thinking about creativity limits our own creative understanding and therefore restrains the many ways we might think about what creativity is and how we support the development of each child's creative potential.

How Do We Experience Creativity or Act in a Creative Way?

Understanding creativity is one thing. Being creative is another. And what does "being creative" mean for young children? How does creativity actually work? That is, what is going on when someone or some child is creative? What we find is something contradictory.

Neuroscientists have detected two sets of cognitive processes occurring during creativity that seem totally different from one another. The first is one of deep absorption, imagination, and loose filters, with an openness to whatever thoughts may come. The second is deliberate reflection, evaluation, and strong filters. Both processes seem to be connected to creativity (Kaufman 2020, 114). We will discuss the neurological activities associated with creativity in much greater depth in chapter 5. The point we want to make here is that creativity involves at least two very different types of thinking.

The Four Ps

Educational scientist James Melvin Rhodes (1961) set out to define creativity and, unable to settle on a single definition, developed the four Ps of creativity: People, Processes, Products, and Press (or Place). Essentially, Rhodes says creativity is this thing that happens when *people* engage in *processes* and create *products*, all within a specific context or *press*.

If we apply the four Ps to nurturing creativity in young children, this suggests four areas of intervention. First, in the domain of *People* (who is creating), we intervene directly with children, exposing them to experiences that acknowledge who they are as creative beings. We design these experiences so children become more aware, more comfortable, and more eager to express themselves in creative ways. Most children don't need to be taught how to be creative; they just need to be allowed (and to allow themselves) opportunities to be creative. The educator nurturing creativity in children can focus on the individual child and look for how creativity is evident in their daily routines and behaviors. Those instances where useful and original expression emerges from the children themselves—not just imitating what someone else does or following some rote instructions—should be acknowledged and valued. That helps those sparks of creativity to catch fire. This is why early childhood educators are taught to ask open-ended questions, to use open-ended materials, and to allow time for a child to work out how they will respond. Of course, parents, family members, and other caregivers are also essential nurturers of creativity in children when they acknowledge and value it. Educators and caregivers can encourage parents and other family members to support creativity.

Second, we can pay attention to *Process* (how they are creating). Are there things we can do that can lead children into creative engagement? Creativity comes about as the individual does something, moving through a set of steps: the *creative process*. The focus of the second P is the verb, the doing part: being creative. Educators who value and nurture creativity are attuned to creative acts and use each moment as an opportunity for nurturing creativity, responding with comments, acknowledgment, praise, encouragement, questions, and extension. Educators can also teach children about the creative process. One process described by Graham Wallas in his 1926 book *The Art of Thought* includes four steps: preparation, incubation, inspiration, and verification (quoted in Rhodes 1961). One can imagine how planning a creative activity for young children could intentionally move through this process to maximize its effect.

The third P, *Product* (what are they creating) is what is produced by any act of creativity. It may just be an idea. It may be a new way of playing with a toy. It may be a way to share a toy and avoid a conflict. It could also be a new block design, a new painting, a new way to dress up, a new way to kick a ball. Those products become one more thing for educators to pay attention to, to capture in a portfolio, to analyze for unique characteristics and value, or to add to an individual child's gallery or hall of fame.

Finally comes *Press* or *Place* (where are they creating), the final P. Rhodes was thinking about surroundings that "press" a person to create in a certain way. The final P explores the situation, environment, or context where creativity is taking place and the extent to which it influences, supports, or hinders the creative act. We will talk about the many dimensions of context or place in chapter 3. A key point we make is that we are talking not only about a classroom or home or library setting, but the relationships among those environments and the contexts that shaped the environments themselves. Context also encourages us to remember that creative learning is part of most experiences children have inside or outside a classroom or other official educational space. Anything you do to set up your environment with interesting materials or to plan activities is focusing on press or place. By paying attention to the context, we are tending to the fertile ground from which creativity more readily emerges. Digging deeper into the many sides of creativity helps you find abundant opportunities to explore, nurture, and enjoy the creativity of your children.

Accessing Creativity

As we just talked about, process is one of the four Ps of creativity. Deepak Chopra (2017), the controversial advocate for alternative medicine, has outlined a more detailed creativity process. Chopra contends that "every child that is born is infinitely creative and that all of us have access to infinite creativity" (2:28). Broadly understood, we completely agree. Maybe not so much that "infinite" part. But we do believe that creativity is central to the functioning of human behavior and the growth of young children. If this bold claim pushes us to think more deeply and act more decisively to recognize and support all creative expression in young children, we are on board.

He goes on to describe a nine-step process by which we access "infinite creativity."

1. **Intended vision:** Have a clear vision of what you would like to create.

2. **Gather information:** Consider what you currently know as well as what is currently knowable about what you would like to create that you could find out.

3. **Analyze information:** Build your understanding of that information, considering what is relevant or not for your purposes.

4. **Incubation:** Rest in a state of pure awareness, letting go of preconceived ideas and trying to be fully present in the moment. Let go of how we typically think about things and become open to unpredictability. When we do this, it leads to . . .

5. **Insight:** Realize an original or new idea. This is the novelty we have talked about as endemic to creativity: something that comes to us from a silent, unconscious, or preconscious place within us, just popping into our heads. That leads to . . .

6. **Inspiration:** Bring a spirit or energy to the insight; essentially, give it life. *Inspire* comes from the Latin *spirare*, which means both *breath* and *spirit*, so we are breathing new life into this original, fleeting thought.

7. **Implementation:** Do something with this inspired thought. Give it some form of expression, thus making it real or more real than merely an idea.

8. **Integration:** Connect the creative expression—that new and original idea—to consciousness, our thinking, our worldview, and the reality around us as we experience it.

9. **Incarnation:** Bring the creative expression to life so it is sustainable on its own. We all know that new ideas are very fragile and can die from too much or too early exposure. We must protect its tiny life like a baby until it can live on its own. This is our understanding of an "incarnated" creative idea—one with flesh and bones that exists in the material world.

As we understand these nine steps, in practice steps 5, 6, and 7 could happen instantly, in less than a second. After all, thought is instantaneous. Steps 5 and 6, moving from insight to inspiration, many times may be a single step. But *insight* and *inspiration* are not synonyms, and the difference in their definitions gives us a clue to the subtle difference. Using standard dictionary definitions, *insight* means to "understand the inner nature of things, especially through intuition." *Inspiration* means "breathing in," literally to breathe into or to place the spirit into, and commonly it can mean "any stimulation to a creative thought." The connection between understanding and its stimulation of an original thought represents distinct actions that influence one another. From the void (step 4—incubation) emerges these insights, and from these insights emerge a creative or inspired idea.

Creativity in the Human Experience

Creativity is a uniquely human process. We want to talk about creativity, nurture it in young children, and even write about it because creativity is a central part of the human experience.

Vlad Glăveanu and Ronald Beghetto (2021) note that you can't study human behavior without tripping over creativity. As we started writing this book, we kept seeing creativity everywhere: daily problem solving, planning a meal, watching a TV series, taking a walk, facilitating a meeting with colleagues, and teaching young children—all involve the meeting of the next moment in a fresh way that helps us take the next step.

We may do all these things by rote. We can walk away from problems. We can make the dinner we had last night. We can zone out in front of a screen. We could walk mindlessly around the block. We could follow a scripted lesson plan. Yet even here, you almost can't stop yourself from being creative. In those moments of doing a daily routine, our minds frequently wander. In those moments, creative ideas seem to come unbidden. This is the "default mode network" that seems to free the mind to access more random association and connections and thereby yield original thought.

Glăveanu and Beghetto (2021) challenge the standard definition of creativity as originality plus effectiveness (much as we define it above). Instead, they argue that a definition should start with "creative experience." That experience involves the "principled engagement with the unfamiliar and a willingness to approach the familiar in unfamiliar ways" (75). In other words, creativity is about how we approach reality and therefore is connected to all our experiences with reality. It suggests that the novelty is not just in our unique ideas but in engaging with unfamiliar experiences or unfamiliar approaches to more familiar experiences. That idea, they say, surfaces several habits of thought that end up being very significant to creativity: open-endedness, nonlinearity, perspective-taking, and future orientation. Psychologist Scott Barry Kaufman (2020) calls one of the precursors to creativity the cognitive trait of "open to experience." He says that individuals who exhibit various behavioral traits that might be considered creative also seem to score higher on measures of openness to experience.

Before we leave the idea of creativity as an essential human experience, let's not forget to state that creativity is fun and satisfying. Evolution allowed for creativity to spur endorphin production, which stimulates pleasure centers. Engaging in creative activity relaxes us, stabilizes our breathing and heart rate, and makes us feel more connected (Benson 1975). It's at least one reason why children naturally want to play. It's fun! Our brains, it seems, are wired to tell us that creativity is good and good for us.

The implications of these ideas are profoundly relevant to anyone who wants to teach children to be more creative. How does this change what we do as parents/guardians or early childhood educators?

- It means that there can't be cordoned-off times for "creative arts" if creativity is happening all around us and inside us all the time (even when we sleep, we dream, right?). We can no longer have "creativity units" but instead look at each unit as a new field for creative endeavors.

- It means that we must think of creativity as associated with many types of experiences, maybe even with every experience. We nurture creativity by thinking through the creative dimensions of the experiences we design for children. We can take new approaches to daily routines or introduce new objects or new ways of playing with objects.

- It means identifying and valuing behavior that shows an openness to cause-and-effect sequences, when children see things from different perspectives or reorder them in a new way, or think about future possibilities, however rich and absurd. We want children to value their ability to do these things by finding satisfaction in using these skills or enjoying the experiences in which these behaviors are evident.

- ◉ It means looking at every child to gauge how they manifest an openness to experience. Psychologists Alexander Thomas, Stella Chess, and Herbert Birch (1970) were among the first to identify three specific temperaments for children: *easy*, *difficult*, and *slow to warm*. "Easy" children may be readily open to new experiences because they are readily adaptable to a changing environment. Children with a "difficult" temperament can be more rigid and may react negatively to new experiences but also may crave a greater variety of change in their environment. The "slow to warm" children are generally fearful of new experiences and take time to feel comfortable enough to respond naturally. If openness to experience is a prerequisite for creativity, educators can support creativity by individualizing how experiences are offered to children, how children are supported during experiences, and how children are provided with skills to cope with and respond to new experiences that encourage prolonged engagement and help them to be more open and not avoid something simply because it is new.

It seems true, as well, that creativity is part of how we define human beings. The ability to think original thoughts seems to be a uniquely human capacity. When you consider the great moments in early human history—the invention of the wheel, the first cuneiform writing, the development of agriculture or beer, the Lascaux cave paintings and *Venus of Willendorf*—all were signs of human creativity.

Creativity is kind of a divine spark and energy that exists in us. Maybe it compels us to do things; maybe it sits and waits to be activated. (We explore this idea in chapter 4 when we discuss the *élan vital*.) We make this connection, as others have, between creativity and the divine because it also points to the importance of creativity. Religions function, in part, to point to matters of ultimate importance. From a Jewish, Christian, or Moslem perspective, if God is important and central to human life, and creativity is a key characteristic of who God is and what God does, it must mean that these religions point to creativity as a central value of life, deeply rooted in the meaning and purpose of existence. It is as if they are saying, "Nothing happens until you create." And if you don't believe in God, what is the big bang but the very first act of creativity: highly unique (nothing else was there!) and immeasurably useful (nothing would exist without it!)?

In sum, as human culture has evolved and humans have tried to make sense of the world around them and their place in it, somehow creativity has been recognized and placed on a very high pedestal indeed.

In the act of creating things, of making and fashioning things, we bring something useful into our world that has never been there before in exactly this way. The drive to be creative is what brings into being inventions and solutions without which our species would not have survived. Scientific knowledge and logic play an important role, but creativity is always present: spurring curiosity, seeing patterns, inspiring "what-if" questions, imagining new possibilities.

What this means for teachers of young children, whether parents, caregivers, or early educators, is that to nurture creativity in young children is to make them *more* of who they already are. It is to acquaint them with something fundamental in their nature. If what we are writing about creativity is true, we must consider these questions:

- How then should our approaches to child development change?

- How can we reprioritize creative activity as a central task within early childhood education?

- What do we need to add to professional development and parent/guardian education to ensure that parents, caregivers, and educators know what they need to know about creativity?

The website scarymommy.com includes a definition for creativity that brings these lofty ideas down to earth and makes them practical for those who care for and nurture young children:

> Using our imagination to come up with ideas or make something new—is one of the most valuable qualities human beings can have. Innovative thinking will serve our kids well in whatever endeavors they choose, and the more we encourage creative activity during their formative years, the more comfortable and confident they'll feel in sharing their ideas with others. (Reneau 2017)

We hope our book will help you take "one of the most valuable qualities human beings can have" and make children "comfortable and confident" in sharing their unique manifestation of this quality. And we will do that by digging into what makes creativity *creativity* at its essence, then revisit those central ideas at the level most relevant for parents, family members, and early educators of all types.

Conclusion

In this chapter, we jumped right into a central problem of creativity: its definition. By exploring this and poking it from all sides, we have broken open the piñata and the candy has spilled all over the floor. If you feel we have created more chaos than meaning, more questions than answers, we have accomplished our purpose and have hopefully spurred you to read further. We also explored the creative process to open up the many ways we can support each step of the creative process. That helped us explain how creativity is experiential, so subtle and commonplace that we often miss it when it is most present, hiding in plain sight. We discussed the many sides of creativity by looking at not only what it is but what it isn't. And we have connected the idea of creativity to the very soul of human existence. Yes, it is *that* important.

We will end each chapter with some provocative "think about it" questions or thought experiments. This idea is grounded in a central premise of creativity, which is that creative questions have multiple possibilities, not a single answer. These questions are designed to open readers up to a wider understanding for themselves and challenge conventional approaches.

Think about It

- What is your personal definition of creativity? Make sure it describes how you experience creativity.

- Which of the creativity myths did you think was true? Where did that idea come from?

- When did you feel most creative in your life? In your work (as an educator or parent/guardian or whatever your work role is)?

- Find some time in the next two weeks to walk through Chopra's creativity process (see page 17). Note anything new you learned or experienced.

- Finish this sentence: "I want to read this book because _____."

Creativity and Child Development

Chapter Two

Bouncing on the knees of giants

Erik Erikson, the famed developmental psychologist, is credited with writing, "In the end, the power behind development is life" (see Santrock 2009, 72). Erikson promoted the idea that humans develop in stages. We argue in this chapter that creativity is central to development. In the previous chapter, we unpacked what creativity could mean. Now we want to talk about its relationship to child development and make a bold claim that creativity sits at the heart of how and why children develop. Perhaps creativity, as a keen element of life, is the power behind development.

Growth and development require perpetual new starts, arrivals, and creations to manifest themselves and to move forward. In chapter 1, we mentioned how creativity is considered a divine attribute by many religions, and we even suggested that every creative act is an echo of the big bang. The implication of that radical idea is that good early childhood education builds on the natural creative impulse that acts in and through children. We will explore this idea in chapter 4 when we discuss how creativity is a life-force. But right now, we want to make sure we ground our ideas in what we know about child development. We can then focus on how understanding creativity and its many aspects helps us be more effective educators and caregivers, whether we are teachers, parents, or other caregivers. We can embrace an approach to early childhood education that is life-affirming and dynamic.

This chapter will explore what we know about child development as a grounding theory of the early childhood education field and how those ideas connect to creativity. We will explore the work of some pioneers in the child development field to discover what they said about creativity and how it helps us understand their conceptual contributions to the field. What becomes evident is that creativity is directly relevant to development. Our guiding question for the chapter is "How do we think about creativity for young children?" Our answer is, always, from the perspective of child development.

What Is Child Development?

Most directly, child development puts together two ideas: *child* and *development*. A child is a human of a certain age; for our purposes, we use the understanding of the National Association for the Education of Young Children (NAEYC) that "young children" are children from birth to age eight. *Development* stems etymologically from an earlier word, maybe Celtic or maybe early German, that means literally "to unwrap." When we "envelop" something, we wrap it up. When we "dis-envelop," we unwrap it; we disclose it and it shows itself as it is. So child development is the unwrapping of children, unfolding into their truer selves.

As Rathus (2008) explains, child development is a field of study with the goal of understanding the physical, cognitive, and psychological growth processes of a child. The purpose of this study is to better understand human nature, the origins of adult behavior, and the prevention of developmental problems (5). The guiding question is "Who are children as part of the human life cycle?"

To dig into the creativity–child development connections more deeply, let's look at the core principles of child development, well summarized in NAEYC's (2022) position statement on developmentally appropriate practices (DAP), and then some creativity ideas that seem connected to or embedded in those principles. These nine core principles represent a consensus among scientists and early childhood experts, especially as found in a series of reports published by the National Academies of Sciences, Engineering, and Medicine (NASEM 2015, 2016, 2017, 2018).

We think the connection between these principles and creativity is clear and direct. Table 1 summarizes how we see the connection between these principles and creativity.

Table 1 shows that how and why children learn and grow parallels how and why they are creative. What drives child development drives creativity. If so, that means creativity must be connected to something central about the unfolding of children in the developmental process. When creativity plays such a central role, how educators, families, and caregivers can support, nurture, and enhance the creativity within each child should be a central concern and central task of all parents, guardians, and teachers of young children.

Table 1. Child Development and Creativity

Principles of Child Development and Learning (NAEYC 2022, xxxii–xxxvii)	Key Creativity Concepts (discussed further in this chapter of the book)
"Development and learning are dynamic processes that reflect the complex interplay between a child's biological characteristics and the environment, each shaping the other as well as future patterns of growth" (xxxii).	• Creativity is a dynamic process. • Creativity reflects a "complex interplay" between nature (biological characteristics) and nurture (environment). (Chapter 5: The Neuroscience of Creativity)
"All domains of child development—physical development, cognitive development, social and emotional development, and linguistic development . . . as well as approaches to learning are important; each domain both supports and is supported by the other" (xxxii).	• Creativity is present in all domains, not just the fine arts. • Learning in any domain enhances creativity in that domain and others. (Chapter 7: Creativity as Curriculum)
"Play promotes joyful learning that fosters self-regulation, language, cognitive and social competencies as well as content knowledge across disciplines. Play is essential for all children, birth through age 8" (xxxiii).	• Pretend play facilitates cognitive processes and emotional regulation, which are important in creativity (Russ and Kaugars 2001). (Chapter 7: Creativity as Curriculum)
"Although general progressions of development and learning can be identified, variations due to cultural contexts, experiences and individual differences must also be considered" (xxxiv).	• Developmental progressions shape how creativity is expressed, with creativity tending to be more or less present depending on age and environmental/cultural context (Runco 2007, 41–43). • Creativity drives with forward movement but often in fits and starts. (Chapter 3: Creativity in Context; Chapter 4: Creativity as a Life-Force; Chapter 6: Creativity and Neurodiversity; Chapter 9: Creativity and Diversity, Equity, and Inclusion)
"Children are active learners from birth, constantly taking in and organizing information to create meaning through their relationships, their interactions with their environment, and their overall experiences" (xxxiv).	• Executive network and default network processing show constant activity in the brain as part of creativity (see page 71). • Wondering is learning. • The act of meaning-making is a creative act. • Children develop their natural creativity by having experiences that require them to think or act creatively. (Chapter 3: Creativity in Context; Chapter 5: The Neuroscience of Creativity; Chapter 7: Creativity as Curriculum)

continued on next page

Table 1. Child Development and Creativity (*continued*)

Principles of Child Development and Learning	Key Creativity Concepts
"Children's motivation to learn is increased when their learning environment fosters their sense of belonging, purpose and agency. Curriculum and teaching methods build on each child's assets by connecting their experiences in the school or learning environment to their home and community settings" (xxxv).	• Belonging, purpose, and agency all provide essential support for creativity in young children. • Creativity is sparked by experiences in school, home, and community settings. (Chapter 5: The Neuroscience of Creativity; Chapter 7: Creativity as Curriculum; Chapter 8: Creativity in Formal and Informal Settings)
"Children learn in an integrated fashion that cuts across academic disciplines or subject areas. Because the foundations of subject area knowledge are established in early childhood, educators need subject-area knowledge, an understanding of the learning progressions within each subject area, and pedagogical knowledge about teaching each subject area's content effectively" (xxxv).	• Creativity benefits from domain-specific and domain-general approaches (see pages 96–97). • Teaching creativity includes directly addressing creativity and teaching creative processes but also teaching in creative ways. • Children's creativity is enhanced by having experiences (in any subject area) that require them to think or act creatively. (Chapter 7: Creativity as Curriculum)
"Development and learning advance when children are challenged to achieve at a level just beyond their current mastery and when they have many opportunities to reflect on and practice newly acquired skills" (xxxvi).	• Addressing challenges calls on creative thinking and skills. • Creativity is taught by offering to children provocations or challenges that require solutions. • Improving creativity means practicing being creative. (Chapter 7: Creativity as Curriculum)
"Used responsibly and intentionally, technology and interactive media can be valuable tools for supporting children's development and learning" (xxxvii).	• Technology and interactive media can be important tools in the informal learning arena to encourage creative thinking and enhance children's creativity. (Chapter 8: Creativity in Formal and Informal Settings)

We believe two self-evident truths about creativity:

1. All children are creative.

2. When children express their creativity, they are expressing something unique and fundamental about who they are.

The first truth echoes the idea of "commonality" in the DAP statement (NAEYC 2022, xxx), namely, that however children differ, they share several things in common. We assert that one of those things is creativity. The second idea echoes "individuality" (xxxi), which underscores that each child is unique in their characteristics and experiences. These two ideas play off the old learning paradox of different and the same. Any two things are similar based on one way of thinking about it and different based on another way of thinking about it. So are the two things different or the same? How can they be both? Creativity is a container in which both can be true. Creativity contains paradox.

One week of *Mister Rogers' Neighborhood* programs featured a musical during the Neighborhood of Make-Believe segments titled "Josephine the Short-Neck Giraffe." As the title suggests, Josephine is a giraffe with a short neck, and that makes her unhappy because she is different from the long-neck giraffes. Gradually, as she meets other animals who struggle with their differences—a snake that can't hiss and an elephant with stripes—she learns that when she is with friends, she feels good about herself. Giraffes are not only defined by their long necks. It all depends on how we look at giraffes and how we think about them. In the Neighborhood of Make-Believe we can think in new ways, like giraffes having short necks or short-neck giraffes pretending to have long necks. We can pretend to be anything we want. Make-believe allows for anything. A realm of make-believe or pretend is a creative realm that thrives on "useful newness," if we can coin a phrase from our working definition of creativity. We need a Neighborhood of Make-Believe to incubate new ideas. It was a new idea that liberated Josephine from her sadness. Creativity drives the process and makes it possible.

Creativity and the Child Development Pioneers

To take our exploration of creativity and child development one step further, we look at the works of five child development pioneers. These are a few—by no means all or even the most important—of the more well-known and influential theorists who, while having specific ideas about child development and education, also had ideas about the creativity of children. Each contributed a key idea or theory that continues to shape our understanding of how children grow and learn. We will explore these theorists in chronological order: John Dewey, Maria Montessori, Jean Piaget, Lev Vygotsky, and Erik Erikson. The following is a greatly simplified and unfairly condensed summary of their thoughts, but we hope it offers you ways to attach what you might already know about their work and ideas with what we are saying about creativity.

John Dewey (1859–1952)

John Dewey was an American philosopher and early pioneer of educational psychology. He is best known for his idea of the student as an active learner and not, as was often thought, an empty vessel in need of filling up. That meant students should be active and engaged, not passive recipients of knowledge delivered through lectures. He challenged the ideas of the philosopher John Locke, who saw children as the proverbial *tabula rasa*, or "blank slate." Instead, following American intellectual traditions of pragmatism, Dewey emphasized education that helped students adapt to and shape the world around them (Santrock 2009, 3). As he wrote, "The only true education comes through the stimulation of the child's power by the demands of social situations in which he finds himself" (Dewey 1998, 229).

Many consider Dewey a proponent of constructivist education (for example, Eby, Herrell, and Jordan 2009), a person who sees education as emphasizing and facilitating the student's active construction of knowledge and understanding. Learning is about building and making something, a product of creative activity. Dewey's description of how education should be done includes many of our recommendations for encouraging and supporting creativity, such as hands-on learning, opportunities to explore on one's own, and learning about one's own life. Education should include practical knowledge as well as traditional academic subjects, and we should be teaching to all the domains of child development, including the intellectual, social, emotional, and physical.

Dewey did not develop a formal theory of creativity, according to Ralph Hallman (1964b), so Hallman did it for him. Hallman was a creativity and educational theorist and philosophy professor who taught at Pasadena City College. His influential article "Can Creativity Be Taught?" (Hallman 1964a) is worth the read. He answers the question with a resounding yes. Hallman compiled several key ideas from Dewey's voluminous writings, including three we think are closely related to creativity: (1) the child as an active learner, (2) the role of **experience** in learning, and (3) a **holistic** view of education that focuses on practical skills.

Creativity is seen as a sign and function of the **active learner**. Unless there is a creator, there is no creation. Dewey's ideas seem to be saying that creativity is a kind of ongoing dialogue between people and the world around them. Active engagement in the world is vital, ongoing, and essential for creativity. And that is mediated through **experience**, the second idea.

Hallman shows a close relationship between Dewey's emphasis on **experience** and creativity. Creativity is a form of human experience. Creativity accumulates new and useful ideas over time to create culture and civilization (see Hallman 1964b, 274). Creativity also combines and integrates things into new wholes. Hallman says that for Dewey, "it is the imagination which is responsible for the actual fusing together of the disparate qualities which arise in primary experience" (277).

Hallman tells us that Dewey's book *Art as Experience* understands openness as receptivity and surrender. It is when we are in a relaxed, reverie-like state that our creativity can be its most spontaneous. Dewey writes,

> Indeed, that is safe to say that "creative" conceptions in philosophy and science come only to persons who are relaxed to the point of reverie. The subconscious fund of meanings stored in our attitudes have no chance of release when we are practically or intellectually strained. (quoted in Hallman 1964b, 279)

Freeing ourselves from the practical or intellectual strain is necessary for us and for young children to be creative. Having freedom from the mental strain of direct thinking and from other distractions (including at times the teachers!) brings us to spontaneous awareness of new ideas—which is another term for learning itself. We clearly learn by paying attention, but we can also learn by not paying attention.

Dewey's **holistic** view of education begins with the idea that learning takes place all the time, not just when an educator is teaching. There is still learning going on when children are practicing a practical skill. The connection back to creativity comes when Hallman tells us that "all thought is creative" and makes the point that in *Nature and Experience*, Dewey is telling us that "science is an art and is as creative as artistic productivity" (1964b, 277). Hallman describes Dewey's use of the term *imagination* as a place where opposites can be brought together—*activity* and *passivity*, *the self* and *the environment*, and *older memories* and *new meanings*—in creative work, just as they are in Fred Rogers's Neighborhood of Make-Believe. The creative act, Hallman writes, unifies "separate subject matters into a common expression" (1964b, 284). Therefore, in the heady world of Dewey's big ideas about *experience*, *nature*, and *education*, *creativity* is equally at home.

Maria Montessori (1870–1952)

Maria Montessori was an Italian physician and educator famous for an approach to learning that is still evident in the many schools that bear her name. She profoundly believed in encouraging children's self-directed learning because they already possessed the knowledge they needed. She once stated, "The child, a free human being, must teach us and teach society order, calm, discipline, and harmony" (Montessori [1949] 1967, 126).

As a medical doctor, she had an interest in pediatrics early on and was exposed to children living in deep poverty and suffering from severe neglect. Discovering that they responded to her treatments pushed her to learn more, which shaped the rest of her life. Borrowing the ideas "education of the senses" and "education of movement" from two French doctors, she developed what she called the "Montessori Method." The features of the Casa dei Bambini, or Child's House, that she began in 1906 are now commonplace in many early childhood classrooms and included such things as hands-on learning, tables rather than individual desks, center time marked by individual choice, and circle time. Her success led to two more *casas*, and her original approaches to education gained popularity. In 2023 there were five thousand Montessori schools in the United States (AMS 2023).

The Casa dei Bambini was a radical upending of conventional ideas about children and how to teach them. Previous education philosophies held that children's cognitive abilities were inelastic, and they had to be controlled and schooled for true learning to take place. That learning was focused on what adults thought was important, like basic reading and arithmetic skills. Montessori's program was new: for starters it was a "house" and not a school. Montessori constructed the houses for maximum movement, with small-size furniture that was comfortable and light enough for children to move around themselves. They were taught to take responsibility for the "house" and its objects. She wanted beautiful objects of high quality because they speak to the soul of children (De Stefano 2022, 98). Children enjoyed cleaning the house more than playing with the toys brought by the wealthy women who supported her program (94). She introduced a communal meal, a feature still required by Head Start. She emphasized the practical learning necessary for life, like how to blow your nose or button your apron. As biographer Cristina De Stefano writes, "Children have almost no more need of a teacher. They do everything on their own, enacting what Maria will soon call self-education" (104).

In our estimation, the Montessori Method is surely a way to teach creativity. *The Montessori Method* (Montessori [1912] 1964), among other sources that describe Montessori's method and strategies, shows us at least seven ways her approach supports and nurtures creativity.

1. *The Montessori Method removes many of the barriers to creativity present in many educational settings.* The whole point of the Casa dei Bambini was *not* to be a traditional educational setting, with its endless rewards and punishments that destroyed the spirit and cramped the creativity of sensitive children— as Montessori wrote, like "butterflies stuck with pins, fixed in their places" (De Stefano 2022, 60). Instead, "every detail was for their autonomy" (94).

2. *Montessori materials are multifunctional.* Montessori describes in detail exactly what kinds of materials should be used to encourage self-education (Montessori [1912] 1964, 185–212, 233–45). Objects, as well as common experiences, are designed to be used in a variety of ways and therefore encourage divergent thinking, a cognitive skill associated with creativity.

3. *Montessori materials are multisensory.* Multisensory materials activate more than one sense as children engage with them, increasing information processing and knowledge retention. Montessori ([1912] 1964) writes, "Pedagogy is not designed to *measure* the sensations, but *educate* the senses. . . . My objects . . . are adapted to cause the child to *exercise* the senses" (167–68). Then she states definitively, "*The education of the senses* must be of the greatest *pedagogical* interest" (215).

4. *Children direct their own learning.* Montessori insists that we, as adults, do not direct their learning, but rather the children are now teaching us! Early in *The Montessori Method* (Montessori [1912] 1964), she writes, "The fundamental principle of scientific pedagogy must be, indeed, the liberty of the pupil;—such liberty as shall permit a development of individual, spontaneous manifestations of the child's nature" (28). That level of freedom avoids constraints on individual creative expression (the "child's nature") while eliciting creative responses to identify needs and interests that direct a child's learning.

5. *Freedom of expression.* The same Montessori principles described in point 4 equally apply to freedom of expression, almost literally in its acknowledgment of "spontaneous manifestations" (28).

6. *Collaborative learning.* Montessori's use of tables and chairs versus desks encourages children to interact and learn together. Further, Montessori's preference for multiage groups assumes they are learning from one another (Montessori [1949] 1967, 226–27).

7. *Creative play time.* Chapter 7 of *The Montessori Method* ([1912] 1964) includes a sample daily schedule. The schedule is for elementary-aged children and includes an hour of "free play" followed by an hour of "directed games" and an hour of intellectual exercises that are all open-ended explorations. There is, in addition, "simple gymnastics," which might be described today as controlled gross-motor activities.

Beyond these seven theoretical ways, a recent meta-analysis of Montessori Education research found moderate to high effects for cognitive abilities, social skills, motor skills, academic achievement, *and* creativity (Demangeon et al. 2023). Educators and parents or guardians could do worse than to look at Montessori education as a place to nurture and support creativity.

Jean Piaget (1896–1980)

Piaget was the first name we thought of when it came to child development theories that address creativity. Jean Piaget was a Swiss psychologist best known for his cognitive-development theory (Rathus 2008, 18). Though he studied philosophy, logic, and mathematics, his doctorate was in biology. His interest in how children think came from observing his own three children (Coon 2006, 115). He wanted to understand how children formed concepts of the world and how those ideas prepared them for changes within the external world. What most interested him was their mistakes.

By paying attention to the wrong ideas children developed about the world around them, Piaget was able to notice in a series of experiments that children's reasoning contains ideas that no one directly taught them, including mistaken ideas. He concluded that children must be learning things by their own cognitive devices, creating their own ideas and actively constructing their own knowledge. To explain how this happens, he developed an understanding of how children's thinking works and changes over time using a vocabulary of key concepts (Santrock 2009, 40–41):

- *Schemas*—A schema is a singular concept a child may have about the world. These mental representations or ideas become the building blocks of knowledge. Piaget thought that children create *schemas* as they interact with the world (40).

- *Assimilation* and *accommodation*—Children use or adapt their *schemas* to make sense of their surroundings, and they do this in two ways: *assimilation* and *accommodation*. When children *assimilate* their *schemas*, they add a new schema to an existing body of schemas. When children *accommodate* their *schemas*, they adjust their existing *schemas* so the new *schema* will fit.

- *Organization*—Piaget believed that children seek to make sense out of the world by organizing their experiences into what he called *schemas*. The "grouping of isolated behaviors and thoughts into a higher-order system" Piaget calls *organization* (41), that is, the organizing of schemas.

- *Equilibrium* and *disequilibrium*—When children try to create a "higher-order system," they frequently encounter cognitive conflicts (what Piaget calls *disequilibrium*). They attempt to reconcile that conflict and seek *equilibrium*. As children assimilate or accommodate new ideas, they move back and forth between states of *disequilibrium* and *equilibrium*, always striving to achieve equilibration.

The cycle of equilibration–disequilibration–equilibration produces cognitive growth, the development of new ideas that are ever more sophisticated and complicated. The trajectory of that growth for Piaget (per Santrock 2009, 42) can be tracked along four stages of cognitive development, with suggestions of broad time periods in children's ages: sensorimotor stage (birth to two years), preoperational stage (two to seven years), concrete operational stage (seven to eleven years), and formal operational stage (eleven to fifteen years).

The *sensorimotor stage* features cognitive activity expressed through sensory or motor activity (Rathus 2008, 190–91). Piaget describes six substages within the sensorimotor stage. The first stage begins with simple reflexes. But at later substages, more cognition is associated with movement and stimuli, as children pay attention more and more to their bodies and their movement, and then to their immediate environment. Gradually in this process they are establishing schemas that help with reaching goals (such as being fed, getting changed, or crawling to a desired toy).

In the *preoperational stage*, children represent the world in words (language) and images (drawing, symbols). It's called "preoperational" because children are not yet using operational thinking or logical thought. They know how to count but not how to add and subtract (Aspiranti 2011).

At this stage, children are conceptualizing the world and expressing their reaction to it with ideas more than with their senses or body movement, as in the sensorimotor stage (Santrock 2009, 42). The preoperational stage is often divided into two substages: *symbolic function* and *intuitive thought*. Symbolic function represents a substantial advancement in cognition for young children. Early in the preoperational stage (two to four years of age), children start to use language and symbols to represent their world, and this finds a common and highly developed form during pretend play. Intuitive thought (four to seven years of age) uses a set of highly reliable mental shortcuts that shape children's understanding of and behavior in the world. These are considered "intuitive" because, while often firmly established, they are not thoroughly considered, like an intuitive understanding that is taken for granted. For example, if you asked why it rains, the preoperational child might respond, "To make puddles."

Piaget's theories add to our understanding of child development in several ways (as suggested by Santrock 2009, 47). First, his thoughts about *assimilation* and *accommodation* set the stage for our conventional teaching wisdom about building on prior knowledge. When we teach, we first want to solicit what is already known and then teach by adding to that knowledge. Second, he saw *play* as an essential way in which children experiment and express where they are cognitively. He thought of it as child's work, not as child's play (Piaget [1945] 1962). Third, he helped us identify a few *thinking problems* that, when resolved, suggested an important advance in cognitive abilities. For example, the idea of object permanence helps us distinguish between two important levels of cognitive ability. If you can see something and react to it but then not react when it isn't there, that is one thing. But if you can remember that something was there and may still exist, that suggests some mental representation of the disappeared object. Similarly, young children are often confused by the law of conservation, which holds that the weight and mass of an object do not change when its shape or arrangement does. Smash some playdough from a ball into a pancake and ask a child if you have more or less playdough. Children of a certain age will often say less (Rathus 2008, 300–301). Another thinking problem might be errors caused by egocentrism, thinking all things are happening because of you. Fourth, his acute assessment of the invisible world of children's thoughts helped us see children as *active, constructive thinkers*, not passive or empty in any way.

Each of these contributions by Piaget suggests a role of creativity in child development. Table 2 elaborates on this suggestion.

Table 2. Piaget and Creativity

Piaget's Contributions to Child Development Theory	Links to Creativity
Assimilation and *accommodation*	Creative thinking lies in the interaction between assimilation and accommodation. This implies that imagination and a playful attitude are important attributes to facilitate creative thinking (Ayman-Nolley 1999).
Play, especially pretend play, is essential to child development	The quality of pretend play—more elaborate and complex, lasting longer—relates to preschoolers' creativity and socioemotional skills (Russ 2006).
Use of *thinking problems* (e.g., object permanence, conservation, or egocentrism)	Problem solving is one way to unleash creativity.
Children as *active, constructive thinkers*	Constructive thinking is creative thinking. It is bringing new and useful ideas front and center to address cognitive challenges.

Children's thinking, Piaget seems to believe, is a creative process, and thus creativity cannot be disentwined from their cognitive development. Others have also identified and written extensively on this connection (for example, Feldman 1974; Sawyer 2003). Their key takeaway is that Piaget's theory of cognitive development assumes creative activity in the creation of schemas and the reorganization of knowledge itself. How that happens, Piaget writes, is "the great mystery of the stages," adding that "the crux of my problem . . . is to try and explain how novelties are possible and how they are formed" (quoted in Sawyer 2003, 13). Piaget also made some striking statements that underscore the value and centrality of creativity. Tania Stoltz and colleagues (2015) quote him as saying, "Education, seen from the current viewpoint, consists of attempting to transform children into the kind of adults existing in the society to which they belong. . . . Whereas for me education consists of producing creators" (65). Eleanor Duckworth quotes him as saying, "The principle [*sic*] goal of education is to create men who are capable of doing new things, not simply of repeating what other generations have done—men who are creative, inventive, and discoverers" (Duckworth 1964, 499). Overall, it is hard to underestimate the impact of

Piaget on our thinking about creativity and young children because so much of what we take for granted in our understanding of child development comes from ideas started or promoted by Jean Piaget.

Lev Vygotsky (1896–1934)

Because he had lived in the Soviet Union, Lev Vygotsky's work was not accessible during the Cold War for several decades after his tragically early death at age thirty-eight. When his ideas became known, they struck a responsive chord for many in the child development field, especially confirming what experience had shown about the importance of social interactions in the learning and development of young children. For example, peer-mediated instruction (using other children to aid instruction or other interventions) is now an evidence-based, common, and effective instructional intervention, especially for children with autism (Odom and Strain 1984; NPDC 2015).

Vygotsky is best known for his sociocultural theory, which asserts that children learn in conversation with other people, notably parents, caregivers, peers, and the wider culture. His natural conclusion was to recommend more social interaction as a way to increase knowledge and learning in young children. As he explored the idea further, he developed additional concepts: the *zone of proximal development* (ZPD) and *scaffolding*. ZPD refers to skills that are just out of reach of a child's ability, an optimal place for growth. There, the self-development of a child, usually driven by curiosity and an innate desire to grow, seems stuck until some guidance or assistance by adults or peers helps them take that next step. That moment is the fulcrum of development, where the magical unfolding of the learning child is taking place. One thing that helps children take that next step in learning and development within the ZPD is scaffolding. *Scaffolding* is a metaphor describing a temporary support structure offered by those nearby to help children learn. A final contribution of Vygotsky was his belief that language plays a critical role in development, especially the idea that children vocalize what they are doing to aid their thinking. Both Vygotsky and Piaget could be labeled constructivist, but they differ greatly by Vygotsky's conviction in the centrality of the social context for learning and the construction of knowledge through social interactions (Santrock 2009, 53, 55).

As a constructivist, Vygotsky's ideas about ZPD, scaffolding, and social learning imply creativity because they all require the creation of new knowledge. Vygotsky's emphasis on social learning reminds us that the task of learning new things through creative thinking is stimulated and aided by others in the environment, both adults and children. Implementing Vygotsky's ideas about scaffolding and working within a ZPD should be done by engaging the children's creative potential. We should be prepared to engage children's creativity by pushing them to creative solutions that fall within the ZPD by scaffolding or relying on peers for creative ideas or prompts, until there is a creative breakthrough and the child uses their creativity to address the next step forward in their learning or competence in completing a task.

Tania Stoltz and her coauthors (2015) write that Vygotsky believed that "creativity is inherent to the human condition, and it is the most important activity because it is the expression of consciousness, thought and language," intertwined with its social and historical context (67). Creativity becomes a way for humans to make sense of their lives, drawing from their context and reflecting back their interpretations and feelings. It emerges in the lives of children as they interact with one another (again the emphasis on sociocultural influences). Therefore, all the expressions of creativity in young children are, in part, products of their society and culture.

Francine and Larry Smolucha (2012) present a Vygotskian theory of creativity based on Vygotsky's idea of scaffolding and ZPD. They write that for Vygotsky, "creative imagination develops from spontaneous lower psychological functions such as dreaming and trial-and-error problem solving" (64). Creative imagination involves new constructions and does not rely on old ideas recovered from memory. As thought matures, thinking is consciously directed by using internalized verbal guidance (self-talk), a step that is supported by and mimics scaffolding strategies by adults or peers. Gradually, the self-guided private speech turns into fully internalized speech and habitual thinking patterns. In this way, the creative imagination makes use of fundamental ideas such as scaffolding and the role of language in articulating thinking.

Creative imagination first appears, for Vygotsky, in the play of young children (Ayman-Nolley 1992). As Vygotsky observed children playing, he was fascinated by object substitution, using an object to represent another object, such as a block becoming a phone or a leaf or a restaurant bill. Children make clear use of their imagination to conceive of the object substitution but also as they see an object as something that it is not, even in the face of the object remaining the same visually. It is a high-water mark of creativity. But Vygotsky also noticed that this is a learned skill, often taught by older children or adults who explained what they were doing, further confirming his ideas about the centrality of social learning.

Vygotsky's ideas about object substitution and the importance of pretend play encouraged Elena Bodrova and Deborah Leong (2007) to create a curriculum called *Tools of the Mind* that explicitly teaches children about object substitution in pretend play. Through modeling and brainstorming, and limiting realistic toys, educators ensure object substitution emerges during pretend play (Smolucha and Smolucha 2012, 68). Notice the emphasis on learning through social interaction with, in this case, adults.

In laying out Vygotsky's theory of creativity, Smolucha and Smolucha (2012, 64) underscore the importance of figurative thinking for the creative imagination. Object substitution is a good example of figurative thinking, as is the use of metaphors or what they call "visual isomorphisms" (two different things that look alike or share a common shape and can therefore substitute for one another). They define figurative thinking as "the visual process of seeing correspondences of shape or function" (77). All this higher-level thinking—objective substitution, use of visual isomorphism, figurative thinking—are the products of creative thinking. They take us beyond the literal to a more "creative" way to look at the world. Inspired by Vygotsky, the authors encourage caregivers and educators to model and encourage figurative thinking in children.

Erik Erikson (1902–1994)

If Dewey is the philosopher, Montessori the doctor, and Piaget and Vygotsky the cognitive scientists, then Erik Erikson is the psychologist. He is best known for his theory about the stages of the human life cycle. Though Piaget also wrote about stages, he was specific to stages of cognitive development. Erikson was talking about the psychological well-being of people as they matured from infancy to old age.

In *Childhood and Society*, first published in 1950, Erikson lays out his "Eight Stages of Man" or life-span development theory. He understands human beings as moving through development in eight distinct stages. Each stage requires people to address certain "developmental tasks," and our progress through life is marked by "developmental milestones." At each stage, we face a "psychosocial dilemma," an identity crisis, if you will, and our ability to resolve that crisis predicts our ability to move to the next stage of development. At this moment of crisis, our path forward seems less certain, yet if we move through it, we develop confidence and skills to resume our developmental journey. The ability of a person to successfully progress from one stage to another basically determines whether they are psychologically healthy (Coon 2006, 130).

These dilemmas are psychosocial—that is, they are about how individuals relate to and interact with other human beings and society (hence his title *Childhood and Society*). The crisis to be resolved at each stage revolves around challenges in our relationships with the wider society. Our pattern of attachment and subsequent ability to form close relationships with others lies at the heart of the developmental work of advancing through the eight stages. What Erikson stresses is how the stages build on one another. Children who struggle with attachment to a caring adult early in life may wrestle with relationships for the rest of their lives (Rathus 2008, 226). The eight stages with their associated dilemma are summarized in table 3 (Coon 2006, 130; Santrock 2009, 75).

Table 3. Erikson's Developmental Dilemmas

Stage (Age Range)	Psychosocial Dilemma
Infancy (0–1 year)	Trust vs. Mistrust
Toddler Years (1–3 years)	Autonomy vs. Shame and Doubt
Early Childhood (3–5 years)	Initiative vs. Guilt
School Age (6–11 years or until puberty)	Industry vs. Inferiority
Adolescence (12–18 years)	Identity vs. Role Confusion
Early Adulthood (19–29 years)	Intimacy vs. Isolation
Middle Age (30–64 years)	Generativity vs. Stagnation
Old Age (65+ years)	Ego Integrity vs. Despair

Since we are talking about early childhood, let's zoom in on just the first three stages. But do take a second to see, based on your current age, what psychosocial dilemma you are facing now. This may help you better understand the scope and depth of these dilemmas and how they affect your own and everyone else's psychological life.

The first stage's psychosocial dilemma is trust versus mistrust. Whenever you hold a baby in your arms, does he or she squirm or relax? Is the baby comfortable there or anxious? Infants make an immediate assessment: *Can I trust this person or not?* That's the first crisis a baby must face. Repeated exposure and interaction with a few caring adults who are warm, nurturing, and responsive teach a baby to feel safe and to trust that the world is an okay place. The more often a baby experiences a positive resolution to these challenges, the less they fear. Conversely, when babies are treated negatively or ignored, mistrust develops (Santrock 2009, 75). The first major task in life is to be able and willing "to let [a primary caregiver] out of sight without undue anxiety or rage" (Erikson [1950] 1963, 247). In the end, the infant must come to see the world as trustworthy or be developmentally stuck.

The second stage (years one to three) is a time to wrestle with autonomy versus shame and doubt. Here, according to Erikson, the toddler is focused on exploring and asserting their independence. Such things are possible because a toddler is now walking at this age and soon will be talking. The so-called "terrible twos" is a manifestation of that emerging strong will, which is beautiful and necessary for a child. They begin to see that they can assert themselves. It makes them feel powerful, but it also causes problems. Not all adults are happy with the ways a child chooses to assert themselves. The conflicts that come out of that may result in shame and doubt: shame because they caused a bad reaction (a parent or other caregiver got angry, yelled, or punished them) and doubt because all the emerging confidence at being more independent is quickly extinguished. As the child resolves this dilemma, they enjoy their autonomy and the sense of self it represents.

The third stage (years three to five) introduces a more advanced aspect of autonomy versus shame, initiative versus guilt. *Autonomy* is now *initiative*, or purposeful behavior. No caregiver should miss the fact that initiative at this stage is what pushes a child to want to do more and know more. But initiative does not appear without bringing along guilt, "guilt over the goals contemplated and the acts initiated in one's exuberant enjoyment of new locomotor and mental power" (Erikson [1950] 1963, 255). So these two very powerful forces are at war within the psyche of the child: the power of being able to do stuff and the guilt associated with doing stuff (sometimes understandable when actions are in disobedience but also at times for irrational reasons). Successful adjudication of these forces leads to characteristics we would associate with any mentally healthy child: confident that they are lovable, safe, getting along with others, effectively managing emotions, and looking forward to their future with hope and optimism.

Erikson saw play as an essential activity for young children and a creative act. He wrote,

> You see a child play, and it is so close to seeing an artist paint. . . . You can see how he solves his problems. You can also see what's wrong. Young children,

especially, have enormous creativity, and whatever's in them rises to the surface in free play. (*New York Times* 1994, para. 29)

In *Childhood and Society*, Erikson ([1950] 1963, 211) defines play as "a function of the ego, an attempt to synchronize the bodily and the social processes with the self." Play is a way children can reconcile the dilemmas at the heart of Erikson's developmental stages. Play can be used to solve problems or work through psychosocial dilemmas. What is peekaboo but playacting separation anxiety? Essentially, Erikson says that play is a creative way we move through stages of development. Play becomes the stage on which creativity can perform.

The chapter "Toys and Reasons" in *Childhood and Society* begins by showing how play allows children to create an environment where they have control and can succeed, a clear defensive posture in a world where they control very little and success is intermittent. He contrasts children's play with adult play, the latter being recreation and a step away from work versus children's play, which is their work. Erikson thought children's play is "an infantile form of the human ability to deal with experience by creating model situations and to master reality by experiment and planning" (Erikson [1950] 1963, 222). This pretend play and the creation of imaginary spaces allows a safer way, with lower risk, to navigate the dilemmas, making it more likely that they can live safely (and trustingly) in the real world. Erikson calls these spaces the *autosphere* (for solitary play), *microsphere* (for parallel play), and *macrosphere* (for associative or cooperative play), to describe how big the realm is and who can live in it. Creativity comes to bear in the creation of these spaces or spheres, driven by the individual's need to reconcile the psychosocial dilemma that emerged as children move from one stage to another. For Erikson, creativity plays an important role in allowing development.

In the final section, Erikson connects play with identity formation. As a child grows, new abilities form new identities. A child who learns to walk comes to see herself as "one who can walk" (235). Such mastery is often accomplished during play. This seems to us a particularly important insight when it comes to challenges adults face with children's behavior. A key function of that behavior is to communicate, but often underneath some immediate message is a child's deeper desire to express who they are, to be recognized and valued as their true self. What a dilemma it creates, then, when the expression of an identity manifests as annoying or undesirable to parents and other caregivers! Can this child be accepted for who they are, however they are showing up at a particular moment! No wonder Mr. Rogers was forever telling his viewers, "I like you just the way you are."

Conclusion

Beneath the ideas, conjectures, and theories of these pioneers, we see the theme of creativity front and center. We began by asking how we should think about creativity for young children. First we look at what we already know about how children grow and learn. And then we think about that through the lens of creativity. What looks different? What comes into focus? What recedes into the background?

We hope that shining a light of creativity off five early childhood trailblazers has given you ideas for how you can think about creativity in young children. But it is important to root your thinking in the soil of child development, what we know about how children grow and change during the all-important early years. And despite the wide array of views and opinions about creativity and child development, none of our five exemplars contradicted the idea that all children are creative and that their creative expression is unique and special to them.

This exploration surfaced many themes and ideas that we will revisit in the chapters that follow, like the creative drive and its association with development, the emerging thought of young children as creative and creating, and the role of the world around us in shaping experiences that are then processed into information, knowledge, and memory. This last idea perfectly pivots into chapter 3, where we write about how our world is organized and influences creativity. Urie Bronfenbrenner helps us understand the context of creativity, something Dewey, Vygotsky, and Erikson would appreciate. Montessori also thought about context with her focus on materials and the environment. She knew how profoundly they shape how a child develops and learns. The connections are endless and weblike, an apt metaphor for creativity.

Think about It

- What idea about child development is most often misunderstood by your colleagues and friends?

- Which child development pioneer has ideas that you most agree with?

- Do you agree that creativity and child development deserve to be discussed together? Why?

Chapter Three   **Creativity in Context**

An ecology of creativity

··

Fred Rogers once wrote, "When I was a child and my mother and I would read about such events [real-life tragedy, disaster, and violence] in the newspaper or see them in newsreels, she used to tell me, 'Always look for helpers. There's always someone who is trying to help'" (Rogers and Head 1983, 183). So who are the helpers? *Mister Rogers' Neighborhood* not only revolutionized the television industry but also brought attention to the world of early childhood development. Specifically, the Neighborhood showcased the importance of building friends, being empathic, valuing emotions and differences, and being a good neighbor or helper. As an early childhood educator, you're a helper, the families you work with are helpers, and the community you work in is a helper. It is critical to include children as helpers too. They support us by helping us know how best to support them. They help us understand their needs, including their need to develop their creative selves.

This web of helping relationships reflects the central role of environment in individuals' development. Children grow and develop in the context of their environment. And it is in this context that creativity occurs, flourishes (or not), and is uniquely shaped as creative thoughts and actions. To Fred Rogers's point about helpers, is the context helping or hindering the development of the child? What in the context is helping creativity and creative expression?

To understand the context, let's look to the work of developmental psychologist Urie Bronfenbrenner (Bronfenbrenner 1979; Bronfenbrenner and Ceci 1994), who developed the bioecological model of child development and challenged ideas that viewed children as isolated individual specimens rather than people living within the ecological systems of family, community, and the wider world. The chapter will provide a blueprint for how the relationship between ecology (environment) and biology influences child development and give advice for how to apply it to your program or family situation.

From Eco to Bio

In 1979 Bronfenbrenner published *The Ecology of Human Development*, in which he introduced ecological systems theory. The prefix *eco-* comes from the Greek word *oikos*, or house. That is precisely what we are talking about here: the first and main environment for the child is the home. *Ecology* literally means the study of the home, or perhaps our home in Mother Earth. At this stage of his theoretical work, Bronfenbrenner (1979) described the relationship between an adult and a child as unidirectional, where influence came only from adults. He identified four *ecologies* that influence a child's growth and development: the microsystem, the mesosystem, the exosystem, and the macrosystem. The ecological model introduced these four ecologies or environmental systems as a set of concentric circles with the child in the center (see figure 1).

Microsystem

The microsystem is centered around the child, where children develop and foster relationships with those closest to them. The microsystem includes interactions with parents, caregivers, siblings, and individuals within their immediate environment. The phrase "the parent is a child's first teacher" is a nice way to emphasize the centrality of the microsystem. When the relationships children develop are strong, they can lead to healthy experiences. When relationships are uncertain or traumatic, they can lead to negative and challenging experiences.

Mesosystem

The mesosystem is the interaction of a child's microsystems with surrounding environments, such as the neighborhood, home, and school. It describes the realm in which discrete elements of the microsystem interact with and influence one another. As a child continues to develop, they have experiences that impact how they trust, how they respond to difficult situations, and how they interact with others. The elements of the mesosystem are not autonomous; it is essential to strive for positive relationships among all the caring adults who have direct contact with the child as an investment in a child's health and well-being.

Exosystem

The exosystem describes the factors that do not have a direct relationship with children but nevertheless affect their growth and development. Some examples of the exosystem include social services and resources, a parent/caregiver's place of work, and a transportation schedule. The exosystem can have either a positive or negative indirect influence on a child's development that educators should be aware of. For example, the loss of a job creates financial difficulty for the family, and even though the child does not interact in that environment, it will affect their development.

Macrosystem

The macrosystem addresses the wider society. Society includes the broader community's history, traditions, beliefs, policies, and laws, and each of these influence a child's beliefs and perceptions of who they are and the society they reside in. The macrosystem culture encompasses the established society the child is growing and developing in, but it does not always match the microsystem culture. For example, a child and their family who recently moved from a country facing war will develop different beliefs and perceptions than a child who has not always lived in a country that has faced war. Yet it is important to invest in understanding the culture, traditions, and beliefs in the society in which you reside and work.

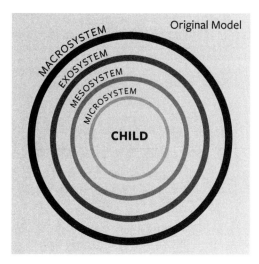

Figure 1. Bronfenbrenner's Original Ecological Model

In 1994 Bronfenbrenner and American psychologist Stephen Ceci circled back to ecological theory to introduce the bioecological model, adding the *chronosystem* as a fifth ecosystem. The addition of the chronosystem acknowledged the dimension of time and the fact that conditions and outcomes change. By adding the Greek prefix *bio-* (or life) in front of the word *ecological*, the focus shifted from just looking at how the environment (the eco) affects people (the bio) to how both the person and their environment influence each other. By including these nuances, Bronfenbrenner and Ceci expanded the ecological model and made it more accurate. They explained the bioecological model as operationalized through *process*, *person*, *context*, and *time*, what they termed the PPCT Model (Bronfenbrenner and Ceci 1994).

The parts of the PPCT Model are interconnected and describe at least four dimensions of the interactive influences of children, their relationships, and their environment.

Process

Process reflects the interaction itself: how it happens and who are the players in the interaction. In the context of early childhood development, the process involves the interaction between a child and the people, objects, and symbols in their environment (Bronfenbrenner and Ceci 1994). On this point, Bronfenbrenner made two key propositions. The first is that

> human development takes place through the processes of progressively more complex reciprocal interaction between an active, evolving biopsychological human organism and the persons, objects, and symbols in its immediate external environment. (620)

Second, he writes,

> The form, power, content, and direction of the proximal processes affecting development vary systematically as a joint function of the biopsychological characteristics of the developing person; of the environment, both immediate and more remote, in which the processes are taking place; and the nature of the developmental outcomes under consideration. (621)

Taken together, these two propositions describe *process*. First, that these fundamental interactions are the context for human development, and second, that the nature of those interactions is shaped by the person and the environment, which is why both person and environment must be taken into consideration.

Person

There are three characteristics that represent the *person* in the PPCT model: force characteristics, resource characteristics, and demand characteristics. *Force characteristics* are traits of a person that impel that person's engagement with the environment. They can include things like curiosity, preference for solo or group interaction, and motivation. *Resource characteristics* are the internal capacities of a person as well as external supports they can access that positively or negatively affect their engagement with the environment. Finally, *demand characteristics* such as age, gender, and skin color act as personal stimulus characteristics. These characteristics trigger immediate effects (hence, acting like a demand) and often shape initial interactions in unusually powerful ways.

Context

Context refers to the original ecological model and the interactive effects of the various ecosystems Bronfenbrenner identified in 1979. However, a new ecosystem was added, the chronosystem, which is described under the next concept, time.

Time

The concept of *time* reflects the transitions, life changes, and societal and culture changes each person experiences. Within the context of early childhood, time reflects temporal-bound experiences, such as when a child's parents divorce, the death of a pet, the birth of a sibling, or going through a traumatic event such as abuse. Each of those positive or negative experiences, though occurring at a discrete moment in their lives, nevertheless persists over time in memory and through their lasting consequences. Those experiences impact the individual's decision-making, their interactions with adults and other children, and their perceptions and beliefs about others and/or society.

What we have been discussing here is a long list of influential variables that shape the context of child development and the context of children's creative lives. There are two important takeaways from this overview.

- First, what influences children's creativity—both their genetic abilities to be creative and ongoing creative activities and expressions—is almost indescribably complex. Rather than throw up our hands, the bioecological model and the PPCT model map out ways to isolate and analyze aspects of this sea of influences.

- Second, using the frameworks of these two models gives us a set of questions and issues we might explore to better understand what is possible when nurturing and supporting creativity in young children. Isolating our questions allows us to yield hopefully very practical avenues where we can stimulate, support, and nurture children's creativity and creative nature. Remember the PPCT Model when you have a child who seems stuck in their development or exhibits their creativity in ways that seem below their natural potential. There may be more avenues to influence their creativity when you think about all the dimensions of the PPCT model.

Making a Creative Environment

If environments are, in some way, creating children, we need to take a long and serious look at those environments. We want to understand what kinds of context best promote creativity in young children. Bita Garooei and Hamid Saghapour (2015) discuss the importance of providing children a free and independent living environment. Remember, this could be a preschool classroom, the children's section of your public library, your living room, or the basement of an in-home child care program. Early childhood educators and family members alike should consider the following when evaluating children's environments:

1. Does it provide children freedom and flexibility, or does it need to be reorganized?

2. Does it fulfill a child's basic needs for safety and security to explore their creative self?

3. Is it free from pressure, allowing for creativity to emerge on its own?

4. Does it foster meaningful social interactions between you as the early childhood educator and each child as well as among all the children?

5. Does it offer a variety of open-ended materials that invite exploration and risk-taking?

6. Does it provide opportunities for you to engage with parents/caregivers?

7. Does it celebrate a diversity of cultures and traditions?

Bronfenbrenner's bioecological model offers an opportunity to understand creativity within the spaces in which a child grows and develops. The environment should allow for both directed and spontaneous learning through a wide variety of activities and experiences: those that include touching and seeing, those that are indoors or outdoors, those done alone and with others, and those that involve physical, emotional, or intellectual challenges (Garooei and Saghapour 2015). Attention should also be provided to the relationship between the adult and the child (alluding again to the microsystem) in support of creative development.

Arthur Koestler (1968, 235) stated that "creative activity is a type of learning process where the teacher and pupil are located in the same individual." The "teacher and pupil" reminds us of the bidirectional relationship between an adult and child, how both teacher and pupil influence each other. Creativity is developed in environments that are open or rigid, leading to experiences that are enjoyable or painful. Creativity embraces it all. Therefore, creative development is a continuous cycle present throughout the lifespan of human development.

To understand the ecosystem of creativity, it is important to first ask what forces drive creativity within an ecosystem. The forces we discovered as part of the research for this book include genetics, life experiences, personal motivation, and interaction with others. Each of these driving forces influences the interactions within each ecosystem.

Conclusion

To summarize and provide a practical application of our exploration of the bioecological model, we developed the following table to summarize the connection between creativity and the four main ecosystems.

Table 4. The Bioecological Model and Creativity

Bioecological Model Layer	Creativity Connection
Microsystem	• The parental or caregiver relationship constructs the space for a child to be creative. • The environment must be positive and nurturing as this influences the child's relationships.
Mesosystem	• A child's creative experiences in a class or other learning environment can conflict with or be reinforced by what occurs at home.
Exosystem	• Creativity can be affected by measures outside of a child's control. The availability of social services in a community due to budget cuts will have an impact on the relationship between a parent/caregiver and child.
Macrosystem	• Children's varying experiences in culture and society can influence how creativity is defined, understood, and practiced. Educators should invest time to learn about the cultural systems in their class. • Children experiencing some kind of trauma (living in poverty, experiencing homelessness, and the like) may not have the same chances as other children to participate in creative experiences. When communicating with the family, it is critical to understand what they are experiencing and not to assume what they have or don't have, in order to assist and support them.
Chronosystem	• Children already have experience once they enter your doors. All experiences—positive or negative—influence a child's development.

Think about It

◉ Go through each of the systems of concentric circles (micro-, meso-, exo-, and macro-) and identify as specifically as you can at least three people or organizations *in your life* who would be part of that system. What did you include?

◉ For each of the people or organizations you noted, how would you describe your relationship with them on a scale of one to five, with one being "I hardly know them" and five being "close and personal"?

◉ What could you do to improve the relationships you have with the people or organizations you noted?

Part Two
Seven Big Ideas about Creativity

Now we are ready to present the heart of the book, seven Big Ideas that we believe will change how you think about creativity and how you understand your role as an educator or parent. We synthesized these ideas from our research, and they cover a lot of ground and look at creativity from many perspectives.

Chapter 4 is a biological viewpoint that quickly turns philosophical. If it is risky to put out ideas that might be controversial, this is the riskiest chapter. You will hear our insecurity in the voice of its narrative. The neuroscience viewpoint is discussed in chapter 5. Ever since the publication of *From Neurons to Neighborhoods* in 2000, the science of brain development has been required learning for anyone working with young children. What happens when we take a scientific look at creativity? Read about it in chapter 5. Then, chapter 6 looks at neurodiversity and its connection to invention. We show how so-called disabilities such as autism and ADHD can be understood and celebrated as unique gifts. In chapter 7, we tackle the unsettled question of whether creativity can be taught, and what role creativity can play as we lay out our learning environments and embark on the adventure of teaching. It is not a coincidence that chapter 8 looks at libraries, as one of the coauthors is a librarian. Libraries are one of many valuable institutions in the exosystem where creativity can be supported.

The last two chapters of this section look at two of the most salient issues in early childhood: equity and trauma. In the aftermath of George Floyd's murder and a global pandemic, no field of endeavor has escaped scrutinizing itself through these important lenses. Given creativity's centrality in everything we do, it has a key role in our understanding of the two Big Ideas in chapters 9 and 10.

Chapter Four   **Big Idea 1: Creativity as a Life-Force**

Evolution as a creative process

In this book we explore the role of creativity in the lives of young children. Throughout, we ground our ideas and suggestions in what we have read in theory and practice and science. This chapter is going to be more speculative, maybe more philosophical. We assert, as the title says, that creativity is a life-force. We are saying that creativity is connected to, and may in fact *be*, the life-giving energy that animates each of us, all of life, and maybe even all of matter.

Are you sure you want to read this chapter?

You will not find this idea echoed in most other books about creativity. Yet something about it felt true and important to us. We hope as you read this chapter, even if you don't agree with everything we say, you take away our core message that creativity is something essential in each of us, and it is absolutely necessary for us to grow and develop. And if it is true for us, then it is true for children. It may be true because creativity is a life-force, or it may be true for some other reason. Maybe it doesn't matter.

We stumbled across the idea of creativity as a life-force somewhat by accident, but its implications suggested something radical, something at the root of what we explore in the book. A life-force is something that resides at the very heart of our being and of all being. It's a big thing to say, maybe too big. But as we explored further, it seemed to us the foundation for a lot of what we talk about throughout this book. It helped us understand why creativity is so important. That excited us, and we wanted to describe our exploration in the hopes that it will excite you too.

When we write about "life-force," we refer to the idea that grounding all of life is an animating energy that flows in and around us. It is an idea that shows up in many forms in religion and sometimes even in science. Maybe it sounds kind of woo-woo, something we cribbed from the latest Star Wars spin-off. After all, it has been hard for Western science to get around ideas that may be more commonplace in the East, for example, the Taoist notion of chi or qi. To be sure, there is a strong scientific reflection that leads us to the idea that creativity is a life-force. But there is also a philosophical or even spiritual sense that is hard to see or understand.

Just because something is hard to see or understand doesn't mean it is not important. One of Fred Rogers's favorite quotes is a line by Antoine de Saint-Exupéry ([1943] 2000) in *The Little Prince*: "What is essential is invisible to the eye" (87). The life-force is invisible, like the wind. We can see its effects small and great in a gentle breeze or a destructive tornado: invisible to the naked eye but profoundly present. More than present, essential. The point is that we cannot rely only on what we see if we want to be aware of what is most important. As Saint-Exupéry also writes in the book, "It is only with the heart one can see rightly" (87). Perhaps creativity can only be seen with the heart.

Evolution and Creativity

We came to the connection between evolution and creativity in our reading of Jean Piaget. Piaget began his career as a biology student. In the early part of the twentieth century, he read the hot book of the time for his field of study, *Creative Evolution* by Henri Bergson. As editors Howard Gruber and J. Jacques Vonéche write in their book *The Essential Piaget* (1995),

> Bergson considered life as an absolute toward which the famous elan vital (life force) tends. This idea was revival of Aristotle's science of genera, according to which every object tends towards its natural local [*sic*] or site. . . . This is the philosophical and biological background against which Piaget developed his ideas throughout his life. . . . For Piaget, the notion of self-organization is centered around the idea of new possibilities opening up the systems. (865–66)

Bergson's concept of the *élan vital* (variously translated as *life-force*, *living energy*, or *vital impetus*) shaped Piaget's thinking about child development. The French words are also English words that add a rich connotation for us. *Élan* in English means an energy infused with enthusiasm, style, or even flamboyance. *Vital* means *of great importance* and is obviously connected to the Latin *vita* or *life*. We cannot help but imagine the innate enthusiasm of young children and understand its deep connection to vitality and life. In describing how this idea of a life-force influenced Piaget, Gruber and Vonéche write,

Piaget conceived of development as an assimilation of the external perturbations by the internal structures of the subject's mind. As opposed to Darwinian selection, Piaget's theory of development is assimilatory: there is no elimination, but a constant opening unto new possibilities. . . . There is an intelligence behind the scene as here is an intelligence behind the hand of the child arranging . . . wooden blocks. (866)

The point here is that Piaget, along with Bergson (maybe because of Bergson), rejected a mechanistic view of evolution as the gradual development of life into greater complexity and diversity of life-forms. Just as Bergson looked at the evolution of human consciousness as part of the same evolutionary process, Piaget saw this life-force as evident in how children express their intelligence and thinking.

This told us that we needed to look into Henri Bergson and *Creative Evolution*. When we did, we were astounded by implications for understanding creativity that were seldom discussed in any of our other research. And the ideas were profound.

In *Creative Evolution*, Bergson (1911) argues that we cannot really explain how evolution works—how it is that animals and plants regenerate themselves over time and also mutate and adapt to changes in their environment, or fail to adapt and die off like dinosaurs or woolly mammoths—simply by virtue of a mechanistic system. Evolution cannot just be a big machine that is mindlessly cranking away and moving all of life forward. Something else is going on to explain how this happens. Along with rejecting the idea, as he calls it, of radical mechanism, he also rejects "radical finalism." What he means is the idea that there must be something implicit in the very nature of animals and plants that moves them toward some final end. Bergson says that can't be how it works because there is too much that changes over time to have all that increased complexity and diversity somehow inherent at the beginning. Furthermore, nothing in the way that things change and evolve suggests it is ending or reaching some final point. It seems to keep going on and on.

Bergson then introduces the idea of the *élan vital* or life-force. What is driving life forward is this creative force, an energy that compels new manifestations, new ways of life expressing itself, new creations. Think about it: how are scientists still discovering new species of plants and animals? It may not be that we never saw them before. It may be that they were never there until now. When you add to this the notion that new forms of life come into being to better adapt to the environment, you have our two poles of creativity: originality and usefulness. This is creativity as evolution.

British management professor Stephen Linstead (2002) explains,

> It is the creative urge, for Bergson, not the Darwinian concept of natural selection . . . that is at the heart of evolution. . . . *Élan vital* is not to be thought of as organismic or personal property, but as immaterial force, whose existence cannot be scientifically verified but is nevertheless implied by all scientific endeavour, and provides the imperative that continuously shapes all life. (103–4)

There is a lot to unpack here. What Linstead first expresses is the idea that *élan vital* is not about natural selection in the evolution of life on our planet but a creative urge. The urge is what we would say is a desire for fulfillment, for full development, which is why we think creativity and child development are intrinsically connected. Linstead asserts that creativity is not "personal property." It is not about individual talent but how the energy of life in the world makes itself known in an individual child.

Since we will be coming back repeatedly in this chapter to the idea of a *life-force*, it may be useful to cement a few more Bergsonian ideas about "vital impetus" and what it is or how it acts. As Bergson understands it, this essential energy flowing through living matter is at the same time constrained by that matter. Energy compels movement and forward action and life itself, but in every case only to the extent that the body can actually complete that action. Energy may flow through an ant, but the ant is still only able to carry what it can carry or do what ants can do. And so it is with creativity as we experience it in young children. We are not waiting for them to become Picasso or Einstein; creativity is at work but within the limits of each individual child's capacity.

The implication for early childhood educators is to recognize the creative energy as something central, important, and essential that manifests itself within the unique container of each child. That is why we can say both that children are unlimited in their creativity and that they are random, chaotic, and immature in their creativity. Both are true. Our job is to increase the capacity of those children to give the creative energy inside them more space in which to work. And then to "educe" (the root word of *education*), or draw out, the individual expressions of the creative energy.

The idea of a life-force should not be new to early childhood educators. Friedrich Froebel, for example, believed there was a life-force that propelled the development of human beings. Froebel created his theory of education based, in part, on this idea of a life-force. In his book *The Education of Man* (Froebel 1885), he writes that it is the destiny of every living thing to develop in its true nature and identity, and that is no less true of human beings. He thought the ideal setting for early childhood education was the *kindergarten*, or the children's garden, where children are planted and cultivated, and then just grow. After all, farmers don't grow crops but only plant and tend to them—the plants grow on their own in response to the environment. Likewise, early childhood educators do not grow children but only nurture their growth. Children grow all by themselves, driven by inner forces.

Froebel believed that what propels us through this development is a self-active life-force. And the self-active nature of this energy is where we get the idea that child development is something that occurs naturally and that our role as early childhood educators is to guide, steer, collaborate with, and (sometimes) get out of the way of children to let them become themselves on their own as they are destined to do. This is why so much of early childhood education is understanding how a child is developing and then working in concert with that movement to support and enhance the inevitable growth forward.

What we postulate in this chapter is that perhaps that self-active life-force is what we mean by creativity. That energy that propels creation forward, starting with the single most powerful expression of energy ever known—the big bang—is still playing out in each person. The life-force fulfills the conditions necessary for creativity: uniqueness (in each person) and usefulness (in perpetuating life). Is it such a leap, therefore, to think of creativity as the power behind evolution, a process of the ever-changing unfolding of the true nature of things?

So what do we make of this in our quest to understand creativity and nurture it in young children? We think the implications are profound. It means that at the very core of life is a life-force pushing life forward, into its next new phase, into its next new expression. And that life-force is creativity, or at least an expression of creativity. And that life-force not only exists in humans but in all living things. Aldo Leopold (1986) argues in his environmental classic *A Sand County Almanac* that human beings are not *over* nature but *along with* nature. He justified that position by proposing that all of life had an animating spirit that propelled it forward. Animals and plants are living things that contain an *élan vital*.

Following this idea deeper, Carlo Rovelli (2014) helps us understand that anything made of atoms (everything, in other words) is made of things that constantly move and gesticulate. Like us, you probably learned in high school that atoms are composed of neutrons, protons, and electrons. What Rovelli tells us is that the electrons are in constant motion, creating electricity. Thus, nothing in life is still. Everything is always moving. And it moves by way of energy that fuels everything, including creativity. So this means everything is moving and vibrating and being creative. Plants and animals, and also rocks, desks, plastic, and concrete. Everything.

So, we wondered, could it be that creativity is the very force that makes up existence and life and evolution and the development of each child? Early in our research, we investigated to see if this was true. We came across nothing conclusive. These ideas are too abstract to be demonstrated or proven. But we became convinced that this idea, however true or not, is still useful. It is useful to consider that everything that is, and is becoming, is an expression of creativity. That idea changes how we look at our lives, the lives of others, the lives of children, and life itself. And in changing how you look at things, you change yourself. Every exploration, encouraged by curiosity, is also a creative act, engendering new ideas at a virtually constant rate. How do we catch that wave?

We have stressed throughout this chapter that we are playing with ideas that are more philosophy than science. One way we can show they are true is if they help us understand ourselves, others, and how we live and move in this world.

Why Do Bergson's Ideas Matter?

We've drawn several conclusions from Bergson surrounding his ideas about creativity as a life-force:

- Life is a creative process.

- Creativity is central to life.

- Creativity is a life-force that pushes evolution and development forward.

- The life-force within us and around us is the same life-force.

- The conflicts between science and intuition, between reason and imagination, stand in our way of understanding how best to teach children.

Let's explore these conclusions in greater detail and discuss their implications for early childhood educators, whether as parents, family members, or educators.

Life Is a Creative Process

Bergson was trying to show that an energy flowing in a progressive and positive direction underlies evolution. That energy is a creative life-force: it gives life to matter, and it pushes matter forward into expressions of life that are ever more complex and more diverse. To live is to create. This makes us bold to claim that life itself is a creative process, and that creativity is the essential fuel of life. That's a big statement with broad implications for anyone interested in nurturing creativity in young children.

First, this understanding of creativity should settle the "why" question once and for all. Creativity is connected to life and is therefore of fundamental importance. Recall in the first chapter how we showed that creativity is important because so many religions identify creativity with God or some other divine character or energy source, like the Force in Star Wars. Bergson never says the *élan vital* is God, but Froebel certainly says it comes from God. What these sources have in common is the belief that creativity is central to existence itself. Creativity is the foundation on which we understand ourselves and our life on earth. Perhaps, then, creativity is not just a domain in our state's early learning standards but the basis on which all education and child development resides. The care and education of young children is about recognizing and honoring a sacred life-force that is animating everything a child does and is and will become.

Second, we should look at creativity not as a talent or even a kind of consciousness but as the energy behind life. Thinking of creativity as energy helps us frame all children's energy as potentially creative. Something new and useful is about to take place. Where is it? How can we find it? How can we give it time and space to come into the light?

Third, and maybe less obvious, is the idea that if life is a creative process, being creative or nurturing creativity is not up to us. We are not responsible for making children creative. Our job is to notice their creativity, name it, and then get out of the way.

Creativity Is Central to Life

If creativity is central to every child, it means that all expressions of creativity—from artistic to problem solving to challenging authority—are a window into the creative energy that is present in children at all waking moments. The role of educators is to support or collaborate with this creative and evolutionary force that is shaping the child into who they will become. In concrete terms, you might do the following:

- Look for expressions of newness. They are an opportunity to see creativity.

- Expect the unexpected. If life is moving forward through a creative force, don't be surprised when it brings you new things. Embrace it and ask how it might lead to creative growth.

- As much as possible, align with the energy the children show up with. This often feels impossible, when it is time to go outside, be in a circle, get ready for bed. One reason countering behaviors emerge at these times is because you are inhibiting creative energy, and young children, with underdeveloped executive function, are at the mercy of that energy. Hopefully you can see the energy's positive source and look for redirection opportunities that still allow it to express itself.

- Understand that disruption is a necessary component of creativity, leading to new ideas, new direction, and new learning.

- Design activities that are both physical and cognitive. Don't treat them as separate things: all physical activities are cognitive activities, and vice versa.

Nurturing creativity in young children can happen at virtually any waking moment. Imagine a daily schedule in the life of children: where might moments to nurture creativity present themselves? Consider waking up, getting dressed, having breakfast, traveling to child care or preschool, the events at child care (circle time, center time, free play, outdoor play, snacktime), traveling back home, dinner, family time spent reading or playing, changing into nighttime clothes, brushing teeth, and nighttime rituals.

Each of these moments could nurture creativity if you do the following:

- Encourage curiosity and exploration.

- Add materials to the space where these events occur that inspire children to be creative (for example, bringing toys in the car or bath).

- Pay attention to what the child is focusing on during that time. Lean into that with questions and conversations that add information to feed their inquiries.

- Respond to activities by emphasizing what children are doing and how.

- Say to children often that making mistakes is helpful learning.

- Think about the overall schedule and ensure there is unstructured time.

Creativity Is a Life-Force That Pushes Evolution and Development Forward

We argued above that evolution is development. The word *evolve* literally means "to roll out." Recall how we mentioned in chapter 2 that the word *develop* means "to unwrap." *Develop* and *evolve* are describing the same thing—the ongoing and progressive coming into being of something.

Bergson proposed in *Creative Evolution* that there is an energy flowing in a progressive and positive direction that underlies evolution. And if that is true, then child development is also driven by the *élan vital* or life-force. It moves life forward, transforming life in the direction of newness and adaptability and greater complexity and flexibility. The life-force transforms children to be more fully developed across the classic physical, cognitive, social-emotional, and linguistic domains. Please don't ask us to prove to you that this is true. Rather, ask yourself, "*If* this is true, how might it change the way I think about child development and creativity?"

Creativity may be the force that propels the evolution of life forward. But it is also the force that propels the development of individual children forward. Piaget was getting at this when he thought of development as the assimilation of "perturbations" or mental uneasiness. That is the flow of development: equilibrium, disequilibrium, re-equilibrium. The causes of the uneasiness are assimilated. Though tears may be involved, this process is learning, developmental growth, and energy moving life to greater complexity and diversity. The energy driving the process is creativity. If so, can there be any part of teaching young children that is not about creativity?

We think it makes sense that the way life evolves on our planet is how we as individuals evolve: forever putting out new actions and ideas. If they are useful and achieve a desired purpose, they become a new part of you. As new parts are added, you grow and change, and the cycle begins all over again. Doesn't that describe creativity?

These ideas align with traditional understandings of child development. When you look at the nine principles of child development as laid out in the fourth edition of *Developmentally Appropriate Practices* (NAEYC 2022), as we did in chapter 2 with respect to creativity, we see a similar pattern linking child development to a life-force. As we have said in this chapter, that force, like child development, is dynamic, all-encompassing, life-giving, joyful, continuous, unfolding, and following an internal logic of its own.

Understanding the creative life-force that flows through every child makes a mockery of any special category that seeks to label children, such as "gifted and talented." Of course children differ. They have different capacities and opportunities to express the creative energy inside. But all children have pulsing through their cells a creative energy that is propelling them forward into life with greater complexity and diversity. That forward movement is true of evolution, it is true of development, and it is true of the growth of knowledge and learning. In every case, we are all moving from an initial state to a more advanced state.

The Life-Force within Us Is Also around Us

The *élan vital* that Bergson writes about is present in the entire evolutionary movement of life on earth, in each individual, and in how we think and learn. We should appreciate how creativity, as this life-force, makes us alive. It makes us human and makes children human. Sometimes children appear more human than we do because their expressions of that life-force are purer, less inhibited and constrained by social norms or behaviors. The nurturing of creativity must begin with a recognition of, maybe even a reverence for, the life-force in us and all around us. The life-force is creating all the time. Our cells are creating. Plants and animals are creating. At an atomic level, there is movement and energy and creating.

Being aware of this energy and movement, having a reverence for life, is the first step in nurturing creativity. We observe and acknowledge the life-force all around us, in children and in the world. This is one reason why outdoor learning is so important (Kinsner 2019). We are not learning about the outdoors; we are discovering our kinship with it. Like is meeting like.

As educators and parents/guardians supporting our children's development, we are collaborating with this force that wants to impel children forward in their growth. We must understand and value the *élan vital* as our coteacher and collaborator, know its strategies, techniques, and goals, so we can work in coordinated and complementary ways with it, bringing our curriculum, instruction, and assessment into harmony with it. If we can do that, we find that we are not doing all the work. Let the *élan vital* do the teaching for you. The life-force or creativity does the developing. Your job is to change, vary, and shape the circumstances and experiences, and to observe and document carefully what is happening. Much of teaching, therefore, is about discovering what is happening and determining how you can play a supportive role, using a light touch in method and approach.

The Conflicts between Science and Intuition, between Reason and Imagination, Stand in Our Way of Understanding How Best to Teach Children

A final implication of understanding creativity as a life-force is that it gives us a way to reconcile many of the paradoxes and contradictions in our field. Bergson realized that it was not simply a mechanism that was moving evolution but a dynamic energy that had to account for the variety and evident progression of the evolutionary project. He ultimately adopted a both/and approach that can give us some confidence that the polar opposites in early childhood education may be reconciled in the end. As Michael Vaughan (2007) argues, so much of nineteenth-century science was rooted in ideas of materialism and mechanism. This was what Bergson was pushing back against. "Those sciences," Vaughan writes, "that attempted to explain consciousness in purely physiological terms and those that attempted to explain life in purely physical and chemical terms are subject to extensive critiques in Bergson's work" (7).

Science and philosophy have different methods, but they both are trying to understand the world and our life in it. When they are put together, they can move us forward through discovery and invention. A logical idea may be true, but it needs scientific validation. A scientific fact is the beginning of our understanding, but it is almost never the final word. Teaching children to be learning beings means giving appreciation to insight and empirical detection—time for both and reflection on both. Children need time for imagination as well as time for reasoned inquiry.

The wisdom of taking a both/and approach in this and many other dichotomies in early childhood education returns us to the underlying idea many of us learned as "the whole child approach." Early childhood education understands that its work is not just stimulating knowledge learning but providing experiences that stimulate growth across all domains. The significance of this "approach" is that however adults may divide and compartmentalize a child's characteristics, they are fundamentally and primarily integrated into a single, whole child. It's impossible to parse out cognitive learning from social-emotional learning or physical learning from communication. Pulling out different domains and characteristics can be helpful for targeted interventions and to measure changes in development, but we must remember to put everything back together.

Conclusion

We warned readers at the beginning of this chapter that we were going to venture into a land of speculation, conjecture, and association. In fact, we have taken a creative approach to thinking about creativity. Our purpose here was to invite a broader consideration of creativity as somehow embedded in the very functions of life itself. Aristotle thought, very practically, that life was the capacity for self-sustenance, growth, and reproduction (Kenny and Amadio 2024). If we are living, we are growing. And growth, that movement forward, is driven by a life-force. We ask in this chapter: What if that life-force is creativity itself? If so, that would mean creativity is the energy that makes us grow and develop. It is the force that propels us into the next moment, into something new that has never existed before. It means that creativity is central to life.

This speculation was a genuine discovery for us. What turned it into a chapter and a Big Idea was how fundamental these ideas are and how exciting the implications. We could see the energies of young children as part of their life-force and therefore part of their creativity. We could imagine nurturing creativity as working with that energy to support a child's ongoing development and learning. We could see learning and creativity and development so intertwined they become inseparable. We can understand that the first step in nurturing creativity is to acknowledge the life-force that flows through us, the children in our care, and the world around us.

So we invite you to pick up where we left off, to explore the implications and rethink creativity and even early childhood education. How does your understanding of creativity change? How does your ability to see creativity in young children change? How do those changes affect your teaching and caregiving practices and how you might nurture creativity in young children?

Trust us, the rest of the chapters are quite different—less speculative and philosophical—but equally fascinating. Keep reading. Keep thinking. And keep noticing your every movement as a creative act.

Think about It

- Where do you see the *élan vital* in the lives of children you know? How does it manifest itself? How would you describe it?

- Next time the unexpected happens, reframe it immediately as something new and therefore something creative happening. How can you go with its energy so it leads you into something new *and* useful?

- All learning is creative because learning requires the individual construction of knowledge or insight. Check out a recent lesson plan (or just something you wish your child knew), and ask yourself: "What kind of creative process might be embedded in the learning I wish to take place?"

- The force driving life forward is invisible like the wind. We only "see" it by how it affects those things around us. Take a moment of quiet, focus on your breath, and ask yourself: "How is the life-force within me pushing me forward? Where is it taking me?"

Chapter Five

Big Idea 2:
The Neuroscience of Creativity

Networks and connections

The brain is one of the greatest mysteries of the human species. Over the centuries, it has attracted cross-disciplinary study among researchers as varied as neurologists, psychologists, and educators. As we mentioned in chapter 1, the idea that some people are creative and some are not is a myth. On some level, we are all artists. We are all creators. We need our collective creativity for our survival. We are in a new time when the study of neurology allows us to explore in detail the brain functioning of creativity (Park, Kim, and Hahm 2016, 110).

The first big idea was about the energy that is driving us forward in our development. It was global, universal. Now we want to ask: what's going on inside?

Creativity is a cognitive function. That means it is about something going on in the brain and its networks. In this chapter, we discuss why brain functions have more to do with the connectivity among different functional areas of the brain than they do with the areas themselves. Then we look at two important networks: the default network and the executive network, and their roles in creativity. Finally, we explore two additional neurological constructs that are related to creativity: divergent thinking and personality. Throughout, we pause to consider what this new knowledge may tell us about how best to nurture and support creativity in young children.

Brain Connections and Neural Networks

Although the brain does not include a creative area or a creative lobe, somewhere in all that gray matter, creativity is occurring. It does not occur somewhere specific in the brain but all over the brain. So creativity is not about an area of the brain but about how the brain is wired and connected. Originally, researchers thought about creativity as a function occurring in some part of the brain, as seems to happen with functions such as visual processing, executive function, and memory. More recently, researchers have suggested that the neuroscience of creativity is about brain *connections* (Beaty, Seli, and Schacter 2019). Likewise, recent research has shown that the phenomenon of memory cannot be adequately described without explaining brain connections.

We believe understanding the neural connectivity that is creative thinking is essential if we are to improve our abilities to nurture and support creativity, with its invaluable contribution to human development. We want to provide just enough information to explain clearly and thoroughly our understanding of the neuroscience of creativity. Bear with us if the going gets tough. We promise to show the relevant and practical connections of this information to the care and education you provide to young children. As you read this chapter, remember that creativity is how the brain works together, how it is connected (i.e., connectivity) and how it connects (i.e., flexibility) (Beaty 2020).

Recent advancing technology has improved how the brain is studied, most notably with brain imaging that allows us to see which parts of the brain are activated under particular circumstances. Sun-Hyung Park, Kwang Ki Kim, and Jarang Hahm (2016) reviewed theories of creativity from a neuroscientific lens. They listed the specific brain imaging techniques that provide a functional brain image and show electrical signals that indicate which brain areas are active during creative activity.

A few areas of the brain to understand within the context of creativity include the prefrontal cortex (known as the site of reasoning and executive function), the amygdala and hippocampus (known as the sites of emotional memory), and the brain stem (where gut responses that happen without thought or feeling occur). Each area does not work independently from the others. Rather, they rely on a communication system. Have you ever had the opportunity to complete an electric circuit? You connect wires together to ensure that electricity flows from some source of energy to some device so that it properly functions, for example, lighting a light bulb. Those connections are like the communication channels between discrete parts of the brain. That communication causes the activation of an area of the brain to support a specific function. Just as complete circuits are necessary to light a light bulb, circuits are needed to connect parts of the brain. It turns out that those connections are more important to creative functioning than any specific area of the brain.

So why do we say the connections are so important? Creativity is a complex process, and we should expect that any complex activity uses more than one part of the brain (Sporns 2013). Even the discrete parts of the brain like the cerebral cortex or amygdala are themselves dense clusters of neural webs—that is, networks of neural connections. As the brain grows during the first three years of life, the number of neurons and therefore neural connections explodes: more than a million new neural connections form every second in the first years of life (Center on the Developing Child 2015). These connections are stimulated by the experiences children have. The more stimulation, the more connections.

Play is a noteworthy example of exercising these all-important neural connections. Stephen Siviy (2016) writes that when a child plays, their brain is activating the prefrontal cortex along with the amygdala and the hippocampus, connecting executive function and reason with emotions and memory. Play connects thinking and feeling, one reason it may promote healthy development.

When people are creative, a number of brain networks are activated. Two main networks dominate: the default network and the executive network. Sometimes these networks work together in the brain, sometimes one after the other.

Default Network

The default network is the neural system the brain defaults to when you are doing nothing. The default network brain areas show increased activity when a person isn't focused on what is happening around them. They're daydreaming. We often don't notice when our default network is operating, because to pay attention to it would be to engage parts of the brain that are not part of the default network. It is the brain functioning that occurs when you are doing "mindless" daily tasks like taking a shower, drifting off to sleep, or driving to work as you do every day. Your mind wanders and you think about something other than what you are doing.

When people are in a default state, the brain does not stop working, but rather different parts are activated. Even though cognitive activity in this mode seems passive, the brain is working a lot, specifically the medial prefrontal cortex, posterior parietal cortex, and temporoparietal junction. The temporoparietal junction is where the temporal and parietal lobes meet. It is where the brain incorporates information from the thalamus (a relay station for general connectivity and processing) and the limbic system (involving emotions, memory, behavior, and smell) as well as from the visual, auditory, and somatosensory systems (Guy-Evans 2023a; Guy-Evans 2023b). The point of identifying these brain areas is simply to stress that when you are in a default state, your brain is still active—you're just not thinking about it. It's like "back office" work. This is not part of the operation where clients are engaged, where executives meet and strategize, where goods are produced, or where services are delivered. This is where paper gets shuffled, records get filed, and accidental connections are made around the water cooler. In short, it doesn't look like a lot is happening, but it *is*, and it is important for creativity.

What does the default network look like for young children? You may be thinking, when are children *not* in the default mode? It's true they are more often in default mode than adults. That's because when we are not in default mode, we are instead in executive mode, which depends a lot on the prefrontal cortex. We are focused and getting things done (like a good executive!). The young child's brain has a much less developed prefrontal cortex, so they tend to be in the default state. Maybe that's why children seem to be more creative than adults. While it is frustrating if you are trying to get children to do something or pay attention or sit still, never forget that important things and rich prospects for creative work happen while they are in the default mode. Giving unscheduled time or opportunities for free exploration can provide special time for the default network. Even letting children be bored is good, because boredom is another feature of the default network. With a little time and patience, creative ideas that capture their interest often emerge.

The default mode is about daydreaming and wondering. Fred Rogers wrote a song that asks, "Did you know that it's all right to wonder?" (Rogers 1979). In it, he asks this question and two others: "Did you know that it's all right to marvel? . . . Did you know when you wonder you're learning? . . . Did you know when you marvel you're learning?" This is Mr. Rogers's full-throated endorsement of the default network, wondering and marveling about the world. The song's pivot on the double meaning of wonder (to be curious about or ask questions and to be awestruck and amazed) is exactly the movement from default to discovery.

Gregg Behr and Ryan Rydzewski (2021) took the title of their book *When You Wonder, You're Learning* from Rogers's song. They write that the song was inspired by time Fred spent with his grandfather, who never tired of answering his questions or supporting young Freddy's curiosity. Behr and Rydzewski mention research that shows how curiosity primes the brain for learning. They suggest that curiosity is nurtured when adults pay close attention to what children are curious about. In a later chapter on creativity, they suggest having "What now?" time when there is no clear agenda and no distractions. Just sit together and ask, "What can we do together during these next thirty minutes?" (70). See more ideas in the sidebar below.

In your practice, think about whether your learning environment (classroom space, library/museum space, or in-home learning space) allows for wondering and daydreaming. Ask yourself,

1. Does the learning environment allow children time to wonder?

2. Is the learning environment more structured, more unstructured, or a little bit of both?

3. Is the learning environment set up for collaborative opportunities for children to problem solve together?

Besides daydreaming, wondering, and curiosity, another word we can add to default network experiences is *exploration*. Scott Barry Kaufman (2020) writes, "Engaging in exploration allows us to integrate novel or unexpected events with existing knowledge and experiences, a process necessary for growth" (93). Providing children the opportunity to explore results in new experiences for them. Exploration connects to a personality trait strongly correlated with high levels of creativity: openness to experience.

Our key point is that the default network, while passive on the surface, is quite active and very useful for creativity. Kaufman (2020, 110) actually prefers the term *imagination* network to *default* because that name highlights its role in creativity.

Here are five ways to encourage daydreaming and wonder in your environment:

1. Take children outside to wonder and explore the environment around them.

2. Build in pause time throughout the day for children to rest from thinking.

3. Create a journal for children to write down, draw, or dictate to you what they are wondering or pondering.

4. Integrate yoga and mindfulness activities that encourage children to rest their brains from thinking.

5. Leave out paper and crayons and encourage children to draw what they are wondering.

As important as the default network is, it never operates by itself. Creativity comes through the default network working together with the executive network. Remember when we said that the default network helps explain why we get our best ideas in the shower or driving to work or right before we fall asleep? These creative ideas seem to pop into our minds when we are thinking about something else. Thank the default network for that. But when we think, "Wow! Cool idea!" we have shifted to the executive network.

Executive Network

The executive network is also a neural system of connected brain areas, but it engages different parts to perform different functions. Executive network functions are goal-directed tasks, problem solving, and abstract reasoning. When this network is activated, the lateral and parietal prefrontal cortex parts of the brain are the most active. When you look at a diagram of these brain networks, you can see that some of these areas overlap (see figure 2). Sometimes the same part of the brain is active when performing two radically different functions: daydreaming and abstract reasoning. It goes back to our main point: we have to pay attention to how parts of the brain are connected. The bottom line is that when the brain is engaged in acts of creativity, both networks are engaged, switching back and forth. Flexible thinking—going back and forth and engaging different networks in rapid succession—makes for powerful creative thinking.

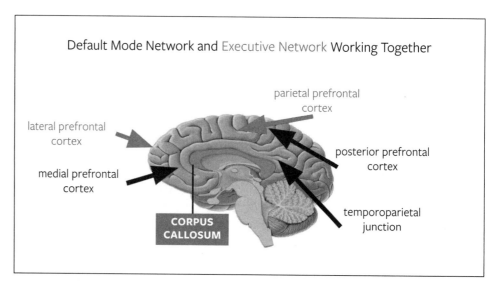

Figure 2. Default Mode Network and Executive Network Working Together. Gray arrows indicate executive mode. Black arrows indicate default mode.

Executive function helps young children manage behavior, prioritize actions, and follow directions. If you know some younger children who can't do these things, it is because their executive network is still developing. Some experts call executive function the brain's control tower (Center on the Developing Child 2011). Strengthening the capacity of this network is essential for functioning in social environments like school. It involves not just management of emotions but active decision-making, like making the choice to "use your words." Play and games (think Simon Says or Red Light, Green Light) aid in the development of executive function because success in the game requires you to decide quickly to stop or go while paying attention to the traffic signal. A lot has been written about executive function and its importance, and many early educators and caregivers are already doing a lot to encourage its development (see, for example, Galinsky 2010*).

Brain Networks Working Together

The default and executive networks work together when we are creative. Some of the research around this is fascinating. Melissa Ellamil and her colleagues (2012) asked fifteen undergraduates to design and evaluate book cover illustrations. When scanning their brains, they found that creative generation (coming up with ideas) was associated with use of the medial temporal lobe and that creative evaluation (evaluating the ideas) was associated with joint recruitment of executive and default network regions. You might expect that the default network connected with creation and the executive network with evaluation, and that did happen. But what was interesting was that the evaluation piece employed both networks. The authors conclude, "What creative individuals may share in common is a heightened ability to engage in contradictory modes of thought . . . and deliberate and spontaneous processing" (1791–92). Mental agility is key.

Or take Charles Limb and Allen Bruan's (2008) study of jazz improvisation. They looked at brain activity while musicians played prepared and improvised jazz music. Their study shows that both networks are used when playing each type of music, but improvisation relies more on the default network. This study was replicated with rappers with the same results (Liu et al. 2012). These researchers noted that the engagement of the executive network seemed to be

---

* Galinsky's book (2010) contains excellent suggestions for building executive function skills, which we think would do well in supporting the development of creativity. See especially chapter 1 and pages 41–62 on skill building for focus, self-control, cognitive flexibility, working memory, and inhibitory control.

around intention to act (such as performing). These creative acts activate many parts of the brain—for example, those that deal with motivation, emotion, and motor function—not just the default network. What these studies tell us is that both networks are active at different times for different functions but are coordinated in the brain for a single purpose. The interplay between the networks is as important as what the networks themselves are doing.

At this point in the chapter, let's summarize our thinking about why this matters to educators and caregivers interested in creativity. Boosting, supporting, and encouraging creativity is not only—or even mainly—about engaging in so-called creative activities. Nurturing creativity means doing "regular activities" (any activity) while being aware of their creative dimensions and adjusting the circumstances so creative thinking is needed or rewarded. You can also design activities where both default and executive networks come into play. By doing so, you engage these two important brain areas *together*. You are combining the executive network with the default network, intuition with reasoning, focus with letting your mind go.

Creativity and the Generation of Ideas

Creative people are good at generating new ideas. One sign of that ability is the presence of divergent thinking. J. P. Guilford stated, "To live is to have problems and to solve problems is to grow intellectually" (1967, 12). Guilford looked at the two ways we solve problems by our thinking: convergently and divergently. We are either narrowing down a specific solution to the problem (convergent thinking) or widening out to consider lots of different kinds of solutions (divergent thinking). Divergent thinking emphasizes originality. In contrast, "convergent thinking is oriented toward deriving the single best (or correct) answer to a clearly defined question" (Cropley 2006, 391).

One can see how both these approaches are needed to solve any variety of problems. Some problems have only one solution, and convergent thinking will help you find it. Other problems have many solutions, and divergent thinking will help you come up with those. The route to those two ends goes in different directions. Divergent thinking is most associated with creative thinking, though James Kaufman (2016, 23) points out that convergent thinking requires us to select the best solutions from among a set of alternatives and thus seems like a creative act.

For our purposes here, suffice it to say that divergent thinking is part of creativity, and we can equally stress divergent as well as convergent thinking in our teaching. It seems a healthy habit to think of problems as having multiple answers and to imagine different possibilities when faced with challenges.

Creativity and Personality

Personality as a psychological construct has been analyzed increasingly under the microscope of neuroscience as technology and diagnostics have improved. Therefore, as we look at the neuroscience of creativity, we ask how our ideas about personality might inform our understanding of creativity. Personality is a "pattern of characteristic thoughts, feelings, and behaviors, that distinguishes one person from another and that persists over time and situations" (Phares 1986, as quoted in Runco 2007, 280). The two keys of this definition are the words *pattern* and *persist*. In a sea of possible human behaviors and brain processing, when certain characteristics show up with regularity or consistency, we have the makings of a personality. Temporary mood swings or a quixotic outburst don't count. So, what are the characteristics identified in personality that connect to creativity? When we asked that question, it led us to the Big Five model of personality.

The Big Five personality traits began with psychologist Gordon Allport, who in 1936 identified over four thousand personality traits (Allport and Odbert 1936). Following Allport, psychologist Raymond Cattell used a statistical method called *factor analysis* to see how various personality characteristics clustered with one another. In the 1940s, he developed a construct that had sixteen personality factors (Cattell 1978). In 1949 psychologist Donald Fiske and colleagues narrowed it down to five personality traits (Fiske 1949; Vinney 2018):

1. Surgency (or extroversion)

2. Agreeableness

3. Conscientiousness

4. Emotional stability (vs. neuroticism)

5. Openness/Intellect

Think of these as dimensions that could be assessed along a scale or continuum for each person, some exhibiting more of a trait, others less. That composite describes their personality. Each of these is important, but the trait of openness/intellect supplies key reasons why some individuals may be more creative than others. When tests identified individuals with specific characteristics associated with the openness/intellect trait, these people also tended to score higher on creativity tests. The personality trait openness/intellect includes a predisposition to engage with aesthetic and sensory information (openness) and a predisposition to engage with abstract or intellectual information (intellect), combining into a trait labeled *cognitive exploration* (DeYoung, 2015). It may be helpful to think of openness/intellect as a continuum between inventive/curious and consistent/cautious.

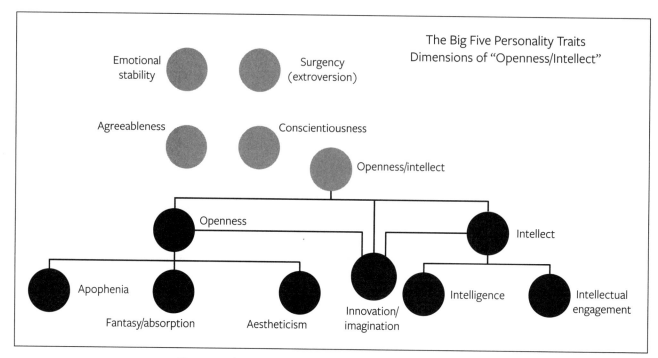

Figure 3. The Big Five Personality Traits

Figure 3 unpacks all the relevant characteristics or traits associated with openness/intellect. Notice how innovation/imagination lies between openness and intellect, as if it must draw on both to be realized. Notice too how it is the only characteristic that combines both these aspects. People with the innovation/imagination characteristic explore the world in two ways: "What can I perceive?" and "What can I intellectually figure out?" Those two approaches are themselves made up of a cluster of behaviors or thinking patterns. Openness is associated with characteristics like apophenia (the tendency to connect things or see patterns in things that are not related or are random), fantasy/absorption, and aestheticism (preference for artistic expression.) Intellect is high when a person exhibits strong traits of intelligence and intellectual engagement (Oleynick et al. 2017). We said earlier in this chapter that creativity and intelligence are related, but not completely. The diagram now provides a model for what is missing, namely, cognitive exploration and openness to experience. So we have three arrows all pointing to Innovation/imagination, or basically, creativity. Scott Barry Kaufman spins this a bit differently but perhaps more compellingly. As he explained to Sam Harris (2020) in a podcast interview,

Intelligence I view as the . . . ability to apprehend and perceive what is. . . . I define imagination as the ability to apprehend and perceive what could be. . . . I actually view creativity as the combination of both intelligence and imagination. So creativity is having the ability to apprehend what is and really learn and understand the real, true nature of the world without any prior beliefs or biases. But we have to go beyond that for creativity. We also have to have that foresight into what society could be, what humans could become. (6:17)

What we find interesting and important in this figure is that it describes creativity as the combination of two unrelated things, perhaps not unlike *newness* and *utility*. We can see at the lowest levels of the figures more aspects associated with creativity (e.g., apophenia, fantasy/absorption, aestheticism, intelligence, and intellectual engagement). Understanding all these dimensions of innovation/intelligences provide educators with additional levers to pull in identifying and nurturing the creative impulse in children.

The broader point here is that the openness/intellect trait, and its association with creativity, explains and expands our understanding of creativity from a psychological perspective. Seeing these larger, more universal traits as themselves made up of other kinds of traits, helps us understand creativity as something that originates with an openness to new ideas and therefore an exposure to new ideas. And yet that alone is not sufficient according to these personality inventories, because it also includes the "intellect" part, which fosters a level of critical thinking and problem solving. As well, openness allows us not to get caught into ruts, but instead, because we tend to be open and accepting of new experiences, we are more resilient and adaptable. When we shut down or insist there is only one way of seeing something or believing something, that is the very impulse that works against creativity. Intellect because the essential tool to navigate our understand that enables change and integration of new thoughts into our current mindset. We hope you see how in the collision between *openness* and *intellect* in the label we put on this Big Five trait there is the root of our creativity definition: newness and utility. And here it is buried in this thread of scholarly inquiry around what are the fundamental dimensions of the human character.

Take a moment to reflect on the following examples that connect openness/intellect to an early learning environment. As you reflect, think about if/how children participate in the following activities:

- A child is able to generate new ideas from piecing together building blocks.

- A child is curious about how something such as a clock works.

- A child gravitates toward artistic activities such as craft time.

- A child has a high need for using their active imagination, for example, enjoying making up fictional stories.

- A child enjoys activities that are culturally focused, such as learning dances from across the world.

Also reflect on connections to cognition exploration. Think about the following as you assess your program environment:

- Do you offer children opportunities to explore their surroundings?

- Do you offer children opportunities to wonder and ponder freely?

- Do you offer children opportunities to make their own decisions and choices to help them explore different problem-solving techniques?

Openness/intellect plugs into inquiry-based learning. Inquiry-based learning is an active learning process that encourages children to engage through questioning, testing, and exploring ideas (Lee et al. 2004). Independent investigation is what cognitive exploration looks like when it is put into practice. And if you think young children are too young for independent investigation, read *Young Investigators: The Project Approach in the Early Years* (Helm, Katz, and Wilson 2023) or *The Project Approach for All Learners: A Hands-On Guide for Inclusive Early Childhood Classrooms* (Beneke, Ostrosky, and Katz 2018). Also check out our case study of Kids World in chapter 11.

We contend that inquiry-based learning connects to creativity through questioning, reflecting, evaluation, and construction. Ask yourself:

- Do my students have the opportunity not only to ask questions but also to carry on discussions?

- Do my students have the opportunity to discover where to access the knowledge they need (with emphasis on the available resources in the learning environment)?

- Do the resources they locate help them answer questions they are pondering and also lead to new questions for them to explore in the future?

- Do I ask my students *why* they answered a question the way they did or *how* they solved a problem?

- Do I provide students the time to evaluate, rediscover, assess, and analyze?

A study from Ju-Hui Wei, Hsueh-Hua Chuang, and Thomas J. Smith (2022) draws attention to the importance of school culture in supporting children's openness to creative solutions. This fits our belief in the importance of context (such as the bioecological model) where the relationships among educators, student, family, and community shape and are shaped by school culture. Clearly, psychological safety in that culture is paramount. School culture needs to be open to creative problem solving and solutions. Educators and children don't solve problems when their solutions are disregarded.

In our research, we discovered the following tips and resources to continue to support creative development:

- **How to Nurture Creative Minds (Resource from Bright Horizons)**. Some of the tips Bright Horizons suggests include spending time outdoors, implementing verbal activities, adding downtime, and asking thought-provoking questions. *www.brighthorizons.com/family-resources/nurturing-creativity-and-imagination-for-child-development*.

- **How to Nurture Creativity in Children and Yourself (Resource from HealthyChild.com)**. Some tips include allowing for creative freedom, setting an example of a creative person in action, focusing on values not rules, and making sure you have a vision. *www.healthychild.com/the-top-10-ways-to-nurture-creativity-in-your-children-and-yourself*.

- **How Families Can Support Creativity at Home (Resource from Scary Mommy.com)**. This website recommends making sure supplies are easily accessible, giving children free time and space, asking questions about their creations, and role modeling what it is to be creative. *www.scarymommy.com/nurture-childrens-creativity-home*.

Conclusion

Key to creativity from a neuroscience perspective is its use of connections and flexibility in the brain. That tells us a lot about how to nurture and support creativity in learning environments. Backed by brain science, administrators need to recognize creativity's centrality to learning and development. To do this effectively, administrators and educators should work together to support and foster opportunities to incorporate creativity into the curriculum. In addition, administrators need to lean on educators, children, and families in developing a creative ecological system (as discussed in chapter 3).

Think about It

- When in your typical day are you in default- or executive-mode thinking?

- Creativity is when openness to experience meets the intellect. How might you support the development of those two traits in the children in your care?

- Ask your children what questions they have about the world. Then follow the recommendations in *Young Investigators* to design experiences during which they answer those questions for themselves.

- We included a number of reflective questions in this chapter to help you think more deeply about how these ideas can inform your caregiving and education tasks. Look them over again, especially on pages 69, 75, and 76, and see how you would now answer them.

Chapter Six

Big Idea 3: Creativity and Neurodiversity

How neurodiversity drives human invention

Statistically speaking, one in ten children could be diagnosed as having a disability (Zablotsky et al. 2023). What qualifies as a disability, or what is sometimes referred to as an *exceptionality*, varies considerably. When the US Congress passed the Individuals with Disability in Education Act (IDEA) in 1975, the law specified with great clarity what constitutes a disability, allowing qualifying students to receive special education funding. A child has the right to receive special services if there is a learning disability or a health impairment, which can include physical and mental disabilities. For a child to be eligible for services, they must have a specific plan to address their specific disability. It must be based on a credible and substantial assessment or evaluation. And the plan must be implemented, as much as possible, in the setting the child would be in (home with a parent or caregiver, at child care, in preschool) if they were not receiving special educational services.

Some of the most common disabilities reported are neurological conditions—things like autism spectrum disorder (ASD) and attention-deficit/hyperactivity disorder (ADHD). More recently, the educational field has begun using the term *neurodiversity*. Nicole Baumer and Julia Frueh (2021) define the term as "the idea that people experience and interact with the world around them in many different ways" (para. 2). The term is meant to highlight the fact that different forms of neurological processing do not necessarily signal a deficiency. Indeed, some neurological differences allow individuals to exhibit exceptional abilities.

Our research uncovered that neurodiversity may be a key, or even *the* key, to major breakthroughs in human invention. Human invention requires creativity. We conclude in this chapter that neurodiversity is linked to some of the most important forms of creativity, those that have led to extraordinary progress and inventions throughout human history. This conclusion leads us to wonder how children who present with neurodivergent thinking in classrooms, in libraries, in child care environments, and at home may be harnessing the ability to make important contributions to society because their brains operate differently than others'. In nurturing creativity, do we take seriously the children who think differently and therefore do not fit into predictable patterns of thought, sensory processing, and behavior? Do we consider that they may need support for their true gifts to become apparent?

There are many forms of neurodiversity, but in this chapter we will look at two common ones: autism and ADHD. We will explore ideas about the relationship between these neurological conditions and creativity. We will also unpack what we think are the implications of the relationship between neurodiversity and creativity. Through a personal story by Zach, we will discuss how we often "support" children with disabilities in ways that inhibit creativity and creative expression. We conclude with some thoughts about how best to support children who exhibit some of the behaviors and idiosyncrasies of these conditions.

Autism

The American Academy of Pediatrics (AAP) describes autism spectrum disorder (ASD) as a "neurologically based disability that affects a child's social skills, communication and behavior" (AAP 2023, para. 1). It is a developmental disability that interferes with a child's social skills, including how they interact and communicate with others. The idea of a spectrum suggests a range of symptoms and severity of those symptoms. ASD is found in 2.5 percent of children. Young children who have been diagnosed with ASD display a range of symptoms that appear as antisocial, such as not paying attention to others, not making eye contact, not using facial expressions, or not reading or understanding the facial expressions of others. They may be very fussy or very quiet and have difficulty establishing and keeping friendships (Rosenblatt and Carbone 2019).

Unique brain circuitry may explain behavioral differences as well as creative expressions. As we learned in chapter 5, brain circuitry explains creative thought and the emergence of new ideas. What if genetics predisposes some of us to have unique brain circuitry, emerging as part of an evolutionary process that ensured that human beings survived during their first one hundred thousand years on earth?

Our first exposure to this idea came in an interview we listened to on *The Psychology Podcast*, hosted by Scott Barry Kaufman (2021). He interviews noted autism researcher Simon Baron-Cohen. In the episode, Baron-Cohen describes why he believes that autism drives human invention. He explains that while the use of tools by early hominids (that is, our evolutionary ancestors between apes and ourselves) has been established by the archaeological record, their level of innovation was relatively simple and static.

The archaeological record shows that once *Homo sapiens* emerged on the scene about seventy to one hundred thousand years ago, we see the rapid increase of more sophisticated tools. (Recall that the Latin word *sapiens* means *wisdom* or *intelligence*. Human beings were the smart hominids.) Baron-Cohen says that "generative invention" came about because of "a cognitive revolution in the brain" (Baron-Cohen 2022, 3:20, 3:38). This change in brain circuitry allowed for what he calls the "systemizing mechanism," a brain connection that makes it possible to identify IF-AND-THEN patterns in our daily lives. If you can identify these patterns, then you can replicate them in some way to confirm that the pattern is trustworthy.

Observing a pattern allows us to do two things: (1) repeat the pattern to confirm that we are getting the same results; and (2) change the IF (the input) or change the AND (whatever operation we are doing), and then see how the THEN (the result) is different. Typically, we change either the IF or the AND, not both, so we know exactly what is causing the change we observe in the results. If a new result occurs, Baron-Cohen says that is an invention.

Simon Baron-Cohen uses the examples of making a shell necklace, a bone flute, and a bow and arrow. Each of these inventions or creations can be described using the IF-AND-THEN pattern.

- *If* I make a hole in ten shells *and* pass a thread through the holes of all the shells, *then* I will make a necklace (71,000 years ago).

- *If* I attach an arrow to a stretchy fiber *and* release the tension in the fiber, *then* the arrow will fly (70,000 years ago).

- *If* I blow down this hollow bone *and* cover up one of the holes, *then* I will make a certain sound (40,000 years ago).

In the case of the bone flute, when two holes were covered, the sound changed, giving us another IF-AND-THEN pattern: *if* I blow into the bone *and* I cover up two holes, *then* I get a different sound. Baron-Cohen is saying that when these inventions show up in the archaeological record, their emergence suggests a neurodivergence was occurring in the brains of these *Homo sapiens* that allowed them to recognize the patterns of systemizing in ways their hominid forebears couldn't do. The new ability makes possible inventions that multiply and progress at a rapid rate, with cave paintings, sculpture, agriculture, and on and on.

To prove the links between pattern recognition, the systemizing mechanism circuitry, and autism, Baron-Cohen (2020; 2022) did a study with six hundred thousand people. Each of these individuals was tested using a questionnaire to assess the number of autistic traits they manifested. What he found was that those individuals who worked in STEM (science, technology, engineering, and math)-related fields were more likely to exhibit autistic traits. He built on this dataset by having subjects take two additional questionnaires, one to assess empathy and another to assess systemizing traits. The sample was divided into five groups running along a continuum between more systemizing or more empathy traits. What they found was that individuals with more autistic traits based on the questionnaire were far more likely to be among the systemizing or extreme systemizing groups. Using some additional genetic mapping data, he found that genes associated with systemizing and genes associated with autistic traits were more likely to overlap in a single individual, suggesting that some genes associated with autism were also allowing higher systemizing and pattern recognition.

It stands to reason that different brains allow people to think differently, and that these differences invariably result in original thoughts. We recently had a chance to talk with a father about raising his adopted son who had been diagnosed with both autism and ADHD. He told us that Noland (not his real name) was challenging to raise because he had an extreme temper that operated on a hair trigger. If Noland did not get what he wanted, he could be very violent, throwing things and destroying objects. The father also told us that Noland had early alpha-betic and numeric knowledge, could count to one hundred in preschool, and was reading before kindergarten. Above all, he was fascinated by machines and trains. He would line up his toys in rows and loved playing with marble mazes and Lego bricks. He was very visually oriented. Here we see the same correlation between autism and systemizing that Baron-Cohen talked about.

Noland's father said that only through slow trial and error were they able to find the right level of medication, behavioral therapy, and environmental adjust-ments for Noland to function. Eventually school was too much of a struggle, so Noland's parents homeschooled him while still receiving support from the local school district's special education services. His father was quick to praise the school for its support, so much so that he, a former advertising executive, became a full-time special education aide in the same elementary school Noland had attended. But Noland's interest in trains remained unabated even at age seventeen. He and his father once drove across several states to retrieve a discarded signal bell Noland had observed on a YouTube channel dedicated to railroad crossings. Patterns and systems continued to light up special parts of Noland's brain through his teenage years and into young adulthood.

Noland's experience reminds us that we cannot treat the connection between neurodiversity and creativity too idealistically. We do not suggest that neurodiversity comes without real challenges nor that creativity inevitably comes to the surface so that it renders the socioemotional adjustment in relationship to others or education experiences inconsequential. Autism is a serious issue and can still be disruptive to individual and family life despite having the potential to trigger high levels of human invention. But Noland is, arguably, a creative genius. And we need a world where that is recognized and celebrated.

Nurturing Creativity in Autistic Children

Some professionals in the field advocate for using a strengths-based approach in supporting children on the autism spectrum. Laurent Mottron (2017), for example, says that the focus by early interventionists on three issues—socio-communicative behaviors, a lack of consideration of autistic language development and learning modes, and a negative view of repetitive behaviors and restricted interests—is not helping young children who present with autistic symptoms. Instead, he encourages interventions that work with and support the way children with autism communicate rather than making them communicate in more commonplace ways. For example, he says some of these interventions that focus on rigorous behavioral training such as requiring eye contact are unnecessary if we conclude that eye contact is not essential for communication. All communication exchanges require some level of accommodation on both sides of the dyad. He argues that children with autism can learn to communicate, but it may not be in the same way as other children. So what? We can build on where the child is, moving with their development. And why, he asks, is there such a fixation on changing the behavior of children with autism who only want to do one thing or focus on one topic area? Trains and machines helped unlock much of Noland's potential. Why should that be changed?

Mottron (2017) points out that the current approach to treating a child with autism is based on changing them—making them conform, suppressing repetitive behaviors, and intervening in "obsessive" interests. Discussing Mottron's article, a Harvard Medical School blog post (Harvard Medical School 2017) suggests that we appreciate the difference between *typical* and *functional* and that we should be leveraging difference rather than trying to extinguish it. It may be the case that what is most annoying and challenging to you as a caregiver or educator is holding the secret for reaching the child who may seem unapproachable in other ways. The blog post ends with a quote from autism expert and animal rights activist Temple Grandin (herself an autistic person who often speaks of preferring animal companionship). "The focus," Grandin says, "should be on teaching people with autism to adapt to the social world around them while still retaining the essence of who they are" (para. 12).

ADHD

Edward Hallowell and John Ratey's (2011) best-selling book on ADHD, *Driven to Distraction*, opens with the sentence "Once you catch on to what this syndrome is all about, you'll see it everywhere." They immediately go on to describe behaviors we see all the time in people we meet, such as being manic or hyper or "creative but unpredictable," connecting ADHD with creativity from the very beginning of their book (3).

Pediatricians Mark Wolraich and Joseph Hagan (2019, 8) define ADHD as "developmentally inappropriate attention and/or hyperactivity and impulsivity so pervasive and persistent as to significantly interfere with a child's life." ADHD is more common than autism, affecting as many as 9.4 percent of children, making it among the most common "chronic childhood disorders" (Wolraich and Hagan 2019, 3). And that only includes those formally diagnosed with the condition.

What would cause ADHD to interfere with a child's life? For one, the symptoms of inattention, impulsiveness, and hyperactivity can make children hard to manage and make it a challenge to maintain routines of daily life. Children diagnosed with ADHD typically must have three characteristics that present themselves: (1) they exhibit inattentive, impulsive behavior that is not age appropriate; (2) the behavior leads to chronic problems in daily functioning; and (3) the behavior is the child's usual way of acting (Wolraich and Hagan 2019, 8).

Key to this definition is the phrase "developmentally inappropriate." That means these behaviors fall outside the scope of what is typical for a child of a given age. That's why ADHD is not usually or should not be diagnosed for any child under the age of four. Symptoms of attention-deficit disorder, such as fidgeting, squirming, having trouble waiting for a turn, having a poor sense of physical boundaries, exhibiting destructive behavior, or showing symptoms for hyperactivity disorder, such as spaciness, daydreaming, and the slow processing of information, are typical behavior for many young children. Behaviors are not issues until they become issues for someone. When that line is crossed between "That's just who they are" to "Is something going on with them that we need to do something about?" is not always obvious. And who gets to decide that line has been crossed is often unclear and hotly contested.

The causes of ADHD are largely genetic and are lumped in with variations in children's temperament. Environment undoubtedly plays a role, but as we have learned in recent years from neuroscience, that role is often to trigger a genetic predisposition. ADHD, like autism, is present in children along a continuum of expression from very mild symptoms to quite severe and disruptive behaviors. One reason doctors think it is genetic is that it seems to be related to the unusual presence or absence of certain brain chemicals. When medications are prescribed, they often bring symptoms under control effectively.

The use of medication for ADHD and autism is commonplace. While we agree that overmedicating or needlessly medicating is wrong, the reality is often complicated. We are not de facto opposed to medication when it can be effective and improve daily life. But because creativity often presents itself through idiosyncratic behavior and thoughts, and because creativity is driven and releases itself through discrete energy, it seems to us that any medication that reduces energy or slows down brain functioning should be of concern, especially if we are trying to nurture and support creativity. Carefully observant family members and educators should look for how medication might be interfering with creative expression and activity and look for ways, in consultation with doctors and pediatricians, to avoid this undesired side effect. Whatever supports and aids the overall positive development and functioning of a child—and we say that in the context of everything written in this book—including any and all creative expression that balances novelty and utility, is the central goal.

Amid these clinical perspectives on ADHD, as well as other neurological disorders, we would do well to recall Mark Wolraich and Joseph Hagen's (2019) note to parents and family members: "Don't forget to appreciate and encourage [a child's] unique strengths and abilities . . . and to communicate that to your child" (14). This must be the first and most important step when beginning the journey of life with a child with neurodiversity. We can and should be practical. We should develop behavioral plans. We should teach replacement skills and behaviors that can be used instead of current actions that are destructive or harmful to self or others. But none of these interventions will be terribly effective without the rock-solid foundation of a trusting, nurturing, and responsive relationship between a child and a caring adult.

Six Reasons Why ADHD Can Support Creativity

Edward Hallowell and John Ratey (2011) explain several characteristics of ADHD minds, some of which lean more toward distraction and difficulty with focused attention, others with hyperactivity, and some with both, that might positively influence creativity.

1. A person with inattentive ADHD often has more trouble than most in screening out information. That can mean they notice more things than others do because their stimuli filters do not work as well.

2. Taking in more stimuli means processing more experiences in the brain. A higher level of outside stimulation means people with inattentive ADHD are often more used to chaos than other individuals, so they are open to letting disjointed ideas linger or be miscategorized in their minds.

3. Because individuals with inattentive ADHD often live with irrational connections longer than other individuals, these tendencies mean their minds generate more novel ideas and perhaps give them greater attention and focus. Idea generation is the cornerstone of creativity, and the ADHD mind is like an idea machine running at high speeds.

4. Individuals with hyperactive ADHD may respond in extreme ways because more stimuli are entering into their consciousness and not being filtered. It is easy to see why these unusual thinking patterns can lead to unusual levels of creativity. Overemphasized reaction to stimuli creates more and prolonged interactions and connections, all generating new ideas and considerations.

5. Hallowell and Ratey (2011) talk about how individuals with hyperactive ADHD are often impulsive, but add, "What is creativity but impulsivity gone right?" (219). Creativity is, in fact, impulsive in and of itself, so persons with ADHD may feel more at home with impulsive thoughts and be more inclined to go with the creative flow than others who snap back into purposeful or executive-mode functioning and forgo the benefits of that impulsivity.

6. There is, conversely, a tendency of some people with ADHD to be hyperfocused or hyperengaged to a degree some might think of as extreme. Hyperfocus is ideal for creative thinking. A focused flow state, as Mihaly Csikszentmihalyi (1990) describes it, may seem the very opposite of an attention deficit. Baron-Cohen (Kaufman 2021, 13:00) reminds us that Thomas Edison's compulsions to invent led his wife to put a bed in his lab so he could keep working day and night on his creative ideas. Such rapt attention is consistent with creative thinking.

Table 5. ADHD and Creativity

ADHD Trait	Positive, Creativity-Based Frame	Supportive Interventions
Trouble screening out information	Child is capturing it all and taking in the bigger picture. They may have greater brain flexibility because they can tolerate chaos and let disjointed ideas linger. Their minds may generate novel ideas and give more ideas greater attention.	• Help focus by asking questions about what is being observed to slow down rapid changes in attention and encourage deeper reflection. • Catalog what is being taken in so you and the child can appreciate all of it. • Reduce distractions by simplifying sensory input such as background noise or visuals with lots of movement and color.
Overemphasized or exaggerated response to stimulation	Child is eager to be engaged. Child exhibits excitement and positive energy.	• Catalog types of stimulation and typical responses. Teach and coach acceptable ways to respond to specific stimuli. • Provide time and space for exaggerated responses as frequently as possible.
Hyperactive/impulsive behavior (fidgeting, leaving seat, in constant motion, running around, climbing on furniture)	Child shows enthusiasm. Child learns with their whole body and learns best when the body is in motion.	• Allow child to stand while working or playing. • Keep the schedule moving along. Keep activities under five minutes. • Provide more opportunities for whole-class movement activities.
Difficulty with task initiation or completion	Child is thinking "big picture" and wants to do a lot and be involved with everything and everyone. This is a big thinker and big-hearted child.	• Break tasks into smaller chunks. • Visually map out each step in the task. • Help the child focus on completing one step at a time. • Encourage and praise every step in the process.

Disabilities and Creativity

Because of this disability/creativity connection, teaching and supporting creativity requires us to pay attention to how children with disabilities are treated, especially with respect to nurturing their creative potential. Despite the clear advances in addressing the needs of children with disabilities that IDEA represents, the pathway to educational success for someone with a disability is a rocky road indeed. Coauthor Zach tells his story about how children with certain test scores or who are diagnosed with a disability are frequently channeled into "special education." These programs can become a prison where creativity is not recognized and the pedagogical approach is rigid, not allowing for the freedom to explore and express oneself.

Here is Zach's story. We caution that the story includes the mention of suicide, and that may be triggering for readers.

Zach's Story

The word *disability* has been part of my vocabulary since kindergarten because I have a learning disability. This is my story. This is my truth. To begin, the early years of being diagnosed with a learning disability were confusing. I was placed in occupational therapy to work on motor coordination, and I attended speech therapy to work on oral-motor functioning. To help accommodate my learning needs, my parents placed me in a Montessori school, where I thrived in an environment that focused on giving students choice in their learning. However, we eventually moved away and faced financial hardships, and my days in a Montessori classroom ended. As I entered public education, it was difficult for me to understand why I was removed from my class and placed in a new classroom, Special Education. As I moved on to other grades, these accommodations were written for me:

- Assistance in preparing for tests with an early emphasis on both reading and math

- Extra time on tests

- Assistance in working through test anxiety

- Permission to work on math and English assignments one-on-one with the special education teacher or an associate

- Assistance in creating a plan to complete assignments in a timely manner

Now these accommodations may seem minimal. However, I became frustrated with how my educational journey took shape. The main reason was because I thought I did not belong in a special education classroom. I expressed this to my mother and father, both of whom also have a disability. They always told me to advocate for myself and stood by my side. In middle school, I began to attend my IEP (individualized educational plans) meetings. I was mature enough to understand that these meetings were about me and my educational journey, and now I had a seat at the table. Once, I advocated that I be removed from special education and be added to the gifted and talented program. I did not believe I was meant to be in special education. However, what cut deeper than anything else from this meeting was being told that more funding is given for students who are in special education than students in the gifted and talented program. As a sixth grader, I did not know whether that was true. My parents continued to advocate for what was best for me as a learner, but regardless, I was asked to remain in special education.

I remembered an experience in reading class, I believe in sixth grade, when the accelerated reading (AR) tests were used to assess comprehension. I have loved reading and visiting public libraries since early childhood. I loved challenging myself by reading books such as *Moby Dick* and Shakespeare plays such as *Hamlet*. Of course, some of the content in these types of texts was advanced for my age. However, I enjoyed the challenge. On a particular day in reading class, I was interested in reading *The Incredible Journey*. The teacher indicated that based on my comprehension tests, the book was beyond my reading level. I was given a book at the fourth-grade reading level. I was puzzled and upset.

It is important for me to mention that I now do not fault this teacher for doing so, as they were basing their actions on the comprehension tests they were required to use. This experience caused me to stop reading for pleasure, and I became depressed.

It was not until the summer between eighth and ninth grade that I took a positive turn, all thanks to driver's education. At this time, I completed a driver's education class so I could get my permit. The only accommodation I got was extra time on each test. Everyone has to learn to drive the same, without accommodations. I was nervous throughout the class until the final day, when I passed with a C+. I was walking on clouds and knew that change was coming in the upcoming school year.

As I entered ninth grade, I, my parents, the special education teacher, and the principal met to discuss my future in special education. At the end of the meeting, it was decided that I would work toward graduation without special education. Although it was challenging, I was able to maintain passing grades that year, and in the end, I was moved out of special education. It was during this time that I discovered how using storytelling could be a creative way for me to accomplish much of my coursework. For example, in history class we were asked to choose a famous author, research them, and then come dressed up as them. I chose John Steinbeck. Although it took me time to put together the research, becoming Steinbeck was easy and enjoyable. I was able to take the information I learned about him and create a dramatic performance in which I become Steinbeck through and through. Through this experience, I learned that a strength I have as a learner is to articulate information by using narrative skills such as storytelling. I was elated. It changed my confidence as a student and as a young adult. However, these feelings didn't last.

Geometry was a required course in tenth grade, and it was a challenge for me. I would later learn that I have a visual-spatial impairment that makes it difficult for me to see three-dimensional objects on a flat-plane surface such as a piece of paper. To complete my assignments and tests, I asked to see and touch dimensional objects (such as a tissue box) or to walk about a surface (like a tabletop). However, my request was denied, and I was required to memorize every proof. I failed the course. I was devastated. At a later meeting, the teacher, the special education teacher, and my parents concluded that I should be put back in special education to help me pass math. Although my time spent in the special education classroom was limited, it harmed my self-perception and mental health a great deal.

At this point, it is important to remind you that this is my story based on my memory. I say this because I am not pointing the finger of blame at a specific person or persons. Rather, I am pointing at the educational system. During one of my last IEP meetings, the results of my ACT scores were discussed. I was asked about my plans after high school. I said, "I am going to college." It was explained to me that based on my ACT scores and the challenges I faced throughout school that college might not be the best option. Despite this explanation, I was determined to at least try college. I would decide for myself what I could and could not do. In the summer of 2006, I entered a community college. My challenges continued for a while, and I attempted suicide. But my self-advocacy grew stronger, I further developed my skills as a storyteller, and I discovered that a career in public libraries was the best fit for me. In 2020 I graduated with my doctorate in education. Although I could spend time sharing my college experience, we are not focusing in this book on the college learning environment. Instead, it is important for me to leave three lessons I learned that connect to points we've made in this book.

Lesson 1: Notice how the focus of educators and the system was on what I could not do and which part of school requirements I was failing. There was no focus on my clear abilities and interests, as I was an ambitious reader and talented storyteller. Fixing injustices like this requires, first, seeing what is happening.

Lesson 2: Words are powerful. It is important to be mindful of our words and statements. As a person with a learning disability, I was hurt a great deal by some of the words and statements said to me, so much so that I attempted suicide. Choose your words and statements wisely.

Lesson 3: To identify sources of creativity, specific opportunities should be provided for children so they can discover them for themselves, and then teachers can see them. We talk later in the book (chapter 8) about creative spaces: what they provide and where to find them. The bigger lesson is that learning is ongoing and everywhere, but the educational system in my case wanted to see it in only specific, limited ways. Within the bioecological system, partnerships between each ecosystem are important for an individual's healthy learning and development.

Lesson 4: Advocacy for creative learning is imperative. It is the responsibility of educators to advocate, to encourage parents and caregivers to advocate, and to encourage children to advocate for their learning. Children should have a voice in their education.

Lesson 5: When educators and caregivers focus on innate creativity and its connection to individual identity, self-worth, and self-esteem, they help students make progress across educational requirements. No one succeeds at school if they think they are a failure. But if there are things they like and do well, they can blossom with the right amount of support.

Supporting Creativity in Children with Neurodiversity

Children on the autism spectrum or with ADHD have a differently functioning brain than their neurotypical peers. It is not inferior, just different. Knowing the positive aspects of these differences may help us understand how to identify the giftedness behind neurodiversity and support it. Looking at our own individual idiosyncrasies, whether clinically diagnosed or not, it is not hard to see how they are both gifts and curses. They allow us to do things others can't, but they also make us annoying or confusing to others. Like folks on the autism spectrum, when we are lost in our thoughts, we find it harder to connect to others, can be unresponsive to requests, and may act unfriendly if we are experiencing something as an intrusion into our lives. When we are distracted or manic, we may be unproductive and feel frustrated, but we could also be highly productive and manage multiple crises simultaneously. Use your own experience as a guide to how best to support creativity.

The following are a few suggestions for supporting creativity in the children who are neurodivergent:

- **Be open to children's brains working in different ways.** Remind yourself that different isn't bad. Different is not something to be fixed. It is something to manage and leverage. Focus on being flexible and adaptive while promoting healthy development and learning.

- **Look for the strengths in neurodiversity** as it shows up in your learning environment or family life. What new thoughts and ideas are these children expressing? This is about paying attention to what a child can do, not what they cannot do. Consider practicing ways to reframe behavior that you find difficult, and try more supportive interventions (see table 5).

- **Design special learning opportunities and experiences** that exercise those latent skills of pattern recognition and focused concentration. Not all children react in the same way to a lesson plan or activity or experience. Some are very engaged and others not at all. What triggers their interests and what does not tells you important things about their neurology (how they think, feel, and behave).

- **Develop relationships with professionals involved.** If children are presenting with clear and chronic ADHD symptoms, chances are physicians, pediatricians, behavioral health professionals, or special education teachers are involved. You should be partnering with them on behavior management concerns, including how to leverage the child's special characteristics for creative pursuits or ongoing development.

Some Thoughts about IFSPs or IEPs

A well-run early childhood program should be screening all children for disabilities, including autism and ADHD. For an excellent autism screening, check out the free Learn the Signs: Act Early resources on the Centers for Disease Control and Prevention website: www.cdc.gov/ncbddd/actearly/freematerials.html# Resources-Developmental-Surveillance-Screening. Positive screening results should trigger a more thorough evaluation and, if needed, a comprehensive treatment program. Such a program may include referral to early intervention or special education.

Children deemed eligible for special education are required to have an Individual Family Services Plan (IFSP) for early intervention before a child turns three or an Individualized Education Program (IEP) for special education after age three. That plan or program is developed jointly by family members, teachers, and other experts to outline an approach everyone agrees should best support the child in reaching their goals. Children should be involved to the extent that it is developmentally appropriate, at least providing feedback and comments about the plan's relevance and applicability. Encourage plans that involve families directly in supporting children.

Nothing we are writing in this chapter should be interpreted as a replacement for sound practices in addressing children's needs or developmental delays. If done correctly, our suggestions can clarify the kinds of support needed to best help a child. Parents or guardians and educators should not be afraid or reluctant to engage fully in this effort. No one will care about their child as much as they will. That is how it is supposed to work, though we know it does not always happen this way. The Parent Training and Information Centers (PTI) (see https://sites.ed.gov/idea/parents-families) available in each state should be your first call if things are not progressing as you want.

We encourage active engagement by parents, guardians, and teachers in screening, evaluation, and treatment responses. During screening, they should be providing information on what they experience in their interactions with the child. Focus these observations on any patterns you note in the child's thinking and behavior, in a variety of situations. During evaluation, the parents/guardians and educators should ensure that their input was considered and the results make sense to them. Otherwise, they should speak up.

During the treatment phase, when the IFSP or IEP is written, your observations and opinions as a parent/guardian or educator are of central importance, as much as any formal diagnosis made by an outside professional. Your ideas can shape what kind of goals to focus on and what kinds of strategies can be used to help the child be successful, as well as coordinating strategies in child care or school and at home. Adding insights you have about the child's creative potential will help make the IFSP and IEP more relevant to the kinds of support you provide. Your engagement (as an educator or as a parent) does not end with the writing of the IEP or IFSP; it continues with its implementation, monitoring of results, and any revisions needed. Adding a sensitivity to the creative potential of children presenting with neurodiversity is not a cure or management response to a clearly diagnosed disability, but it can make the process more engaging, maybe even fun, and certainly more likely to be successful.

Conclusion

In this chapter, we explored neurodiversity, the idea that people experience and interact with the world around them in different ways. There is no one "right" way of thinking, learning, and behaving. There is no one way to be normal. Differences are not deficits. Instead, we highlighted how characteristics of neurodiverse individuals may be exactly why and how they are creative.

Think about It

As you think about children in your life who may be on the autism spectrum, display ADHD tendencies, or are neurodivergent in other ways, consider these questions.

- Complete this sentence: What I most want to know about children with autism or diagnosed with ADHD is _____. Find an expert who can tell you what you want to know.

- Think about children whom you care for or teach whose behavior is a challenge to you. What are those behaviors? Describe them as specifically as possible. How are those behaviors exhibiting creativity or the potential for creative thought? How might behaviors you see as negative be reframed positively (revisit table 5)?

- Revisit the IEP or IFSP for any children in your care. What are the goals? Do they seem reasonable and appropriate for where you want the child to go, supporting the next step in their development? Is this really what the parents/guardians want? Are there ways you can write in supports for their creativity?

- Make a list of the interests of the children in your care. If you don't know, make a plan to find out (talk to the child's primary caregivers, observe what they spend most of their time doing, and so on). What special events could you plan to feed those interests?

Chapter Seven # Big Idea 4: Creativity as Curriculum

Nurturing creativity by taking domain-specific and domain-general approaches

Can creativity be taught? With all our discussions of neural pathways and life-forces, and a kind of blurry definition, an apparent answer might be no. Conventional wisdom says you either are creative or you are not. How could instructional interventions make any difference? Yet if creativity is as important as we write in this book, being able to teach it would seem crucial.

It is clear from chapter 2 that many child development theorists saw creativity as a key part of children's growth and development, and therefore of their education. Many looked at children's natural curiosity and playfulness as a sign of an intrinsic creative drive. Now we want to flip that around and ask, if children are naturally exploring and learning and being creative, what is the role of the early childhood educator? If they are already doing it, what exactly are we teaching? All education is about changing the way we think about and understand the world, and that cannot help but influence, shape, encourage, and mix it up with creative thinking itself. This chapter is really about where creativity fits into the curriculum and what instructional practices are involved. How could our curriculum and our instructional practices change to invite creativity into the educational process? Knowing what we know about creativity, what do we teach and how?

We begin the chapter by exploring domain-general and domain-specific approaches to teaching creativity. As we unpack that, we will explore where creativity fits into early learning standards, which in turn helps us connect creativity to the main ingredients of teaching: curriculum (what to teach), instruction (how to teach), and assessment (what difference it makes). Connecting creativity to teaching requires us to look at these three areas to ask what should be added or changed in our approach to teaching young children when we place creativity front and center in the practice of education.

Domain-General and Domain-Specific

To help readers understand how to teach creativity or incorporate it into the curriculum, we need to introduce two distinct approaches to thinking about creativity: domain-general and domain-specific. Each suggests a strategy by which an educator might include creativity into their overall curriculum.

First, some definitions of these terms, courtesy of one expert we spoke with who helped us understand the teaching of creativity: Dr. Keith Sawyer of the University of North Carolina at Chapel Hill. Dr. Sawyer, though trained as a psychologist, teaches in the School of Education and is deeply interested in how creativity is taught or how it can be an "educational innovation." He authored *The Creative Classroom* (2019), in which he unpacks what creativity looks like in the classroom, discussing how to teach "creative knowledge," exploring his idea of "guided improvisation" and mastering the "teaching paradox." We will discuss this further in the chapter, but first we offer his definitions:

Domain-general refers to teaching and learning around the idea and practice of creativity in general. A domain-general approach teaches creativity as a unique domain in and of itself. It is as if we could have a unit on creativity and capture the full spectrum of creative thinking and acting. This book is a domain-general approach to creativity since we are talking about this singular mental activity in many of its forms and expressions.

Domain-specific refers to teaching and learning by engaging children in creativity as they acquire new knowledge and skills in any domain. The point is to teach in such a way "that the knowledge that students acquire [through every other learning domain] better prepares them to engage creatively with that knowledge" (Sawyer 2015, 11). This approach could mean thinking creatively about any specific subject matter by thinking outside the box and arriving at unique solutions. The implication here is that any knowledge accumulation or skill development in these areas also nurtures and supports creativity. The skill development aspect is particularly important in what is traditionally considered arts education. Dance, music, painting, sculpture, and poetry are all creative activities, and children's performance in these activities is likely to improve as children learn more skills: how to move your body, how to play an instrument, how to mix paint, how to throw a pot, how to write a sonnet. These, of course, involve subskills and the slow accumulation of expertise and experience through practice that makes someone "good" at these creative endeavors. But as we have stressed throughout this book, artistic pursuits are not where creativity begins and ends.

Sawyer (2015) argues that domain-specific learning is more effective and consequential than domain-general. He points to one study in which creativity was improved by specific training, but only in the domain in which that skill was practiced.

Addressing creativity in specific areas yields more satisfying results. Any learning done in a specific domain, like math or science or the violin, will only enhance and expand creative expression in that field. Learning basic arithmetic, the structure of the atom, or how to rosin a bow all aid creativity. Creative geniuses like Einstein or Bach both mastered their respective fields well before they composed their masterpieces, be it formulas or fugues. But all that domain-specific expertise did not help them be creative in other realms. Knowing my multiplication tables will not help me express my creativity playing the violin. Sawyer (2015, 12) points to a few studies that show creativity training to be effective when it is domain focused, but it is not transferable or generalizable to other domains.

And yet some skills seem domain-general, like being able to get into a default-mode state, cultivating personality traits like openness to experience, or experimenting with feeling more comfortable drawing outside the lines and breaking rules. What seems to be happening is that domain-general and domain-specific skills come into play together with neural processing. A recent study by Qunlin Chen and colleagues (2020) synthesized a few functional neuroimaging studies to discover that across three creative activities (music improvisation, drawing, and literary creativity) there were common neural activations, suggesting that there is a central, domain-general system for artistic creativity. The brain networks were the same even though the activities were different.

In summary, *domain-general* learning around creativity makes creativity the object of your learning, and *domain-specific* uses creativity in the process of learning about a specific topic or subject. Educators of young children should neglect neither.

Thinking about domain-specific topics raises another question: What domains? For the ancient Greeks, it was the nine Muses, each with a different kind of creative pursuit (or domain): epic poetry, history, love poetry, lyric poetry, tragedy, hymns, choral song and dance, comedy, and astronomy. Lawrence Hershfeld and Susan Gelman (1994) conceived of eight "domains of mind": cognitive neuroscience, cultural anthropology, biological anthropology, developmental psychology, education, linguistics, philosophy, and psycholinguistics. Many of us are familiar with Howard Gardner's eight intelligences: interpersonal, intrapersonal, spatial, naturalistic, language, logical-mathematical, bodily kinesthetic, and musical (see Kaufman 2016, 51). There are countless domain lists of this type. For our purposes, focused on early childhood education, we look at the domains of early learning guidelines or standards.

Creativity and Standards

The concept of *domain-specific* should not be new to early childhood educators or families who are aware of early learning standards. Back in 2001, when Congress passed the No Child Left Behind Act that reauthorized the Elementary and Secondary Education Act, the George W. Bush administration invited every state to develop early learning guidelines. These were concrete statements of what the state expected or wanted or were planning to see children know and be able to do. Over the decade that followed, nearly every state did so. While there was pushback and rancor from those who resisted what was seen as an effort by educational policy wonks to push down standards-based education into the play-based, let-them-have-fun early childhood education area, these efforts did result in some coherent structures stating what preschool learning should be about. The research showed clearly that children whose educational experiences were focused on discrete outcomes generally tended to do better with those outcomes than those whose experiences did not. The idea of standards led to greater clarity about what the purpose of early childhood education is.

In Tom's earlier book *Saving Play*, he and coauthor Gaye Gronlund argued that embracing a standards-based approach to learning did not mean abandoning play-based learning, and that recommending specific subject matter did not inevitably mean rigid and didactic teaching. In fact, nothing in the No Child Left Behind Act required its focus on literacy and math to include rejecting blocks and doubling down on flash cards, even though that happened all too frequently (leading Tom and Gaye to write the book). In the context of teaching creativity or creatively teaching, we want to expose all the domains in state early learning guidelines to creative approaches and put play front and center in children's educational experiences. We would argue today that most state early learning guidelines can be a useful foundation for developing curricula that remains open to and supportive of creative approaches.

However, the early learning guidelines got it wrong in relegating creative pursuits solely to areas called things like "Creative Arts," at least in the Iowa Early Learning Standards (Early Childhood Iowa 2019). Iowa divides Creative Arts into three standards: (1) sensory and art-related experiences; (2) rhythm, music, and movement experiences; and (3) dramatic play. Yes, these are indeed creative exercises, but creativity is more than art, dance, and drama. In fairness, Iowa's standards include an Approaches to Learning domain (commonly found in other early learning standards as well) that includes three standards: Curiosity and Initiative, Engagement and Persistence, and Reasoning and Problem Solving.

As we have noted elsewhere, creativity is a bedfellow of curiosity, an impetus for engagement and persistence, and a handmaiden for problem solving. So the standards are not missing this wider understanding of creativity. You could argue that Approaches to Learning is domain-general creativity since it supports all future learning. However, we think the standards avoid putting the appropriate (in our view) emphasis on creativity as a central function in "academic" pursuits.

In contrast, consider the Ohio Early Learning and Development Standards (Ohio Department of Education and Ohio Department of Job and Family Services 2022). Like Iowa, Ohio has a domain called Approaches to Learning, with no overt mention of creativity. Instead, there are two strands: Engagement and Persistence, and something they call Mindset. The latter strand is the development of a "growth mindset," clearly alluding to Carol Dweck's (2008) work, recognizing her emphasis on the growth mindset as key to unlocking potential. Interestingly, one of the standards in the Engagement and Persistence strand is "Engages in new and unfamiliar experiences and activities." That relates back to one of the personality traits associated with creativity, openness to experience. Ohio early educators may want to think about how to enhance that openness by engaging children in new and unfamiliar experiences and activities, then monitoring and modifying them so the reaction of children is wonder and excitement, not fear or indifference. The Ohio standards recognize that openness to new experiences is a prerequisite to engagement.

Creativity is especially pronounced in the Ohio standards in the Creative Development domain, which is broken down into two strands: Artistic Engagement and Expression, and Creativity and Play. The standards include this description:

> The Creative Development domain includes skills related to expression of thoughts, ideas, and feelings through visual arts, dance, music, and dramatic play. Standards in Creative Development represent the integration of skills from other domains (such as language, motor, and executive function). In addition, the arts can be used to demonstrate skills and knowledge across other domains, with research showing the positive impact participation in arts education has on academic and lifelong success. (Ohio Department of Education and Ohio Department of Job and Family Services 2022, 23)

Our first response was happiness to see creativity mentioned explicitly and in a broader context than just the arts. But the description still narrows it down to these topics while acknowledging its obvious link to skills in other domains. The domain title of Creative Development appears to be about creativity in general, but the description implies that creative development is largely artistic development. Our point here is not to criticize Ohio, but to suggest how early educators may want to recognize the limitations on creativity that their state standards are imposing.

Turning last to the *Head Start Early Learning Outcomes Framework*, which includes Creativity explicitly as a subdomain under Approaches to Learning, we notice a series of goals:

Infant/Toddler

Goal IT-ATL 8: Child uses creativity to increase understanding and learning.

Goal IT-ATL 9: Child shows imagination in play and interactions with others.

Preschool

Goal P-ATL 12: Child expresses creativity in thinking and communication.

Goal P-ATL 13: Child uses imagination in play and interactions with others.

(Office of Head Start 2018, 15, 21)

What interests us here is that these goals, which are broad expectations of skills and behaviors believed to be connected to school success, are about the ability to leverage (use and express) creativity for understanding, learning, thinking, and communication. Creativity, in this conceptualization, is a means to an end. Infant/Toddler goal 9 and preschool goal 13 suggest that imagination and creativity are at work in play and that play becomes a context for exercising creativity.

As we examined standards, we saw all kinds of allusions to creativity that suggested a lot of different understandings of what creativity is. This variety and diversity shouldn't surprise us, given the cloudy understanding of creativity in general. However, a lack of clarity and precision is a problem when writing standards, which should be clear and specific if they are to be of any use. We want creativity to be a central part of the educational and child development goals we have for children, in child care and preschool and with caregivers at home. That means creativity needs to be pursued intentionally through standards, curriculum, lesson plans, instructional strategies, and assessment. It needs to be in standards so we can ensure that our curriculum addresses creativity experiences and related skills. It needs to be in the curriculum so our lesson planning includes exercises and instruction that highlight creative thinking and creative expression. And it needs to be in our assessment so we know whether what we did made any difference. This requires intentionality, and it requires a clear understanding of what we want to accomplish.

Ultimately, we think creativity in the standards (as it is included at the time of this book's writing) does not have sufficient clarity and specificity to support educators who want to nurture or teach creativity to children. The problem is that standards lack our expansive definition of creativity and therefore convey the idea that only certain domains are "creative." Our solution is to encourage educators to take a creative approach to all teaching and to do so by engaging the creative energy of children with which they approach all learning.

How to Teach Creativity

This examination should make it clear that standards in and of themselves are not a sufficient guide about what and how to teach. Since content knowledge helps a child engage with the domain in a creative way, virtually all learning provides a richer context for creative thinking, expression, and action. When children engage creatively with a topic, they learn it. Drawing a picture of a butterfly or dancing like a butterfly are concrete ways to learn about butterflies.

How you teach is also important. A creativity approach to teaching has two basic answers: (1) use creative approaches to teaching (whether it is how you set up your environment, how you talk about the topics you want to present, how you engage with children in positive and nurturing ways, how you schedule the day, or how you manage the learning environment), and (2) teach in a way that encourages creative thinking and creative responses from children, soliciting, recognizing, and valuing creative expressions of every sort.

Rather than giving you a list of what you should do to teach creativity, we want to show you how to create your own ideas about teaching creativity. Try this experiment. In figure 4, you will see a list of creativity-supporting behavior based on Sawyer (2015, 9–10), who compiled these behaviors from a variety of sources. Sawyer's list is designed for teachers with older students, but we boiled down and developed ten principles for early childhood educators. In figure 5, you will see a list of domains typical of early learning standard domains and standards. Start with figure 5 (or use your state's early learning guidelines) and pick a domain and standard at random. That will be the learning goal. Then pick an educator behavior at random. Here's our challenge: outline what a lesson or activity might look like if you were trying to help the children in your care reach that standard using the selected teacher behavior. The point is to bring into collision two random ideas and see what it triggers in your thinking. And it also shows how any subject can be approached using the figure 4 behaviors. These teacher behaviors are our best suggestions for how to teach creativity.

Figure 4. Educator Behaviors That Encourage Creativity

These behaviors are based on a list by Keith Sawyer (2015, 9–10). We have adapted them for early childhood educators, reducing the number from 17 to 10. Readers may still want to look at Sawyer's original list for a larger array of strategies as well as to better appreciate how these behaviors support creativity.

1. *Be surprised and open to unexpected questions, ideas, or responses to your lesson plans:* The unexpected catches you off guard and pushes you into uncomfortable territory. Instead of trying to get back to the land of comfort and control, try to roll with it and allow it to take your lesson plan in a new direction just to see what happens.

2. *Foster trust and safety:* Ensure that your educational environment is a safe place to express oneself, make mistakes, and say awkward or wrong things.

3. *Build self-efficacy:* Repeat often the theme of this book: we are all creative. The job of the educator is to help children discover their own creativity and their own identities as creators.

4. *Welcome problems:* When a problem comes up, how can you make your first thought be "Cool! More things to explore and think about"? Encourage questions, and especially don't worry about not having answers. Instead, invite collaboration in solving the problem (see more on this with the discussion of improvisational teaching later in the chapter).

5. *Model creativity:* How are you creative? How do you value creativity, pursue creative arts, and celebrate your own creative ideas? Share that with children and be their example.

6. *Encourage idea generation:* Design your lessons or activities so the knowledge you wish to convey is at least partially coconstructed. Unless children participate in the process of learning, it is just you talking at them. Giving time and opportunity for every child to come up with an idea helps every child be creative.

7. *Cross-fertilize ideas:* When you can, make connections between books, activities, videos, and games. It is the collision of different ideas that generates new ideas.

8. *Allow time for creative thinking and incubation:* Set aside specific time for just thinking. The same goes for projects or center-time activities. If you have a timer to control how long children are at center, make sure it is at least five minutes. Follow it up with reflective questions: How did the time go? What new thing did they learn?

9. *Encourage sensible risks:* Without violating safety rules or encouraging harmful behavior, see how far you can push the envelope in risk-taking and experimentation.

10. *Encourage creative collaboration:* Think about what you can do to work with children to identify and solve problems, to make decisions about what and how to learn, and to work together in play centers.

Moving beyond a laundry list of good ideas, let's consider how instructional practices support creativity. We start by emphasizing two important ideas discussed above:

1. All learning can support and be supported by creativity.

2. When you help children become skilled at something, you encourage them to be more creative with that thing.

With the first idea, we want to point out the reflexive nature of applying creativity to teaching. It moves in two directions (sometimes at the same time!). The first direction is from knowledge to creativity. The more you learn, the more creativity can occur. Fundamentally, creativity is thinking new, original thoughts. It moves from just thinking to expansive acts like imagination and wonder. Then it moves further into action:

- expressing a creative idea

- making something

- implementing a possible solution to a problem

These actions take a new idea or thought (ingredient #1 for creativity) and put it out there for social validation (usefulness, ingredient #2 for creativity). Acquiring new knowledge cannot help but encourage creative responses.

The second direction is applying creative habits to the learning process:

- asking questions

- proposing new ways to think about existing ideas

- making a joke

- drawing a picture

- taking time to think deeply

- getting excited

All these actions stir up our thinking and generate even more ideas. Creativity and learning are inseparable. This is the root idea behind constructivist education, why the great pioneers of constructivist education embraced creativity and practices that provided space, time, materials, and incentives to explore and create. Knowledge is acquired, then also changed and modified, and that new creation is what is retained as learning. Something retained just through memorization will soon be forgotten. How many of us could fill even one page with everything we remember now about what we learned in high school? Instead, the best kind of teaching encourages and makes space for each individual student's own unique construction of knowledge.

This movement from knowledge to creativity and then creativity to knowledge is like a piston driving a cognitive engine: creatively responding to new content in turn generates new knowledge that spurs creativity . . . and so on (see figure 6).

Creativity and the creation of knowledge moves us forward with deeper and deeper understanding of a topic, ourselves, and the world around us. Any learning we do, in turn, increases our capacity to be creative in the domain where the learning is taking place. And it can and should go as deep as our interests, passions, and abilities will take us.

At a practical level, if these two ideas are true—that creativity is central in the learning process and that the deepening of knowledge in a single domain builds motivation, satisfaction, and success in the educational process—then children benefit greatly by educators building reflection time into every lesson. Thinking about it again, analyzing and reviewing what happened and what mattered, is a necessary practice to aid creativity's role in the learning process. That's the thing about education: what matters is what is retained by a child, not what you thought you were teaching them. And by *retained*, we mean what is constructed or created in their minds based on what we said or what they experienced. Formative assessment—incremental check-ins so we can learn about what they are *actually* learning—is vital to all teaching.

Then there is the second idea: helping children learn something gives them a new platform for creative endeavor. Essentially, this means that when children learn anything new, they need to have space and time to make it their own. They need to be allowed and encouraged to experiment with their ideas about this new knowledge or skill they have acquired. If they just learned about butterflies and how they fly by fluttering around, where does that take them? To draw a picture or make up a story about butterflies? To explore further with a book or trip to a butterfly zoo? To dress up like a butterfly and go fluttering around the program space? To teach a friend about butterflies and why they are so interesting? The typical example of this is the child who learns how to play a musical instrument and then can play music. But the examples here show a much wider range of responses.

This second idea is part of the creative energy piston (see figure 6), but the emphasis here is on how an individual child makes a bit of learning their own. That self-possession of the idea can take any form. That's up to the child. But if

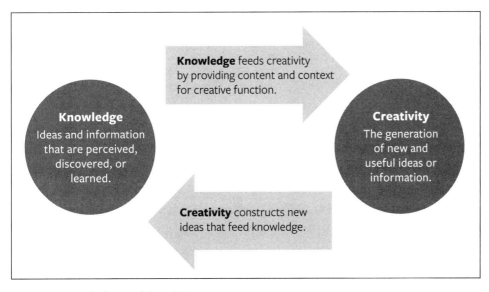

Figure 6. Knowledge and Creativity

they can take the basic concept or skill they learned and do something—literally almost anything—that is a creative act, and it also cements the learning, they have learned something and it is theirs.

Creative Instruction

When you teach in a way that affirms and uses creativity—an approach that can take place any time you teach—you have the closest thing to teaching creativity. Teaching in a creative way provides another dimension by encouraging creative responses in children. It moves children beyond simple responses to ones they actually have to think about. What if you were to end most of your instruction with "Now let's draw a picture about this"? What children choose to draw tells you everything you need to know.

In practical terms, this is what Keith Sawyer's work has been leading to, culminating in his 2019 book *The Creative Classroom*. And indeed, what makes Sawyer's work so valuable is that he is interested both in what has empirically been shown to be effective *and* in concrete recommendations and strategies for teachers. One of his key ideas and a valuable contribution to our thinking is the "creative learning paradox" (Sawyer 2015, 20). This paradox is encapsulated in the title of a book he edited, *Structure and Improvisation in Creative Teaching* (Sawyer 2011), combining two seemingly incongruous words, *structure* and *improvisation*.

Sawyer asserts that educators need to be both planful and open to change, to have clear goals and to capitalize on serendipitous moments, to use skills necessary to achieve concrete learning outcomes and skills that leave questions unanswered, inviting further exploration and growth. He defines three paradoxes:

- *The teacher paradox:* Teacher expertise must weave together a large knowledge base of plans, routines, and structures within improvised classroom practice that responds to the unique needs of the moment.

- *The learning paradox:* In effective creative learning environments, children are provided with scaffolds—loose structures that are carefully designed to guide them as they improvise toward content knowledge, skills, and deeper conceptual understanding.

- *The curriculum paradox:* Good curricula and lesson plans are necessary to guide educators and children down the most effective learning trajectory toward desired learning outcomes. Yet the most effective curricula are those designed to foster improvisational learning (Sawyer 2015, 21).

Two ideas bear deeper reflection: *paradox* and *improvisation*. The idea of a *paradox* is two or more things that don't really make sense together and yet at a deeper level do. We find that people who can embrace paradox without dismissing it as a logical absurdity are often creative in their thinking. And we need that way of thinking about so many issues in life: What is the best way to teach children? How do we organize a society where everyone is treated fairly? How can I do what I love to do and still support myself and my family? The most satisfying answer to these tough questions is found in a paradox where two opposing ideas are both true: by explicit teaching and by letting children figure it out on their own; by promoting liberty *and* justice for all; by finding creative ways to do what we love but also by finding work that is remuneratively rewarding. Sawyer's contradictory notions of structure and improvisation are both true and both implemented in teaching, learning, and structuring education:

- Educators must have learning objectives, lessons plans, and direct instruction, *and yet* they must respond to whatever spontaneously occurs in the learning environment.

- Children should receive concrete information that is organized into coherent blocks of knowledge *and yet* loosely structured enough to allow for their own construction of that knowledge.

- Educators use standards, curricula, and lesson plans to organize time and space in a program *and yet* follow approaches that encourage improvisational learning and radical flexibility for children to take what is learned in whatever direction makes sense to them.

Improvisation literally means "without provision" or "not providing." Some of the earliest definitions of *provisions* meant foresight, prudence, and care, the act of providing beforehand and arranging in advance. That's what improvisation is *not* doing. It is just trusting that what is needed will be there, like the next note on a scale you have never played or a funny rejoinder to a line you have never heard before. It is the paradox of teaching: planning and providing, and then improvising your way through. Every educator, including both authors, will tell you that we plan very carefully for each lesson, and it *never* (never ever) comes off as we had planned. Some improvisational skills to let you move and groove will serve you well.

Sawyer (2019, 44–52) shares rules that comedy groups use when teaching improvisation. It turns out they can help educators too. Improvisation is a collaborative activity, like all learning. Every instructional process involving an educator and child is a matter of coconstructing knowledge together. This collaboration is where the improvisational rules are helpful.

The first and foundational rule is "Yes, and." Everything you do and say includes these two pieces:

- *Yes*—I am aware and accept your response. I am glad the response was clear enough for me to recognize it.

- *And*—Now I will add something of my own that gives you a starting point for another response.

The other rules fine-tune this basic rule.

- *No denial.* Everything you say and do has to affirm what you expressed by saying "Yes, and." You *must* accept what you are given, and only after you explicitly accept it can you add your "and."

- *Don't drive the scene.* Improvisation is a cocreation, two individuals working together to create new knowledge. Everybody works together and contributes equally.

- *Don't endow.* When you *endow*, you assign attributes, actions, and thoughts to the other speaker. That means you are taking too much control and inhibiting the other's creative responses.

- *Don't ask questions.* Wait! What? Questions, like endowments, limit the responses you may receive, since the response is about answering your question and not responding to the situation. Especially don't ask questions that you know the answers to. That's not coconstructing knowledge. But you *can* ask questions to clarify responses or to truly move the conversation into new territory of inquiry and knowledge development.

- *Don't cross the fourth wall.* The fourth wall is the one that divides the performers from the audience. The analogue in education is metacommunication, or communication about communication. When you say something about the lesson plan or the educational purpose, it interrupts the flow of the "scene."

Sawyer's advice was written mainly for K–12 educators. You may feel these ideas make less sense for early childhood educators. We still think his advice can be incorporated into an early childhood educator's repertoire. At a time when many are identifying the need for educators to engage in cognitively complex and challenging interactions with young learners, these ideas of paradox and improvisation may have special salience. For example, the CLASS (Classroom Assessment Scoring System) frequently finds that programs score lowest in the domain of Instructional Support. National Head Start scores for CLASS indicate the average score is less than half of what it is for the other two domains (Head Start Early Childhood Learning and Knowledge Center 2020). The Instructional Support domain includes three areas: Concept Development, Language Modeling, and Quality of Feedback (Head Start Early Childhood Learning and Knowledge Center 2024). Under each of these areas are three dozen observable strategies for establishing instructional support. We think many would be addressed by eliciting creative responses on the part of children, perhaps by using some of the improvisational rules discussed here. The improvisational "rules" give guidance on how teachers can respond to children in ways that encourage analytical thinking and problem solving.

Another early childhood analogue for Sawyer's ideas is found in *Powerful Interactions* (Dombro et al. 2011). Its recipe for "powerful interactions" involves a three-step process: (1) be present, (2) connect, and (3) extend learning. The book has many suggestions for how to mix these ingredients together, and the "Yes, and" rule covers quite a few.

In practice, younger children may be put off by the additional burden you place on them to be cocreators. Here is where you trust the creative forces in children. This is not a magic formula, and additional support, scaffolds, and encouragement may be needed for them to step up to this role and use those creative forces. By now you know what it looks like when they are engaged and being creative. Keep experimenting until you see that. A week of practice may be necessary. Curious readers may want to explore what Amy Laura Dombro and her colleagues (2011, 67–129) wrote in the section under the third step (extend learning), where the authors discuss how to respond to curiosity and inspire imaginative play.

Another creative teaching strategy is to focus on what is already of interest to the child. So often educators are frustrated because they can't get children attentive or engaged. Recall that educators are trying to stop current engagement in whatever children are focused on, and then get their attention enough to explain what the desired focal point is, and then get them to understand what they must do to be focused on that focal point. That is a lot to ask of children. And some educators and parents/guardians are asking them to do that *most* of the time. No wonder habitual ways to get children's attention are doomed. How can you deliver the same results by working with the energy of children rather than against it? How can you engage with the children *where they are* before you get them to where you want them to be?

Yet another creative teaching idea is that of constraints. As we mentioned when listing creativity myths in chapter 1, constraints do not inhibit creativity but rather expand it. The famous example we used was *Green Eggs and Ham.* Think about how you can construct creative challenges with constraints. Paint a picture of a butterfly going to school. Think of a story about how a girl is about to get eaten by a dragon but she escapes. Of course, encouraging a child to paint whatever or write whatever they want is fine. But when they're stuck or don't paint much or imagine stories much, try providing some kind of constraint to harness their creativity.

There is also benefit in teaching children a creative process that helps them address challenges or solve problems. You could provide explicit instruction to children for a developmentally appropriate version of the Chopra process from chapter 1 (see page 17). Alternatively, here is a basic one from James Kaufman (2016, 20–24):

1. *Problem construction:* uncover the problem

2. *Incubation:* sit with it; engage default network processing

3. *Intimation:* something breaks through (Kaufman notes that steps 3 and 4 can be combined, or step 3 can be eliminated)

4. *Illumination:* the creative solution appears—the aha moment

5. *Verification:* the idea's usefulness to address the problem is confirmed

Could these steps be turned into a social story for young children? Or repeated as a program-wide activity? Or established as a classroom behavioral norm or expectation? Wouldn't that be creative teaching?

Your best approach to creative teaching may not be changing how you teach at all. It may simply be realizing what you are already doing. Many good practices that educators do commonly are based intentionally or accidentally on things that encourage creativity in children. Margaret Adams and Jie-Qi Chen (2012) describe four types of creativity that typically occur: exploring and experimenting, making, inventing, and "creating wholes" (350). *Creating wholes* means finding or making parts, then putting them together or integrating them to produce a coherent whole. Adams and Chen say it is the most sophisticated type of creativity because it involves both divergent and convergent thinking. Almost any activity or center in a program could be a place for all four of these types of creativity. Imagine a table with manipulatives. Children can explore and experiment with objects, moving them around, making patterns. They could make something out of the objects. They could invent a use for the objects. Or they could use them as part of a larger project where math shapes, say, could be cars or people or houses in a play town. In general, educators can see what forms of creativity emerge from whatever they have set up or planned, or they can intentionally design features or provide instructions that encourage these types of elaborations.

Sally Blake and Duane Giannangelo (2012) discuss three common early childhood activities—play, problem solving, and inquiry—in which creativity is front and center. The authors affirm that pretend play relies on the same cognitive and affective processes that are associated with creativity, citing research linking play with divergent thinking. Play both elicits creative responses among players and becomes an idea vehicle to express creativity. Observing play can tell educators a lot about the creative potential of children in their care.

Few problems are solved without some creative processing. Sometimes educators create provocations or challenges that require children to develop solutions (for example, building a bridge with blocks over a railroad track, designing ramps that make cars go faster, filling vessels with water using a funnel). Social conflicts such as sharing a toy, taking turns, and waiting for a teacher to answer a question all trigger creativity. Putting energy into solving the problem rather than lashing out represents creative learning. Overall, problem solving and creativity encompass many similar skills and results.

Inquiry is a key element of almost any STEM subject matter. Inquiry means exploring, asking questions, making observations, and engaging in dialogue with peers and educators. Having learning environments that change over time, such as by introducing new objects and new opportunities for exploration, will spark asking and wondering, driven by curiosity. These three types of activities—play, problem solving, and inquiry—are likely already taking place in your learning environment or even at home. Now we invite you to see them as laboratories for creativity experimentation.

While children are doing this, what is the role of the educator? Adams and Chen (2012) suggest three practices: observing children creating, framing creative activities, and appreciating differences. Your observations of children are your best guide to teaching creativity. If children are naturally creative beings and every child is creative, then at any given moment you should see creativity in action. If you don't see that, then what is getting in the way? Remember that creativity requires some time in the default system, which may mean having fewer distractions and taking time to sit with materials. Sometimes it is best just to watch and not intervene, but sometimes engaging is a supportive gesture and a way to encourage and nurture creativity. Adams and Chen (2012, 352) call that "framing." A frame is not the picture. It accents a picture, gives it definition, and complements the features of the picture. By framing, you provide your support to allow the child to immerse themselves more fully in the activity. Maybe you add something new or take something away or model a unique use of an object. Appreciating individual differences is key here. By definition, children will not be creative in the same way, so you must approach your observation with curiosity and an open mind. What is happening? Where is it going? What new idea is the child constructing in their mind? These three functions are great foundations for all creative teaching. If they do not come naturally to you, consider training opportunities that would allow you to perfect your skills of observation, framing, and appreciating differences.

We want to offer a final suggestion about teaching creativity. The old joke about how you get to Carnegie Hall applies here: practice, practice, practice. Children need to practice creative thinking to make it more commonplace and to increase their fluency in doing it (and so do you!). Remember that creativity is contradictory: both a skill and a habitual way of thinking; how brains typically work and how brains can be trained to work; a cognitive process that is free-flowing and yet focused and intentional. This paradox needs to play out as children experience both sides of creativity. Our suggestion for doing that is practice with a bit of metacognition thrown in. As creativity is elicited through learning activities or experiences that occur during the day, set aside intentional time for children to practice creative thinking and also to reflect on that thinking. What came about as they were thinking? Improving creativity means practicing being creative.

Conclusion

Yes, you can teach creativity. Or maybe better said, educators, parents, and other caregivers can and do play a critical and necessary role in nurturing and supporting creative thinking. Using both domain-general and domain-specific approaches, you can teach creativity by directly addressing the issues of creativity, but more importantly and usefully, by teaching in creative ways and in ways that elicit creativity in the give-and-take of instructor and learner. Children develop their natural creativity by having experiences that require them to think or act creatively. Any lesson can require a learner response, and that learner response can be a creative expression that uses any and all art forms (drama, dance, music, painting, and writing). Of course any thinking about any subject or responding to any lesson where a child is telling themselves what something is or means is a creative act too.

Creative instruction requires educators to reconcile structure and improvisation. It calls for flexibility and openness. Let's stop expecting children to respond in some predictable way to our lessons. Instead, let's be surprised and amazed at how many different responses you can document.

The ideas in this chapter may make you think you have to overhaul your entire curriculum. We are not advising that. Instead, think about your curriculum through the lens of creativity. Chances are you are already teaching creativity. Start by affirming what you are already doing. Then think about any new idea that might be added to your repertoire from figure 4 (p. 102). Like everything else, your teaching practice is an evolving thing. Know where you are. Know your next step. And trust that each step, any step, will take you there. When we teach creativity, we are teaching something as basic as how to think and how to learn, and what creative interests are and how to pursue them. And when we teach all this in a creative way, using creative instruction, the possibilities are endless.

Think about It

Look back through this chapter. Look at what you underlined or highlighted. Read any notes you kept. What are the main ideas you are taking away? Then ask yourself these questions:

- If you were to write a creativity curriculum, what would be the three most important learning goals?

- Looking at your current lesson plans or even just what you did today, what of your teaching might be categorized as domain-specific? As domain-general?

- Reread the teaching, learning, and curriculum paradoxes (see page 106). How have these shown up in your experiences as an educator or as a parent/guardian whose children have educators?

- Write a personal definition of *creative instruction*.

- What about teaching creativity scares you? What excites you?

Chapter Eight

Big Idea 5: Creativity in Formal and Informal Settings

Everyone, everywhere, all at once

Author and illustrator Peter Reynolds, famous for picture books, including *The Dot*, said, "It's very, very hard sometimes to hear your [creative] voice. That voice that's inside of you. And if you give yourself some time and space . . . you'll hear it. And it's a beautiful thing when it happens" (Hahn 2020). Reynolds makes two important points in just a few words. First, each person has their own creative voice. Second, time and space are important for creative discovery. How are these two things happening in early childhood programs? It is critical to provide an immersive and creative learning environment that offers children a space to discover their creative selves. By doing so, we believe children will discover that creativity has a place in their learning and development not only in the classroom or early education program but everywhere. How do we allow each child to hear their own creative voice? And how do we provide time and space for that to happen? That is the focus of this chapter.

What kind of space nurtures creativity? And where do we find such spaces? First, creative spaces should:

- Provide ongoing opportunities for new experiences
- Be able to be navigated and engaged independently
- Emphasize process as much or more than product
- Offer open-ended challenges
- Provide opportunities for social interactions among participants, encouraging and leveraging social learning

- Be accessible to all learners: multisensory/hands-on

- Be multicultural

And where are these creative spaces? Creativity is not just something that happens in early childhood programs—it can happen all over the community. Specifically, we are thinking of three institutions dedicated to informal learning: libraries, museums, and public television. We might also add public parks and playgrounds, symphonies, dance companies, and theater, many of which offer classes and programs designed for young children. Parents, family members, and other caregivers have a responsibility to know what is offered in their community and to create opportunities for children to connect and be involved. We think this is important—not least because one of the authors is a librarian.

What Makes a Space Creative?

Back in chapter 1, we introduced the idea of the four Ps of creativity and mentioned the fourth P as *Press* or *Place*. This chapter asks "*Where* are we creative?" Creativity can take place anywhere, of course. But not all spaces are equally supportive, nurturing, or stimulating. We came up with a list of seven important characteristics of creative spaces. It is probably not realistic to expect a single space to offer all of them, but as you look into your community, look for spaces where these characteristics seem evident.

Spaces cannot make creativity happen, but through their design and their use they can foster creative thinking and making. The space can have a profound effect on our experience and how much or deeply we can have creative experiences. When we talk about spaces, we include not just buildings and rooms but outside areas. We also consider the contents of the space. Early childhood educators have long understood how important the classroom or caregiving environment is to their work of caring for and educating young children. The decision of how to set up the space and what to put into it are important parts of intentional teaching.

Let's explore these seven characteristics in turn. Each may provide some ideas for how to better structure home or learning environments, but we mainly present them to invite you to think about where in your community such spaces might already exist.

New Experiences

A creative space should present new objects, materials, subjects, and activities that can introduce children to unexpected and novel experiences. Consider places in your community that could give children new experiences. A public library often provides a space to play with toys, building blocks, puppets, and puzzles. Further, public libraries offer comprehensive programs, ranging from learning about a culture to going on a nature hike. That newness is exactly the ingredient that can lead to creativity. New experiences, by definition, create new thoughts in a child and elicit original responses. Creative spaces should undergo regular change and frequently introduce new space arrangements, equipment, objects, materials, and things to do. While children like to visit a playground and play on the same equipment, it is also beneficial for them to try different equipment or use a piece of equipment differently. Recall how we mentioned in chapter 5 that a key ingredient in the cognitive makeup of the creative personality was "openness to experience." You test that openness and give children a chance to experiment with being open when you expose them to new experiences. Having a variety of new experiences allows children to choose among a set of options. Watching what choices children make can tell you a lot about their preferences and their openness to new experiences. Teachers and caregivers can also give gentle encouragement to children who are stuck in a rut or afraid to venture into the unknown.

Independent Engagement

Creative spaces should allow for some independent engagement. Where is that possible in your area? Young children must practice and explore their growing autonomy and self-initiated movement. Moving into a new space and engaging with a variety of materials gives children important experiences in self-efficacy and individual power. Even when they are small and very needy, the first movement toward self-direction forms the basis of a lifetime of movement toward being a separate, independent, and whole person. Having some activities that require adult help and supervision is all right, especially if it expands the range of experiences available, but giving children as much autonomy as possible is essential.

Process over Product

Creative spaces do not limit the nature of engagement. We think about this especially when a library or museum or community fair has "kids' activities" with the materials laid out for children to make a necklace or painting or whatever. The best support we adults can offer is to follow along with how the child wants to engage with objects and materials. The final product may or may not look like the prototype; the creative exercise in making the product is most important. However, often missing is the time and opportunity for repeated experiments with the various possibilities the materials represent. Parents and caregivers can provoke additional exploration with a few well-placed "I wonder what would happen . . ." statements.

Open-Ended Challenges

Creative spaces are most engaging when they offer open-ended challenges. Tom remembers going to the Mill City Museum in Minneapolis, Minnesota, where a water table with running water challenges children to create water chutes with enough velocity to move logs down the length of the table. This is creative gold. The challenge is the engagement lure, and the open-ended nature encourages a variety of responses. When we write about *challenges*, we think about the Reggio Emilia approach practice of "provocations," which are educator interventions designed to make children rethink, reimagine, or reengage with materials or processes. It is key to teaching in a child-led way and is only possible when there is more than one way to engage.

Encouraging Social Interactions

Beginning with Vygotsky but continuing through to educational theorists like Jerome Bruner and Albert Bandura, we know well that children learn through social interaction, but this idea is often forgotten or sidelined by our bias to think about teaching and learning as individual experiences. Creative spaces that include opportunities for children to talk and play with each other give an added boost to creative thinking. Creative community spaces should be places where children can gather. Most libraries have a children's area with children's books and often toys and games as well. Extensive programming in libraries (think story times or craft/game nights) offer times to be in the library space with friends. Any of us can remember how different it is to play alone or play with friends. They are both valuable experiences, but a rich creative life includes both.

Multisensory

We engage with the world using five basic senses. Nerve cells send messages from these sensory outposts around the body to collect in the brain for understanding and remembering. Providing experiences that require sight, hearing, touch, taste, and smell expands the variety of stimulation that triggers creative thought and expression. Varying or adding sensory stimulation introduces new experiences and can spark a creative idea or action. Another way to add variety is to incorporate different learning styles, such as visually, aurally, through movement, or through words. Though the idea of learning styles as a fixed preference in individuals is not true, a sheer variety of approaches can enrich any experience (Nancekivell, Shah, and Gelman 2020).

Multicultural

Almost everything about any space, from the architecture to the furniture to the objects and artifacts inside, is a cultural expression. Thinking about creative spaces from a multicultural perspective opens up even more variety. Multicultural artifacts can introduce children to a cultural expression. Most art museums do this naturally. Another perfect example is the Musical Instrument Museum in Phoenix, Arizona, which houses a collection of over fifteen thousand types of musical instruments and sound-making artifacts from every corner of the globe. Creative space designers should be thinking about what obvious or implicit cultural expressions are evident in the space. And as they engage with their surrounding community, they must ask what kinds of cultures should be represented so the space can reflect the multicultural nature of the community. When that fails to happen, creative spaces can unintentionally signal that there is a "normal" culture, implicitly characterizing other cultures as different or "abnormal."

Creative Spaces and Informal Learning

From ancient times, societies have always had creative spaces for informal learning. Informal learning is basically learning that takes place outside of formal learning institutions like public schools. While the term *informal* may connote that the learning taking place there is less serious or less intentional, that is incorrect. Informal learning opens up spaces and times to acknowledge that we are learning all the time and that learning can take place anywhere. Through our research, we discovered the following definitions for informal learning:

1. Shannon Dowling (2020) writes that "in informal learning environments, the ownership of learning lies with the individual to design their own experience, create their learning outcomes, and self-assess" (para. 1).

2. Informal learning is a commitment to lifelong learning, as emphasized by Philip H. Coombs and Manzoor Ahmed (1974, 3), who state it is "the lifelong process by which every person acquires and accumulates knowledge, skills, attitudes and insights from daily experiences and exposure to the environment. . . . Generally [it] is unorganized and often unsystematic; yet it accounts for the great bulk of any person's total lifetime learning—including that of even a highly 'schooled' person."

3. Martin Johnson and Dominika Majewska (2022) state that informal learning learners have "a significant level of influence on the process."

4. Finally, Eric Wiebe and his colleagues (2013) state that students can "direct their study at a depth and breadth that serves their personal needs."

It is apparent in these definitions that informal learning is self-directed and self-controlled. That means it is less structured than formal learning and not the result of direct teaching. Motivation for learning comes less from outside influences and more from the learners themselves. It is independent of setting and more often than not involves some interaction with other people. In fact, this is probably how we do most of our learning. When learners choose how their learning takes place, it becomes more authentic, and therefore it becomes easier for them to learn. You gain confidence as a learner because you control the experience and therefore construct the knowledge more readily because it is your own creation.

We emphasize informal learning for two reasons. First, because we are underscoring the deeper principle that creativity occurs all the time and not just when it is planned for by a teacher. Second, because most communities have sites for informal learning that are often underused and yet can provide a rich addition to the creative life of any child. Informal learning also seems to have embraced John Dewey's theories of education as we discussed in chapter 2 that emphasize hands-on learning, a practical application of knowledge, and building on strengths. Dewey knew that learning is built on previous experiences, occurs through social interaction, and includes a reflection of those experiences. These learning characteristics enable creativity as well as suggest how one might engage with creative spaces. Next time you take a child to a library, museum, or city park, ask yourself,

- "How can this experience build on the last time we were here by doing something more?" [building on prior experience]

- "How can we increase the social interaction among the children present?" [social interaction]

- "How can we reflect on our time in this creative space?" [reflection]

Three informal learning institutions that are present in many communities are public libraries, museums, and public television/digital technology. We will explore each to discover how they can be useful spaces for creative endeavors. What matters in any creative space is not the space itself but how the space allows for experiences of an individual or a group of children that, in turn, promote creative thinking and action. Remember that informal learning environments are diverse and include other settings, such as art groups/councils, community theater, conservation areas/parks, and makerspaces. All can be potential partners in supporting children's growth and development. When we understand and support informal learning spaces, we recognize that learning is a lifelong journey, stretching beyond the classroom or early childhood program.

Public Libraries

Public librarians continue to evolve their roles and responsibilities by providing resources and services beyond book lending (Cabello and Butler 2022). As discussed in chapter 3, development is interconnected between environments, within the *exosystem* that includes the community and neighborhoods, as well as public libraries. A public library is open to everyone. The programs offered by a public library build bonds between individuals across the community (Goulding 2009). Furthermore, the American Library Association (ALA) adopted the Library Bill of Rights in 1939 to provide policies to guide libraries' services. Policy number 6 asserts that libraries are a space for everyone: "Libraries which make exhibit spaces and meeting rooms available to the public they serve should make such facilities available on an equitable basis, regardless of the beliefs or affiliations of individuals or groups requesting their use" (ALA 2019).

Further research from the Urban Libraries Council (2007) identified "the power of place" as one of the primary relationships between public libraries and economic development, meaning that libraries serve as community anchors. Public libraries offer a multitude of program opportunities for children to support their learning and development, such as story time, reading programs, after-school programming, cultural programming, book clubs, and STEAM (science, technology, education, art, and mathematics) programs. These opportunities can be enhanced by a multisensory, exploratory, structured, and/or unstructured learning approach. Furthermore, the spaces in many public libraries have evolved to be more open over time, giving children freedom to learn and explore. Programs offer many a chance to connect and participate in their community, to feel both valued and respected. The public library has evolved to include the space not only inside of the library but also outside, extending experiences to individuals who may not otherwise be able to visit the library.

Informal learning and libraries

The programming offered by libraries exhibits many components of informal learning. As a space, public libraries are a relatively unstructured learning environment. Public children's and youth librarians are charged with providing programming that is educational, is driven by patron needs, makes room for patrons' participation (including planning and implementation), and is less structured to allow for direction changes. Creativity is infused in public library programming through a multitude of endeavors:

1. Including a space, permanent or mobile, with a variety of materials and tools so patrons can be creative

2. Including a space for children to experience play experiences including (but not limited to) art, music, and dramatic play

3. Including a space for creative safety for individuals to create, share, express, and have a civil conversation

4. Offering programming that emphasizes creativity through engagement between individuals, such as an engagement between parents/caregivers and children

5. Offering creative programming that is culturally specific, allowing for patrons to learn, connect, and discuss; developing a collection that is inclusive, representative, and reflecting of the world

6. Mobilizing creative resources (such as books, make-and-take art kits, and media) so patrons may take part in learning, expressing, and creating outside of the library walls

7. Encouraging process over product in creative experiences, such as when librarians provide supplies for children to create projects after a story time program

Partnership with a public library

Partnering with the public library is a powerful way for early childhood educators to enhance creative opportunities in their programs. Partnerships continue to evolve as public libraries ensure they maximize the services, resources, and programs offered to their community. Many public librarians take the initial step to reach out to local schools, child care centers, and home providers; however, if your local librarian has not reached out, we encourage you to do so. The focus for your first conversation should be to understand your needs for their services, including guest readers, books, author visits, STEAM activities, and so on.

We recommend that you prepare to ask the following questions when you first meet with the public librarian:

1. Does or has your library offered outreach programming for educators?

2. If so, what programs and/or services are offered?

3. What is your checkout policy for educators?

4. What resources and materials are available for educators?

5. What is the process for opening a library card?

Specific to creativity, some of the programs you could recommend to the public librarian include the following:

1. Bringing artistic materials for students to create their own mural that showcases who they are as an individual

2. Bringing puppets for students to use to create their own play

3. Offering a story time where students are encouraged to participate in reading the story

4. Providing a STEAM (science, technology, engineering, art, and math) activity demonstrating how creativity occurs not only through art but also in other disciplines. Some ideas for STEAM activities include designing a course for a robot to complete, learning about the colors of the rainbow using celery (www.youtube .com/watch?v=Klug9Foou3s), or using building blocks to design a city.

Museums

Like libraries, museums have been around for thousands of years, yet their purposes have evolved. Even if your community does not have a museum you can visit in person, the power of technology has made museums and resources across the world easily accessible. The following is a list of museum services and resources we found in our research that can be accessed without physically visiting a museum:

- Digital libraries of artifacts such as historical documents, artwork, and/or scientific discoveries

- Live streamed or on-demand educational presentations at no cost

- Educator resources, webinars, and trainings on a diverse slate of subjects for multiple age ranges

- Virtual field trips

- Curriculum on a variety of topics to make the museum come to life within your program or at home

Museums and informal learning

Museums offer a transformative learning experience, transporting visitors to a different time period, to the age of the dinosaurs, into outer space, or to the other side of the world. Regardless of the type, the museum supports the development of critical learning skills, intrinsic learning, and communication skills (as learners reflect on their experience with others). The learners' exploration and learning are driven by their interests. Creativity is also infused in museums by the following endeavors:

1. Museums offer learning through play and play activities as a strong part of the experience of children and families.

2. Museums offer children dramatic and theatrical experiences, for example, by putting on a puppet show related to the museum's theme.

3. Museums offer children investigative experiences, such as participating in an excavation of dinosaur fossils.

4. Museums offer children immersive experiences in other cultures through activities such as music, dance, and cooking.

5. Museums provide a well-rounded perspective on history where learning might include an audio tour, a scavenger hunt, or a hands-on learning experience.

6. Museums offer children the opportunity to dream of future careers specific to their interests. For example, children interested in STEM careers might visit a museum that focuses on outer space and do activities such as constructing their own solar system, launching themselves into space through a simulator, or building and launching a rocket using recycled materials.

Partnerships with museums

Partnering with a museum is possible whether or not it is located in your community. First, do a little investigation about the museum, perhaps searching a website or reading a brochure. Many times these sources provide concrete information about exhibits, programs, and activities, for example, if the museum offers experts who visit classrooms or other learning environments. Then contact the museum to discuss what you are seeking to offer to students that will encourage their creative exploration. We suggest asking the museum educational coordinator the following:

1. Are any of the activities, programs, or events you offer interactive and multi-sensory? What online and/or virtual experiences do you provide?

2. Is there a maximum size and recommended age of students you accommodate?

3. Does the museum provide an extension of activities (such as make-and-take kits) for students and families to complete at home together?

4. How do you believe the museum offers children an enhanced learning experience?

5. What approach to learning do you believe the museum offers to children (for example, project-based learning)?

Public Television and Technology

One reason public television came into being was as a tool for educating young children, with early programming like *Mister Rogers' Neighborhood* and *Sesame Street*. Now the explosion of commercial television and digital content add even more options. But public television's children's programming has historically been produced with a keen eye on a single mission: using television to teach children (CPB 2011). As such, it qualifies within our definition of informal learning.

Nowadays public television offers an astonishing array of programming, though lamentably, almost all is animation, driven by its lower production costs. Nevertheless, if we told you that there was a source with an enormous amount of free educational material, specifically designed for consumption by young children and presenting all kinds of topics and ideas, wouldn't you be interested? A quick review of children's programs scheduled on a local PBS station found programming covering topics such as using math to solve problems, discovering prairie grasshoppers and seahorses, paying fines on overdue library books, struggling with a divorce, living Alaskan adventures, learning about mofongo and volcanoes, meeting Albert Einstein and considering the importance of curiosity, tracing the growth of trees using photos, feeling self-conscious about clothes, setting up a strawberry horchata stand, and changing a broken wheel. What a variety of new ideas, new learning, and new launching places for creative thinking, exploration, and expression! That's just half a day of programming available every weekday through your local PBS station (local stations are available to 99 percent of American homes). Perhaps because it is free, it is more likely to be watched by families of low income (CPB 2011). This does not include the PBS Kids streaming service, which is accessible 24/7.

Public television and informal learning

Watching television is not, per se, a creative activity, but it is an educational experience and can lead to and connect with creative thinking and actions. Research does show that coviewing with adults makes a significant difference, especially the more the adults interact with children during and after viewing (and even before, if they set up the expectation that a child will learn something by watching). Michael Robb and Alexis Lauricella (2015) say the key is to use technology and digital media (including e-books, internet content, and video games) in ways that increase adult-child interaction (77).

One of the things public television, and increasingly other digital content providers, has encouraged and promoted is the active *using* of its programs and technology, not just viewing them. The viewing experience becomes a launching pad to read books or do related activities. To take some dated examples, Fred Rogers visits a crayon factory. Let's pull out a box of crayons and color. Elmo plays with a red balloon. Let's play with a red balloon too. These same utilization strategies can be effective for any digital content or other technology-mediated learning.

None of this should be understood as us advocating for increased media use, and any efforts by parents/guardians and caregivers to limit viewing and screen time is a good idea. Nevertheless, good things can happen as adults support and monitor the use of technology by children. The most recent policy statement on the topic from the American Academy of Pediatrics (AAP 2016) advises not more than an hour a day for children ages two to five years. Its advice to parents

and guardians is to focus as much on quality of content as quantity of screen time, recommending families develop a media plan (https://healthychildren.org/English/fmp/Pages/MediaPlan.aspx) to curtail excessive screen time and focus on high-quality content across a wide variety of media and digital options. These ideas connect to what public television was saying years ago to support the intentional use of television as an educational tool for informal learning.

As we consider the idea of "quality content" and the relevance of all of this in nurturing, supporting, and teaching creativity to young children, we should return to our seven characteristics of creative spaces. In selecting good programming, pay attention to the source (PBS has a good reputation for quality products), but also ask whether the program or digital media content does the following:

- Introduces **new experiences** or new content

- Allows children options to make choices and **engage individually**

- Focuses on **process over product**

- Offers **open-ended challenges***

- Provides opportunities for **social interactions** among participants.**

- Provides **multisensory** experiences

- Provides **multicultural** content

Partnerships with public television

Back in the 1990s, the Corporation for Public Broadcasting began issuing Ready to Learn Grants to public television stations across the country to help parents, caregivers, and child care providers make effective and appropriate use of their children's programming (PBS 2005; CPB 2011). We the authors have a special interest in partnering with public television because Tom used to work under this grant at Iowa Public Television, designing and implementing that outreach work. The pioneering work reached out to the child care community to encourage and support viewing paired with hands-on activities for each episode using, among many programs, *Sesame Street* and *Mister Rogers' Neighborhood*. Today many PBS programs provide printed and online material to support their effective use.

* In our view, many computer, video, and online games, especially in the educational area, are not often open-ended, have a limited number of interactive options, and tend to emphasize one correct answer.

**Technology does not always encourage social interaction. This is why we stress here the importance of "intentional use" and promoting coviewing to add that element to an experience where it might be missing.

We recommend partnering with local PBS stations to learn about the training and resources available to support educators' and families' intentional and educational use of programs. *Sesame Street* has a plethora of resources for all kinds of early childhood topics at https://sesameworkshop.org/resources. Hedda Sharapan, former educational consultant for *Mister Rogers' Neighborhood*, writes a monthly online newsletter for educators called *What We Can Continue to Learn from Fred Rogers*. (Go to www.fredrogersinstitute.org/heddas-newsletter to subscribe.) The February 2023 post explores the topic of how Mr. Rogers encouraged curiosity, a perfect entrée to creative thinking and wondering. For the newer programs, we suggest going to PBS Kids (https://pbskids.org) for links to program-based resources as well as a section just for parents/guardians with tips and ideas. Public television and any technology can be a source of informal learning, but it takes thoughtful and intentional consideration of how it can be used to accomplish your goals.

Parks and Cultural Venues

We dug deeply into three creative spaces that are available to most people in most communities. But we want to underscore a few more. Public parks and playgrounds are wonderful creative spaces, as is any space that can get us close to nature. It's little wonder that nature has been the most important inspiration for human creativity since early humans painted pictures of animals on cave walls near Lascaux, France, seventeen thousand years ago. There are many resources to support immersing young children in nature (see, for example, Sobel 2020 and Daly 2022). Many communities are home to performing arts groups (dance, music, and drama). Many have classes for children. These educational opportunities, outside of formal school, are informal learning options as well. Don't forget them.

Conclusion

The winner of the 2023 Academy Award for Best Picture was *Everything Everywhere All at Once*, a wild film that imagines hundreds of alternative universes, each with a separate story and sequence of events and an alternative version of ourselves. It is literally about everything, everywhere, and all at once because time and space are no longer staying in their dimensional lanes and get jumbled together. This is a creative way to talk about creativity. And in this chapter (and throughout the book), we invite you to imagine with us how creativity is everything and everywhere and all at once.

We discussed creative spaces and informal learning to make a few of the infinite connections between our daily lives, our location at any given time, and the creative possibilities present in our experiences. To conclude, we want to stress that this chapter could have been a whole book, and we are offering only a few examples of how creativity can be everything, everywhere, all at once. Please do not stop here. Explore what can be creative for you and your children in any waking moment. Using our guidelines about what makes for a creative space and what makes for informal learning can complement whatever is happening in preschool or child care.

Think about It

- How would you make your space a more creative space?

- Do you or your program have a partnership with the local public library? If not, what resources from the library could help support you, your children, and families?

- How might informal learning environments benefit formal learning environments such as your classroom/early childhood program?

- Look over your lesson plans for the past week and see if any could have been enhanced by a visit to a museum or by resources from a museum website.

- Look into your local public television station and discover what resources they have connected to a favorite program of your children.

Chapter Nine   # Big Idea 6: Creativity and Diversity, Equity, and Inclusion

How creativity helps us address issues of fairness and belonging

A s we write this chapter, the country is engaged in a protracted culture war. One example occurred in 2022, when the governor of Florida pushed a bill named the Stop Wrongs to Our Kids and Employees (WOKE) Act through the Florida legislature. This bill prohibits schools, colleges, and universities from teaching anything that would cause individuals to "feel guilt, anguish or any other form of psychological distress" due to their race, color, sex, or national origins (Stop WOKE Act 2022, 10). It bars state university professors from providing evidence against the state's voting laws. It outlaws the teaching of institutional or structural racism; that is, the idea that as ordinary functions are carried out, organizations or systems may impact individuals from racial groups differently, whether or not there is a single "racist" individual carrying out that function. With this law, academic freedom and the ability of teachers to have a say over what and how they teach has been compromised. Despite being struck down by a Florida judge who called the act "positively dystopian" and leaving many puzzled over its vague wording and definitions that defy conscientious efforts to obey the new law, Stop WOKE Act efforts have had a chilling effect on the teaching and practice of concepts like equity, diversity, and inclusion (Mudde 2023). In a *Guardian* opinion piece, Cas Mudde (2023) writes that one in four teachers have changed lesson plans due to laws like this.

The culture war drew focus on the theater of early childhood in April 2023 when the governor of Alabama, Kay Ivey, demanded the resignation of Dr. Barbara Cooper, head of the Alabama Department of Early Childhood Education. Ivey heard about the department's use of NAEYC's Developmentally Appropriate

Practices (DAP). In a statement, Ivey said, "Woke concepts that have zero to do with proper education and that are divisive at the core have no place in Alabama classrooms at any age level, let alone with our youngest learners" (Moseley 2023).

What "woke concepts" in DAP disturbed Ivey? There appear to be at least two ideas. First, that early childhood educators should be aware of "larger systemic forces that perpetuate systems of White privilege." Second, that parents who identify as gay, lesbian, or transgender should be treated with equality, dignity, and worth (Moseley 2023). These ideas are commonplace in business and politics across the country, so it is not surprising that many, including Dr. Cooper, were caught off guard by this accusation. Governor Ivey insisted that Dr. Cooper renounce the DAP text and stop using it. Instead of doing so, Dr. Cooper submitted her resignation. So the war rages on and the casualties mount.

Part of what we observe in this conflict is a lack of creativity when examining issues of diversity, equity, and inclusion. Just as creativity has an important role to play in the arts and sciences—indeed across every learning domain—it also has a central role to play in our moral lives. How we apply ideas of fairness to everyday life is a creative challenge. Applying ethical principles to real life requires original thought because rehashing the same old ideas really doesn't get us anywhere. Creativity can help us find useful solutions to problems of social justice or plain old human relationships. In public discourse, conflict requires us to think in new ways about the problem, its causes, and how to reframe it. Can we imagine ways to grab the string ends and pull so the knot is untied rather than tightened, becoming harder to untie? This is creative work.

Therefore, we do not enter this chapter about the intersections of creativity and diversity, equity, and inclusion blind to the challenges these subjects present. But creativity's value is even greater than we might imagine because it can be an essential and often unacknowledged aid in helping us address this important topic. We begin the chapter with definitions for *diversity*, *equity*, and *inclusion* with an eye on their implications and connections to creativity, considering how creativity can help us promote these values. We will ask how equitable access is to outside supports that nurture and promote creativity in young children. We will also offer some recommendations for educators and parents/guardians on nurturing and teaching creativity using an equity lens.

Whenever the discussion rolls around to issues of diversity, equity, and inclusion, defining terms is the first order of business. These terms are often misunderstood and confusing because they are used by different people in different ways. Rarely is a single definition the correct one, and maybe that's not the point. Whatever a reader thinks these terms mean, we want to be explicit about what *we* think they mean. We use words to communicate so our intention and meaning are clear and understood. Because this is a book about early childhood education, we use the definitions from the NAEYC (2019) position statement *Advancing Equity in Early Childhood Education*.

Diversity

According to the Definition of Key Terms section in the *Advancing Equity* statement, *diversity* means:

> Variation among individuals, as well as within and across groups of individuals, in terms of their backgrounds and lived experiences. These experiences are related to social identities, including race, ethnicity, language, sexual orientation, gender identity and expression, social and economic status, religion, ability status, and country of origin. The terms *diverse* and *diversity* are sometimes used as euphemisms for non-White. NAEYC specifically rejects this usage, which implies that Whiteness is the norm against which diversity is defined. (17)

What stands out to us in this definition is the very first word, *variation*: how we vary or are different from one another. The dimensions of diversity are endless. Each of us is unique, but diversity highlights that idea. Difference is controversial, especially when many of us see ourselves as a divided people. Yet within diversity is a strategy to address our lack of unity. Look at a one-dollar bill. On the back are the two sides of the Great Seal of the United States. The back of the seal, on the right side of the bill, depicts an eagle holding in its mouth a script with the words *E Pluribus Unum*, or in English, "out of many, one." Central to how we understand ourselves as a country is this very struggle that we are different and yet we are one. In fact, we could say it is our mission statement. How do we become one when we are so different from one another? That is the value and the challenge of diversity.

Diversity is a reality. How we respond to diversity is a choice that should be guided by ethical and moral values. We think potential responses to diversity are best understood as a continuum that starts with rejecting or othering those who are different from us. Then we reach a neutral point where we tolerate, accept, and accommodate the difference others present to us. But on the far extreme from rejection is embracing and celebrating. Here the differences others present to us are something to acknowledge and frame as a positive contribution to the present moment. In this way, embracing and celebrating diversity builds unity.

Early childhood has not been immune from the challenges of diversity. Consider the most recent statement on developmentally appropriate practices (NAEYC 2022) that repeatedly echoes that tension between having common and essential practices that are important for all children and yet understanding that children are unique and differ from one another in significant ways.

> Educators understand that each child reflects a complex mosaic of knowledge and experiences that contributes to the considerable diversity among any group of young children. . . . Early childhood educators recognize this diversity and the opportunities it offers to support *all* children's learning by recognizing each child as a unique individual with assets and strengths to contribute to the early childhood education learning environment. (xxxi)

Embracing and celebrating diversity are not trendy "woke" concepts for NAEYC but foundational values. Therefore, ideas like diversity, equity, and inclusion can and should play a key role in how we look at all practices related to early childhood education and creativity. Because creativity is, by definition, presenting new and original ideas, embracing difference seems important to nurturing creativity. The unique perspectives individual children bring because of their cultural, racial, ethnic, or genetic makeup (see chapter 6 on neurodiversity) are fuel for creativity.

Simply put, creativity and diversity are connected very deeply. Creativity involves flexibility of thought, an outside-the-box mindset, and a willingness to break rules and conventions to bring "the new" into play. Those skills, or cognitive predispositions, are essential for functioning in social situations marked by diverse individuals. Bringing diverse people together and navigating a world of difference requires creativity, imagining new possibilities that did not exist previously.

Likewise, diversity is necessary for creativity. Bringing together diverse people—of different backgrounds, races, ethnicities, ages, classes, education, and all possible characteristics—more often and in larger numbers fosters creativity. More new and different ideas give more opportunity for creativity to be and become. Consider some statements from a video of Amazon employees (Inside Amazon 2018):

- "Inclusion is necessary for diverse ideas to exist and grow. Inclusion and diversity combined is what allows innovation."—Tania San-Miguel Bounds

- "[Diversity] helps [us] innovate faster, and think bigger."—Eli Yoffe

- "Having diverse teams allows us to think creatively when we're thinking of different ways of solving a problem." —Neha Goswami

- "Diversity brings and encourages new ideas and you never know where you're going to get them."—Mario Marin

If workers talking about work situations testify to the value of diversity in solving problems and being innovative, how could this not also be true of early education programs or families where diversity is invited in and celebrated? When children who are used to eating with knives and forks learn that some people use chopsticks, what a revelation! Or when a father comes in and sings a folk song in a language most of the children haven't heard before, or when a grandmother demonstrates a sari or head scarf or *huipil*. Everything, even everyday and commonplace things like eating, singing, and clothes, can be seen in new ways. Caregivers and educators alike can intentionally introduce that newness and that difference to evoke creative responses.

Equity

The Key Terms section from the *Advancing Equity* statement defines *equity* as

the state that would be achieved if individuals fared the same way in society regardless of race, gender, class, language, disability, or any other social or cultural characteristic. In practice, equity means all children and families receive necessary supports in a timely fashion so they can develop their full intellectual, social, and physical potential. (NAEYC 2019, 17)

This definition reminds us that equity is about fairness. When things are out of line with what we think is right, we react by saying, "That's not fair." Those are almost always equity issues.

In the original full statement, the definition includes an explanation of the difference between equity and equality. The stress in early childhood on individuality makes it clear that every child should not be treated the same even if we have similar (or equal) expectations for success in reaching important developmental milestones. In practice we are not giving every child the same thing; we take a more nuanced approach that does what is necessary to ensure that every child reaches their full potential.

Looking at creativity through an equity lens makes us ask if we are equitably making available opportunities to be creative and to express creativity, and if we are acknowledging and supporting children's unique contributions. If all children are creative, then no single approach to let them express their gifts is acceptable. Creative expression, as we have written throughout this book, takes many forms. And paying attention to how each child is being creative, noting which creative activities they choose, is the first step. Then we provide whatever unique scaffolds and affirmations are the key to creative equity.

Is it fair that only children who love to paint are considered creative? Is it fair that only those who are quick problem solvers be considered creative? Is it fair that only those who show interest in the subject be rewarded or acknowledged, or is there a way to find special subjects or experiences that ignite the intellectual curiosity of each child? These are equity questions.

Everyone is creative, but creative endowments are unique. Given this central fact, we see how it fits with our understanding of equity, when everyone gets the support they need to be successful. Success in the context of this chapter means being creative, exploring one's innate creativity, and exercising one's unique creative gifts. Equity demands that every child's creativity is supported and nurtured, shared as valuable within the family or among the community of learners. The support and nurturing must be provided equitably, fairly, so that we don't see only some children as creative and others less so. This approach says that talented and gifted (TAG) programming is a profoundly inequitable practice that needlessly withholds critical opportunities for creative learning and expression. We are not suggesting that a so-called TAG student should have opportunities taken away from them. That strikes us as zero-sum thinking. Rather, we are suggesting that the goal should be effective differentiation of instruction for all children and an approach to all instruction that emphasizes and leverages creativity.

This last point hits home with Zach, who was in special education through most of his K–12 education (see his fuller story in chapter 6). At an IEP meeting during sixth grade, he requested that he be put into a TAG program because he felt it would best support how he learned, asserting that his struggles were not a learning disability. The request was turned down. Zach says today that it "stifled how I learn and how I understand as a learner. It was not until I got my first master's degree that I realized, wait, I am smart. I can learn. But it matters how you teach me."

When we examine creativity from an equity perspective, our teaching practices and educational policies should change. Equity in the context of creativity means tailoring our environments, lesson plans, and assessments to do five things:

1. Become aware of and make children aware of their creativity as part of the unique endowment they have in just being human. Mihaly Csikszentmihalyi (1996) found that creativity vanishes if it is not recognized. A unique and useful idea is like a tree falling in the forest. Unless it is heard, can it be said to exist?

2. Provide children with opportunities to explore and develop their creative gifts. This includes developing spaces that invite creative exploration. A variety of materials and experiences must be available because creativity is so varied and every child is creative in unique ways, so those opportunities *cannot* be the same for every child. What each child needs to be creative must be discovered.

3. Collect, document, and curate the artifacts of creativity. Maybe it's snapping a picture of the latest block construction or making a note of an interesting comment made during circle time. The point is to treat all forms of creative expression as valuable, worthy of acknowledgment and recognition.

4. Remove barriers that interfere with children's access and opportunity; this is a professional responsibility. Later in this chapter, we will discuss more about removing structural barriers.

5. Practice what Colin Seale (2022) calls "Tangible Equity," a term he coined to describe strategies to make equity concrete and real in everyday educational practices. In his words, this means moving "beyond good people with good intentions" (61). His six Ps—Power, Priorities, Probe, Privilege, People, and Problems—provide step-by-step guidance for educators in dismantling structural barriers to educational equity.

Inclusion

The "Key Terms" definition from NAEYC's 2019 *Advancing Equity* position statement reads:

The values, policies, and practices that support the right of every infant and young child and their family, regardless of ability, to participate in a broad range of activities and contexts as full members of families, communities, and society. The desired results of inclusive experiences for children with and without disabilities and their families include a sense of belonging and membership, positive social relationships and friendships, and development and learning to help them reach their full potential. (18)

Children belong with their peers, and whatever makes them different (such as ability) should not be a reason for excluding or segregating them. It is illegal to exclude children on the basis of race, gender, and ethnicity. Inclusion is a central goal when celebrating differences and pursuing justice.

The DEC/NAEYC (2009) joint position statement on early childhood inclusion focuses on the inclusion of children with disabilities and says that inclusion consists of access, participation, and support. That is what we mean by *inclusion*: everyone has access to learning and experiences, participates and engages at a level to maximize their learning, and is supported individually in whatever way is necessary to ensure that access and participation. Factors other than disability may also limit access, especially in early childhood. Families living in poverty do not have the same access to high-quality education. And even in public education, quality varies based on the tax base of the community.

We like to think about the connection between belonging and inclusion. Being included is a sign that we belong. The opposite of *bias* (another key term in diversity, equity, and inclusion [DEI] work) is belonging. Taking an unbiased view of a person is telling someone they belong and therefore are included.

We must acknowledge three central equity issues facing early childhood education that are at heart inclusion issues: suspension and expulsion of young children from early childhood settings; inconsistent access to teaching and learning for dual language learners; and, as mentioned above, the segregation of children with special needs into classrooms that are separated from typically developing peers (Children's Equity Center/Bipartisan Policy Center 2020). Addressing these larger equity issues will also promote creative equity. Suspended or expelled children likely lose access to the nurture and support of their creativity. Not making explicit and intentional efforts to address language barriers thwarts the best creative instruction. Isolating differently abled children interrupts the rich social learning needed for creativity that is brought about because of the diversity of learners present.

We must fairly include everyone in everything that relates to how creativity is taught, supported, and nurtured in classrooms and early education programs. Do all children have equitable access to every aspect of creativity that shows up in the curriculum? What must change so they do? How can we consider children with special needs, given the tendency of our educational system to place them in self-contained learning environments away from typically developing children? If we are not teaching children in inclusive settings, we are not equitably teaching them creativity.

Fred Rogers (1994) tells us, "What nourishes the imagination? Probably more than anything else, loving adults who encourage the imaginative play of children's own making" (47). In other words, it is the relationships children have that most nourish their imaginations and creativity. Do children have equitable access to those "loving adults"? What about access to other children? Their creative expressions in play, the arts, learning, and making are often more influential on children's creativity than anything adults do. Inclusion, as a function of setting or environment, directly affects motivation to learn and learning itself, and therefore creativity.

Creativity and Culture

Every person, every child, has a cultural identity, which is why an examination of cultural identity is a key part of DEI work. Young children are raised inside of a specific culture that gives them an indelible mark and speaks profoundly about who they are. This hearkens back to our discussion of Bronfenbrenner in chapter 3, where we discussed how the macrosystem has a cultural dimension, which intersects with the family within the microsystem. Culture is present among parents/guardians, extended family, and neighborhood institutions and organizations. In essence, the many contexts that shape who a child is and who they become almost always have a cultural element.

NAEYC's *Advancing Equity* statement (2019) defines *culture* as "patterns of beliefs, practices, and traditions associated with a group of people" (17). Barbara Rogoff, in *The Cultural Nature of Human Development* (2003), argues that one cannot understand child development apart from culture. All child development theory and practice has a cultural component. Culture shapes how children see themselves, who they are, and what they are trying to do.

Rogoff (2003) writes, "Culture is not an entity that *influences* individuals. Instead, people contribute to the creation of cultural processes and cultural processes contribute to the creation of people" (51). This is why recognizing and acknowledging the cultural identities of young children in an early education setting is so important: who they show up as is in no small part who they were raised to be from their very conception. They bring the culture that shaped them. When children are behaving in certain ways, it behooves us as caregivers to wonder how that behavior relates to their upbringing and its cultural context before establishing strategies for addressing it.

Rogoff also argues that these two dynamics—the individual shaped by culture and the individual shaping culture—are "*mutually constituting* rather than defined separately from each other" (51). This means we see the causation moving in both directions. Rogoff helps us understand that even as children are expressing various aspects of their cultural upbringing, they are also ever so slightly, often unconsciously, expressing those aspects in a way that modifies the culture around them. When those changes are positively received and imitated by others, they become "cultural processes." Those processes in turn shape behavior, which also is shaped again by how that new process is expressed. And on it goes. This process is not individual but collaborative.

In this way, the expression of culture and the perpetual way it is changed are products of creativity. And as with all creative activity, it should be acknowledged, celebrated, and encouraged. For example, you may have a big reaction when a child says the F-word, but what do you do when they reply, "What's wrong with that word? My mommy uses it all the time." In these cases, the child is bringing forth cultural knowledge in their own way but has little experience with how cultural expectations change between family and school. Bringing these new ideas into a different setting is an act of creativity as well as a way in which culture is expressed and shared. Caring adults can help support that learning by appreciating and supporting how children understand their world and themselves. With guidance, children learn how to express themselves.

Rogoff (2003) writes, "Culture is not static; it is formed from the efforts of people working together, using and adapting material and symbolic tools provided by predecessors and in the process creating new ones" (51). The ongoing evolution of culture is driven by "people working together"—in other words, collaboration. Rogoff further expounds,

> Communities develop as generations of individuals make choices and invent solutions to changing circumstances. Borrowing and building on the practices of several communities can lead to cultural practices that creatively solve current problems of child rearing and community adaptation. (362)

In nearly every case, creativity comes from, is responsive to, and is an expression of culture. Most cultures use creative expressions to say something about themselves, what's important to them, what is pretty, what is appropriate and valuable. At one level, creative expression might include artwork, food, clothing, or music. At a deeper level, cultural expressions of creativity are embedded in ideas about language, education, health, social relationships, and religion. Another important element is how creativity or creative expression is or is not a value within a culture. Most cultures support positive representations of themselves but are less enthusiastic about negative or critical perspectives. Some cultures are more or less open to certain cultural expressions, say, from young children. That receptivity, that acceptance or rejection, will strongly influence the role of creativity within a child.

If there are barriers to cultural expression, such as allowing a dominant culture to be the default and not identifying different cultures and their various expressions, culture and therefore creativity are suppressed. Creativity is multicultural, and as educators and caregivers, we must be careful not to ignore or suppress creative expression coming from nondominant cultures. We must allow a rich multicultural learning environment if we want diverse, equitable, and inclusive creative engagement.

Basic culturally responsive teaching practices, such as drawing on children's culture to shape curriculum and instruction, collaborating with families and local communities, and promoting respect for differences among children can foster creativity or be adapted to address creativity (Muñiz 2020). A good place to start with cultural responsiveness is establishing close connections and communications with families. It is important for a child's development that they can embrace their culture and express it creatively.

A good case in point comes from Dr. Debra Sullivan's book *Cultivating the Genius of Black Children* (2016). Early in this book, Sullivan writes about how African American culture intersects with certain approaches to learning, explaining distinctive characteristics about Black creative expression that have been identified in the research. She writes,

> Expressiveness can be found in almost every aspect of the African American cultural experience, and high value is placed on creativity, uniqueness, "flavor," and style. Individualism is encouraged. . . . Creative expression is a form of communicating thoughts, ideas, emotions, perspectives, and experiences. Jazz, an African American creation, is a perfect example. The mark of an expert is *not* being able to re-create music exactly as presented on a sheet of paper; it is being able to embroider and embellish the sheet music with your own unique, creative, stylistic flair. (48)

She goes on to discuss what this might mean in a classroom.

> The learning task provided by the teacher . . . serves as a template, a starting point, not the end product. The goal is to take what is presented and make it different, special, unique. Such creative learners often color outside the lines, add more details to the drawing, invent new verses for the song. . . . Unfortunately, many of our learning environments limit such individual expression or eliminate opportunities for creative expression when budgets are strained or restricted. (55)

When diversity, equity, and inclusion meet creativity, there is space for creative expression. Diversity comes through in the varied approaches children take in addressing an assignment. Equity is how these varied approaches are recognized and celebrated. Inclusion is the space we create when we allow for the unexpected, the creative. Too often what is unexpected is perceived as nonconforming, rebellious, and disruptive, and therefore not welcome because we did not expect it. However, a teacher who reframes the effort and perceives the results as something different, special, and unique, as something to delight in, enjoying the surprise and getting curious about why and where it came from, can expand learning dramatically and nurture creativity in students who might otherwise feel shut down or disrespected. (Remember that *disrespect* means literally to "not see again.") The most important thing an educator can do to nurture creativity is to see it, acknowledge it, and deem it valuable.

In a multicultural context, we should ensure that children have the opportunity for creative expression of their home culture (dance, song, stories, food, clothing, and so forth) and then give space and time to showcase those unique, culturally derived expressions for everyone. By doing this, we help children discover a new route to their creative lives.

Structural Barriers to Creativity

As necessary as these practices may seem, the reality is that the barriers to creative expression are all too common among historically disenfranchised students. In a famous TED talk, English author and education adviser Ken Robinson pointed out the contradiction between the pressing need for more creativity in the world and how educational institutions, built on old nineteenth-century factory models, marginalize creativity and the arts by overemphasizing standardized tests and rote learning (Robinson 2006, 2010). Of course, early childhood education has pushed back against this for a long time, but sadly these trends are more likely to be true in poorly resourced schools. Jonathan Kozol (2005) describes visits to schools in Ohio, New York, California, and Chicago. He found those with a predominantly non-white student body focused on academic testing, scripted curricula, and lesson plans, as well as an emphasis on skills related to the technical trades.

Kozol describes a classroom visit he made in which the rigidity of the instruction shocked him. When he spoke to the teacher afterward, the teacher said

> his principal had little choice about the implementation of this program, which had been mandated for all elementary schools in New York City that had had

rock-bottom academic records over a long period of time. "This puts me into a dilemma," he went on, "because I love the kids at P.S. 65." And even while, he said, "I know that my teaching SFA [Success for All, a scripted curriculum] is a charade . . . if I don't do it I won't be permitted to teach these children." (50)

This bleak picture, though dated, illustrates how educational policy that seems to be almost anti-creativity has long been promoted in poorer and minoritized schools. We suspect that things have changed in classrooms over the years, but probably not enough. We are sure readers will be able to describe contemporary learning environments where this is still commonplace. We also know that prekindergarten educational settings are more segregated than K–12 schools (Peiffer 2019). Quality and educational outcomes may vary across these settings as well. For example, Ijumaa Jordan (2022) describes visits to two preschools, one in an affluent community and the other in a lower-income neighborhood. In the former, she found an elaborate outdoor environment with a treehouse and hills to roll down, and a well-equipped indoors with water tables, musical instruments, and portfolios with work samples, anecdotal notes, and family commentary. The lower-income preschool had four classrooms surrounding a small outdoor area with a large play structure that had been built with funds donated by the parents. Playtime was limited to twenty minutes and only "sometimes" were the balls brought out to play. Similar rote learning and a tight control over movement and participation options, as Kozol describes above, were present here. Jordan explains that the push to get play back into kindergarten and early childhood programs "ignores the elephant in the room" because misguided policies fall disproportionately on Black and Brown children (51).

Dartmouth College professor Casey Stockstill (2023) accidentally discovered how segregation was an issue in early childhood programs. In her book *False Start: The Segregated Lives of Preschoolers,* she explains how she set out to simply observe children in two preschools in Wisconsin, a middle-income private school and a Head Start program. The classrooms were, in fact, segregated by poverty and race. The racial and economic disparities in the community were reflected in the classroom. What she observed from two programs that were considered both of good quality was a starkly different lived reality because children bring their socioeconomic backgrounds with them. Enrollment in the private classroom was virtually the same from fall to spring. In the Head Start program, there was a 30 percent student turnover. Kids were showing up after unpredictable evenings. That worked against efforts to create stability and predictability. The private school children were able to sit for longer story hours than those in the Head Start program. Stockstill argues that if the classrooms were made up of smaller percentages of children from lower socioeconomic backgrounds, behaviors could be better managed and creative learning opportunities increased.

We know that children living in poverty are less likely than richer children to play sports in school and take music and art lessons. They are also less likely to be in gifted and talented programs where many schools explicitly encourage creativity and creative activities (Knop 2020). And there is a wider trend to reduce or eliminate "optional" arts programs and even recess in schools, especially those with more limited resources (Miller and Almon 2009). In Seattle Public Schools, white kids get the most recess and Black kids the least (Dornfeld 2019). Mariana Souto-Manning (2017) makes the point that any boisterous behavior on the part of young Black boys is often clamped down, and thus active play is restricted disproportionately. An equity approach insists that play is a right and not a privilege. These systemic barriers to creativity must be dismantled. As educators, we need to ensure that all children have access to instruction that places an emphasis on creativity, understanding its positive effect on cognitive and social development.

Our point here is that instructional practices that inhibit creative expression are more commonplace in schools and programs that serve primarily Black and Brown children. While we know that is not true everywhere or all the time, we are emphasizing how an exploration of creativity from a diversity, equity, and inclusion lens requires that we dismantle policies and practices that make the encouragement and nurturing of creativity less likely. Consider Alabama, where developmentally appropriate practices—which recommend and promote experiences that nurture curiosity, peer community, pretend play, exploration, and creative expression—are deemed "too woke" and therefore may discourage the very things a creativity-centered approach to early learning should include.

Teacher bias may also affect support for creativity in young children. Tuppett Yates and Ana Marcelo (2014) found in their study of 114 preschoolers that teachers who rated children of all races highly along dimensions of imaginative and expressive pretend play nevertheless rated the Black children with lower school preparedness, less peer acceptance, and more teacher-child conflict. The greater the creativity, the more Black children were deemed less ready for school and less likely to get along with peers and adults. Some of this bias contributes to the disproportionate levels of suspension and expulsion of Black children from early childhood programs despite not showing more frequent or severe misbehavior (Gilliam et al. 2016; Children's Equity Center/Bipartisan Policy Center 2020).

Another structural barrier has been standardized tests. Routinely, children of color have scored lower on academic and intelligence tests than white children. Some scholars, notoriously among them the authors of *The Bell Curve* (Murray and Herrnstein 1994), have assumed an inherent intellectual deficit when scores are consistently lower among certain groups. Others have pushed back and questioned the motives and methods of scholars like Charles Murray and Richard Herrnstein, saying that the authors were trying to make the case that intelligence is genetic, which is a small step away from the plainly racist idea that genes must explain this discrepancy. Critics pushed back by stressing that race is a social construction, that genetic differences among races are not at all pronounced, and that there are other, less toxic explanations for the differences among some children of color and white children when it comes to intelligence test results (Ryan 1994).

What is seldom raised in this debate is the research of Paul Torrance, who found that his pioneering creativity test did not have the same racial disparities as intelligence tests. While most creativity scholars say there is a connection between intelligence and creativity, it is not consistent or even a strong association (Kaufman 2023). The Torrance Tests for Creativity Thinking (TTCT) is a classic divergent thinking test, identifying subjects who easily and readily expand their thinking about subjects. When children respond to questions, the test measures the number of ideas generated (fluency), the variation among those ideas (flexibility), how unique the ideas are (originality), and how developed the ideas are (elaboration) (Torrance 1962; Torrance 1965, 269–71, 310–11). The TTCT remains a popular option for measuring creativity in schools and for research. Meanwhile, it is widely acknowledged as not precisely able to capture the full array of creative thought processes, and concerns persist about its predictive validity (Kaufman 2016, 73–74, 215).

As Torrance was assessing his test's validity, he discovered that when he disaggregated scores by white and Black races and between middle- and low-income groups, there was no statistically significant difference. The "intelligence" difference identified in IQ tests did not appear in Torrance's TTCT test (Torrance 1971). In fact, African American children scored higher than Caucasian children in the test domains of fluency, flexibility, and originality. James C. Kaufman (2016, 138) reports on a 2005 meta-analysis involving more than forty-five thousand subjects and writes that it found "very small positive correlations." Kaufman and colleagues found no differences in rated creativity of "poems, stories and personal narratives written by African American, Hispanic American, Asian American and Caucasian eighth grade students" (232).

If creativity is a kind of intelligence, it may be a more universally accessible intelligence and therefore one that is more fundamental to human experience. Creativity may be a way of tapping into intelligence in children that is less accessible through conventional means, such as how well they do in school or on tests of cognitive ability. Knowing that creativity is a common and useful cognitive ability should minimize the inherent bias educators exhibit when they look at academic performance or test results and make assumptions about children's underlying abilities. Creativity becomes a lens that views children more equally, perhaps because creativity is more open-ended than most tests of cognitive ability and yet also requires a certain utility. If we could fairly assess children's creative potential, educators could better prepare them for their unique vocations.

Suggestions for dismantling these barriers should focus on rote learning, less time for recess and play, teacher bias, and standardized tests:

1. *Support all children's creativity.* The central problem of equity in education is disproportionate outcomes that stem from disproportionate treatment and disproportionate expectations. This manifests in the domain of creativity when educators believe that some children are not creative because they do not exhibit certain obvious talents and therefore do not merit support. We dismantle this barrier by not believing this myth. All people deserve support and nurturing of their creative potential, however it manifests itself.

2. *Be aware of individual bias.* We all have biases. We all have things we see and don't see. We all like some things and dislike others. Dismantling barriers begins with taking these common tendencies toward bias and making sure they are not influencing how we treat and teach children. This begins with introspection, knowing ourselves deeply, and ensuring the choices we make as educators are intentional and not harming children. We need to make our implicit biases explicit so we can make more thoughtful educational decisions.

3. *Engage children at a cultural level.* Encouraging cultural expression is a good way to help children experience and celebrate their creativity. We know cultural expression is invariably a creative expression. Using culture to tap into creative impulses can open up new avenues to elicit creativity from children.

4. *Use recognized strategies for individualization.* A popular way to approach individualization is a technology called Universal Design for Learning (UDL) that was developed by the organization CAST. According to the CAST website, UDL "is a framework to improve and optimize teaching and learning for all people based on scientific insights into how humans learn" (CAST 2024, para. 1). This framework allows educators to develop a curriculum that can be individualized and therefore uniquely responsive to a child's specific needs.

Universal Design for Learning (UDL) asks educators to provide multiple means of engagement, multiple means of representation, and multiple means of expression and action. The idea is to overcome the many barriers that keep students from paying attention, understanding the content, and demonstrating their new knowledge. The UDL framework guides the design of instructional goals, assessments, methods, and materials that can be customized and adjusted to meet individual needs.

The CAST website (https://udlguidelines.cast.org) includes the guidelines for the UDL framework as a graphic organizer. The framework introduces educators to a layered approach to teaching and ensures that learners leave with a uniquely internalized understanding of the content. We also recommend Marla Lohmann's (2023) *Creating Young Expert Learners: Universal Design for Learning in Preschool and Kindergarten.*

Conclusion

Creativity is a central way by which we can advance DEI. Its invitation to newness and usefulness are exactly the ingredients we need among young children and adults to sort out and respond to the many challenges surrounding diversity, equity, and inclusion and understand the reality we live in, to face it head-on in all its uncertainty and complexity. There are no easy answers. As Barbara Rogoff (2003) reminds us, "The goal is to learn creatively from each other, to be able to address new issues as well as those with which humans have struggled for generations" (362).

We understand that the act of promoting and nurturing creativity in young children is an act of embracing diversity, advancing equity, and ensuring inclusion. Too often status quo learning environments and situations work against creativity in early childhood education. These barriers must be identified and removed with an intentionality that signals how important creativity is.

The special relationship between creativity and culture opens many opportunities to recognize and invite creative expression that validate the identity of young children and ensure that their culture will be a lasting support for understanding self and the purpose of life. No one expresses this better than Rogoff (2003):

There is not likely to be One Best Way. Understanding different cultural practices does not require determining which *one* way is "right" (which does not mean that *all* ways are fine). . . . Learning from other communities does not require giving up one's own ways, but it does require suspending one's assumptions temporarily to consider others and carefully separating efforts to understand cultural phenomena from efforts to judge their value. (368–69)

Think about It

- Complete this sentence. I always feel like I belong someplace when _____.

- Attend an art exhibit or a musical, dance, or theater performance created by individuals who are not from your cultural background (however you define that). Reflect on the similarities and differences compared to other artistic exhibitions you have seen from your own cultural background.

- Think about the children in your life you care about, whether as their parent/guardian or educator or other caregiver. Write down their name(s) on a piece of paper. Then make a list of at least five "creative endowments" you can identify. What are you doing to support their creativity?

- As an educator or parent/guardian, when you look at the creative life of your children, what are barriers you see that interfere with their access and opportunity? How about other people's children?

- Are you facing opposition or pushback to local efforts that support DEI? How do you respond? Who else or what organization in your community would be an ally in supporting DEI?

Chapter Ten

Big Idea 7: Creativity and Trauma

Looking after our village

Dr. Bruce Perry and Maia Szalavitz (2006, 258), authors of *The Boy Who Was Raised as a Dog: And Other Stories from a Child Psychiatrist's Notebook*, state, "The more healthy relationships a child has, the more likely he will be to recover from trauma and thrive. Relationships are the agents of change, and the powerful therapy is human love." Child development is not a linear process but a complex one that includes both positive and negative experiences. When negative events or situations are extreme or destructive, we often talk about them in terms of trauma. These experiences play an outsized role in the lives of young children because children are vulnerable and often have not built up the psychological defenses needed to survive even relatively small slights. Such trauma can cause physical and psychological damage, affecting children's perception of themselves and others.

Severe trauma is not about isolated cases or a rare instance of abuse from a violent or negligent family member. It is all too common. Consider the following:

- At least one in seven children experience child abuse/neglect each year (CDC 2024a).

- Each day, one thousand youth are treated in emergency departments for physical assault–related injuries (CDC 2024b).

- Sixty percent of children have been exposed to crime, violence, or abuse, either directly or indirectly (Finkelhor et al. 2009).

Or look at the Adverse Childhood Experiences (ACEs) Study. ACEs are ten types of trauma: physical abuse, sexual abuse, emotional abuse, physical neglect, emotional neglect, mental illness, divorce, substance abuse, violence against your mother, and having a relative who has been sent to jail or prison. The study found that 64 percent of US adults reported they had experienced at least one type of ACE before age eighteen, and nearly one in six (17.3 percent) reported they had experienced four or more types of ACEs (Swedo et al. 2023).

Our purpose for including a chapter on trauma is to explore the idea that creativity can be a healing impulse when children are damaged by harmful experiences. We are familiar with play therapy and art therapy, through which creative faculties help children heal and build skills useful in resilient behavior. By understanding trauma, you can incorporate creative expression in the learning environment or at home to help children find socially appropriate ways to express feelings of shame and rage, as well as increase their self-esteem, build resilience, reduce stress, and feel empowered. Creative expression can be incorporated into the curriculum or into home activities through art, music, dance, and drama. This book is about nurturing and supporting creativity in young children, and this chapter is about why that may help children understand, process, and recover from trauma.

What is traumatic or harmful to one child may not be to another child, nor may it seem traumatic or harmful from an adult perspective. Trauma is about what a situation or event does to the child from that child's point of view. One thing that can change how an experience affects a child is whether it is occurring on top of previous trauma or in the context of a family beset with mental health concerns. It soon becomes apparent that the impact of trauma is more important than what the traumatic experience was. Trauma can elicit strong emotions like fear, guilt, helplessness, or rage. It makes it harder to trust. Children become overwhelmed by conflicting emotions. Trauma can cause dissociation, where a child feels cut off from themselves, withdraws, or starts to manifest dramatically different behavior than previously.

The effects of trauma present themselves every day in our early education programs and our homes. Let's prepare for trauma by learning more about how creativity is the mind's way of creating meaning from experiences, even bad ones, and how we can identify and support its innate movement toward healing in ourselves and others. Creativity can create meaning and coherence during chaos and allow us to restore a sense of normalcy, of wholeness and health, of equilibrium and stasis.

Before we move forward with this chapter, we offer this disclaimer: diagnosing and treating trauma should be the work of trained professionals with both the education and authority (licensure) to perform this work. The recommendations in this chapter should not be interpreted as a treatment plan for any specific case involving trauma. They are, instead, general recommendations to guide the thinking of nonprofessionals in considering appropriate action.

What Is Trauma?

The Substance Abuse and Mental Health Services Administration defines trauma as "an event, series of events, or set of circumstances" resulting in physical harm, emotional harm, and/or life-threatening harm and that "has lasting adverse effects on the individual's functioning and mental, physical, social, emotional, or spiritual well-being" (SAMHSA's Trauma and Justice Strategic Initiative 2014, 7) This definition points to both trauma's lasting impact and its comprehensive impact. On this second point, a detailed white paper published by the National Child Traumatic Stress Network (Cook et al. 2003) presents an organization framework for complex trauma outcomes in children with seven impairment domains: attachment, biology, affect regulation, dissociation, behavioral regulation, cognition, and self-concept.

Trauma has a whole-child effect. The signs of trauma show up in dramatic and volatile emotional expression, in thinking and reasoning impairments (think about difficulties engaging the executive network we learned about in chapter 5), and physiological symptoms like pain, sleeplessness, and abnormal behavior, though not always with a clear label. Tom remembers when one of his daughters was two years old, she began to act out in startling ways, like smearing butter on the sliding glass doors leading to the backyard. It was a clear sign that something was not right, but what was the problem? How could it be trauma? Tom and his wife thought about what changes had occurred before their daughter started to act differently. They realized that they had started their daughter in a new at-home child care arrangement. They also knew it was not going smoothly but thought it was worth staying since child care was not easy to find and perhaps things would improve over time. They didn't. This behavior communicated in a way their daughter's words could not. They found another care setting and the behaviors immediately stopped.

Trauma and the Brain

Despite the whole-body effects of trauma, the brain seems to play an outsized role when trauma occurs. The brain is the central control system of the body. When a child experiences trauma, it creates a response in the brain that impacts all the other body systems. Cathy Malchiodi (2015) reports that some experts believe that if the traumatic event is serious enough, the memory of the trauma is stored in feelings or images. The child may not be able to talk about or even understand what happened. However, other kinds of activities like play or artistic expression that engage the default network may allow a child to access the memories (11).

The brain's response to trauma also helps us understand why children who have experienced trauma behave the way they do. Simply put, when a child experiences a terrible episode, the body takes over and starts to activate the limbic system, the brain's emotional regulation network (Malchiodi 2015, 8). This is a survival response that can cause a child to exhibit classic post-traumatic stress disorder (PTSD) symptoms. In fact, the DSM-5 (*Diagnostic and Statistical Manual of Mental Disorders*, 5th edition) has added a "*preschool* subtype posttraumatic stress disorder," which includes more developmentally accurate symptoms for young children (APA 2013, 6, emphasis added). Another condition that manifests is Developmental Trauma Disorder (DTD). Symptoms include having difficulty playing or engaging in creative activities, being wary of adult and sometimes even peer relationships, having diminished ability to calm down by themselves or "self-soothe," and using coping strategies that keep them from "emotional closeness, readiness to learn and imagination" (APA 2013, 7). This is what makes trauma so difficult to address. The very mechanisms that can help a child deal with challenging emotions are not available to them.

Yet another impact of trauma is cortisol toxicity. A traumatic experience raises the level of cortisol, a hormone that is released during times of perceived threat that prepares the mind and body for a fight-or-flight response. When stress is persistent, these high levels of cortisol become toxic and negatively affect brain development, especially in young children whose brains are developing (Gebney 2018).

The specific impacts on development in the brain are telling. For example, the hippocampus, a brain area that creates, stores, and interprets episodic memory, is smaller in adolescents who experienced trauma in early childhood (Humphreys et al. 2020). And the prefrontal cortex, which plays a central role in the executive network, can become deactivated when an individual experiences trauma, affecting areas such as reasoning and decision-making (Bremner 2006). These effects help explain why children respond the way they do to trauma and suggest what an effective healing and caring intervention can look like.

Epigenetics: How Trauma Lives On

Recent research has shown that trauma can change the genetic makeup of the body so the impact of trauma is transmitted from generation to generation. That outside influence on genetic makeup and its expression, determining which parts of the genetic code show up physiologically, is called *epigenetics*. (The prefix *epi*- means "above" or "beyond.") Trauma can have an epigenetic impact on a person by switching genetic expression on or off due to environmental factors. These genetic changes are reversible and do not change DNA sequence (CDC 2024c).

Epigenetics are significant during the developmental period of early childhood. Trauma, including abuse, a parent or guardian with alcoholism, poverty, and neglect, to name a few forms, have an epigenetic impact on how children's genes work (CDC 2024c). This directly affects their learning, their relationships with peers, their relationship with you as their educator, their ability to trust, and their ability to seek assistance in their learning. Understanding epigenetics is important to your relationships with parents/caregivers who may have had traumatic experiences themselves. These experiences may influence their parenting, their interaction with their child, and their involvement in their child's education.

Trauma-Informed Care and the Environment

Our purpose in going into so much detail around early childhood trauma is to make crystal clear the connection between trauma and creativity, as both are neurological phenomena. It follows that healing from such insults on the brain's neurological systems would also involve brain-based intervention. As we consider why creativity may be an effective response to trauma, we begin by defining *trauma-informed care*. The National Child Traumatic Stress Network defines a trauma-informed system as "one in which all parties involved recognize and respond to the impact of traumatic stress on those who have contact with the system, including children, caregivers, and service providers. Programs and agencies . . . act in collaboration with all those who are involved with the child, using the best available science, to maximize physical and psychological safety, facilitate the recovery of the child and family, and support their ability to thrive" (NCTSN 2024). Any response or support to an individual child who has experienced trauma should be done in the context of sound trauma-informed practices.

This means, in part, that learning environments should foster social-emotional well-being; build a community of trust among children, educators, and parents/ caregivers; offer children the safety and opportunity to express themselves; and provide an extended network of professionals to help children deal with traumatic experiences in a healthy way. Everything we talked about in chapter 3 about Bronfenbrenner's bioecological model, which describes the overlapping systems in which a child grows up, is relevant here because it shows us how these multiple influences can help and harm children. It also shows how they can become a web of support.

Trauma and Creativity

"Grimm's Fairy Tales saved my ass," cartoonist and art teacher Lynda Berry told *The New York Times Magazine* (Marchese 2022). Berry had a rough childhood: her father abandoned the family when she was twelve, and she faced episodic poverty and her own struggles with depression. Having creative outlets, both as a consumer and as a creator, was essential to her survival. Creativity can be healing, and her story helps us understand why. She read. She drew. She told stories. She saw movies. She sang songs. It all restored her. She told her interviewer,

> I've found that engaging in this kind of work—anything that adults call art and that kids might call a toy; that contains something alive—seems to make me feel that life is worth living. It's a thing I always say to my students: Art is a public-health concern because it keeps you from killing yourself and others. (para. 29)

Creativity can and should play a central and curative role in the lives of people affected by trauma. The connection is clear. And not just cartoonists think so. Christianne Strang, a professor of neuroscience at the University of Alabama at Birmingham, insists, "Creativity in and of itself is important for remaining healthy, remaining connected to yourself and connected to the world" (Gharib 2020).

Researchers Paula Thomson and S. Victoria Jaque (2018) compared 234 adult professional performing artists with varying numbers of ACEs. They found that performers with four or more ACEs (18 percent of the sample) were more likely to report anxiety and shame-based responses, which one might expect. They also showed disproportionately greater inclinations toward fantasy, demonstrated a creative process that was more intense and more highly valued, and expressed enjoyment in the performance experience, traits the researchers suggest may indicate more creative resilience (Jacobs 2018, para. 4). As well, these performers with high ACEs levels expressed greater appreciation for creativity's ability to change them and help them engage with the world.

When Paula Thomson (2018) examined artists with PTSD, she found that they were more likely to be anxious and experience emotions like shame, anxiety, and depression. Yet their participation in artistic activity helped them reach positive states of mind despite any lingering negative effects. Another study (Hallaert 2019) compared suicide rates between art majors and non-art majors and found that if artists were able to engage in creative experiences that resulted in a "flow state," that characteristic tended to reduce the risk of suicide.

Creativity seems to make a positive difference while still not removing all the negative outcomes of trauma. It may be that trauma itself interferes with creative thinking and processing, even as creative activities deliver a benefit. That is one conclusion that can be drawn from Dori Rubinstein and Mooli Lahad's (2023) nonsystematic literature review, which found that the same brain networks are active during both imagination and PTSD symptom manifestations. In other words, there are crossover effects because they involve the same parts of the brain.

Therapists and other mental health providers are aware of the potential of arts and creativity as a healing tool. Mary Rockwood Lane (2005) describes how art is used in hospital programs. She advocates that nurses use creativity in their caring relationship with patients. Cathy Malchiodi (2015) reports that creative interventions have been developed in almost every kind of creative art. When whole groups of children are involved in creative projects—including children who are recovering from trauma and children who are not—the intervention is nonintrusive without singling out specific children in a way that might be embarrassing or shaming. In her chapter, she lists several recommended therapies based on creative arts, including art therapy, music therapy, drama therapy, dance or movement therapy, poetry therapy, bibliotherapy, play therapy, and sandbox therapy. She describes these interventions as "expressive therapies" (12) because they provide a variety of ways individual children can express themselves, which aids in healing trauma. For children who are trauma survivors, she writes, "Creative expression (1) offers a way to contain traumatic material within an object, image, story, music, or other art form; (2) provides a sense of control over terrifying and intrusive memories; (3) encourages active participation in therapy; (4) reduces emotional numbness; and (5) enhances reduction of hyperarousal and other distressing reactions" (Malchiodi 2015).

Malchiodi mentions an "integrative approach" in which two or more therapies are used, or in which expressive therapy is used in addition to other noncreative forms of therapy. The careful use of these techniques presents children with new tools for healing, acceptance, and integration of trauma effects into their psychological and physiological well-being. Expressive therapies can transform home or early childhood settings into places of healing if educators, parents, and caregivers work with outside professionals to help support healing and recovery.

Beyond healing and recovery, creativity can be a predictor of resilience. A child with a big imagination or one who enjoys engaging in the creative arts has more tools at their disposal to help face challenges in life. Rubinstein and Lahad (2023) report that playfulness enables resilience and coping with traumatic events, for example, pointing to the SEE FAR CBT treatment protocol for anxiety and PTSD. SEE FAR CBT combines Somatic Experiences, Fantastic Reality, and Cognitive Behavioral Therapy, which involve, respectively, focusing on bodily sensations, reimaging narratives in imaginative and fantastic ways, and traditional psychotherapy (Lahad et al. 2010). It is not hard to imagine that our mental capacities for imagination and pretend, which draw on our impulses to create, would have served an evolutionary function in allowing our ancestors to process traumatic experiences and survive them.

We are not suggesting that child care providers, preschool teachers, or families should implement these therapies, which are designed for professional behavioral health specialists. Our point here is that among mental health professionals a growing appreciation for the connection between trauma and creativity is emerging, and it represents another illustration of creativity's unique value and contribution in supporting healthy child development.

Still, knowing these approaches may encourage educators and parents/guardians to explore these options with professionals when providing care to a child who is struggling with debilitating aftereffects of trauma. Behavioral health solutions are best implemented in transdisciplinary teams that include the input and participation of parents and other caregivers, including early childhood educators (Gilkerson et al. 2013). The best thing you can do is to be aware of behavioral health services in your community so you can make referrals. No one expects you to be a health professional, but we do expect you to know where to find one and how to connect families to these vital services.

What follows are specific recommendations for how parents, caregivers, and educators can use creativity to help address children suffering the aftereffects of trauma.

Implement best practices for trauma-informed care (TIC)

Do whatever is necessary to establish safety and trust through the experiences children and families have with your program. (As a parent or family member, make sure the preschool or child care your child attends exhibits these characteristics plainly.) This could include the following:

- Establish relationships with children and families that show them you are a safe, trustworthy person.

- Arrange your space and schedule your time to communicate safety and caring.

- Establish a caring community among your children where the children look out for one another and care about one another.

At a program level, Head Start suggests routine screening, direct action to reduce exposure to trauma and traumatic stress, support for resilience and protective factors, and improving access to community partners and professionals who can assist in addressing trauma (see https://eclkc.ohs.acf.hhs.gov/mental-health/understanding-trauma-healing-adults/understanding-trauma-healing-adults).

Head Start also reminds programs to be attentive to staff who are traumatized by life and by their work with children experiencing trauma (see https://eclkc.ohs.acf.hhs.gov/publication/caring-ourselves-we-care-others).

Enhance creative expression

Infuse the environment with many options for creative expression. Consider the full range of artistic activities (art, music, dance, sensory play, sociodramatic or pretend play, poetry, and story). Think about ways for children to both create and consume all forms. Creative experiences are helpful as preventive medicine. Routine practices of painting, singing, or playing can make these tools more readily available if a trauma event calls for additional coping and healing.

Be a referral resource for parents/guardians

Learn about providers in your community who offer therapy or behavioral health support for children who have experienced trauma so you are ready when such a child shows up. Set up a partnership so the health provider knows you and your program as a place that is welcoming and supportive. For a child who is receiving services, offer to be a place where interventions can be developed and exercised.

Explore other resources

The following resources feature activities to infuse creativity within your learning environment, helping students explore their emotions and feelings. As a reminder, these activities do not replace therapy.

- **Messy Art:** www.creativeplayla.com/messy-art-in-the-trauma-informed-ece-classroom

- **Dr. Jo Nash's Expressive Arts Therapy:** https://positivepsychology.com/expressive-arts-therapy

- **Mental Health Technology Transfer Center Network:** https://cars-rp.org/_MHTTC/docs/Expressive-Arts-Therapy-Toolkit.pdf

- **Diversified Consulting:** www.diversified.world/ourteam

- **Teach Trauma:** https://teachtrauma.com/educational-tools/classroom-activities/

The following are critical resources for supporting yourself, students, and families facing mental health concerns. Please note: Each case is different, and it is your responsibility to take the best course of action, including dialing 911.

998 Suicide and Prevention Lifeline: https://988lifeline.org. Dial, text, or chat 9-8-8.

SAMHSA's Hotline: www.samhsa.gov/find-help/national-helpline. 1-800-662-HELP

National Mental Health Hotline: https://mentalhealthhotline.org. 866-903-3787

National Alliance on Mental Illness (NAMI) Hotline: www.nami.org/help. 1-800-950-NAMI

United Way 211 Hotline: www.211.org/get-help/mental-health. Dial 2-1-1.

Conclusion

We had two reasons for writing this chapter. The first was to add one more argument to why we think creativity is valuable, by discussing its role in helping people address trauma. The second was to provide suggestions for how creativity can be a tool to address trauma in the lives of children and families, to help you be more responsive and more effective as an educator and caregiver. Trauma is a serious concern because its impact can be so destructive and long-lasting.

As early childhood programs have begun to address the traumatic experiences their children have undergone, many are surprised at the extent their staff have suffered from trauma as well. Love and compassion are the best responses to trauma, and the arts can expand that and provide new avenues to reach children and staff and help them respond to trauma in healthy ways. The helpful influences of creativity on trauma are now well established among medical and psychology professionals. We hope this understanding and our recommendations provide you suggestions for program improvement and effective interventions.

Think about It

- Does your school have a trauma-informed focus? If not, what benefits could lie in becoming a trauma-informed school (to you, to your students, and to families)?

- What partners might be available to assist you in implementing a trauma focus in your instructional design?

- How might libraries be a resource to you as you develop new approaches to supporting children who have experienced trauma?

- Stop and reflect on your own mental health. How might it be impacting your service to children and families?

Part Three
Creativity for Real

A lot of this book up until now may seem to you heady and weighty. Maybe too much so. This last part is much different, testing the utility of our ideas. Creativity must fulfill its obligation to be useful if it is to be called creativity at all. We delve into creativity in action and as an imperative in the last two chapters. Chapter 11 includes six case studies where we see creativity in action. Chapter 12 takes a personal look at creativity in the lives of the authors. We find that our own stories tell us a lot about creativity's value and how it can be nurtured.

Singer-songwriter Brian Molko writes, "The more personal you make something, the more universal it becomes, because essentially we're all made up of the same emotional stuff" (Zaleski 2013). We come to a similar conclusion. Creativity is the great synthesizer and uniter, helping us reconcile many opposites, not the least our emotional, social, and intellectual lives.

Chapter Eleven   Creativity in Action

Louder than words

The phrase "Actions speak louder than words" is sometimes traced back to a sermon preached by Saint Anthony of Padua in the twelfth century. After all the theory and philosophy of creativity, what matters is how it shows up in the educational life of children. We hope you understand this far in our book that educational life is not just what happens in schools or child care. Children's educational life is their daily life. It is in the living that things become real and their true nature is revealed.

As we had spent almost three years researching creativity in the lives of young children, we gradually synthesized the seven big ideas that make up the core chapters of this book. But were we right? We had to find out.

We wanted to know if our understanding of creativity was visible in the world. We used our respective professional networks—Zach's children's librarian colleagues and Tom's contacts from his almost thirty years of working in early childhood in Iowa—to identify six sites to visit. We wanted a variety of settings, ages, and geographies. Our hosts were all curious about what we wanted to see. The best we could offer was, "We want to see what we can see about the creativity of children." But, we stressed, do nothing out of the ordinary. We want to drop in as if from a Martian flying saucer.

The six sites were all in Iowa:

- Van Meter Community Schools, Four-Year-Old Preschool

- Newton Public Library

- MATURA Head Start, Winterset

- Kids World Daycare and Preschool, Centerville

- Moore Elementary School

- Pella Public Library

In the end, these became our case studies. We were looking for signs of our seven Big Ideas:

1. *Creativity is a life-force:* Where did we see energy and movement? In what direction was it leading children? What was planned, but then what did children actually do?

2. *Creativity is about neural connections:* Where did children focus during open-ended play or free periods where they could make their own choice? Did we observe default and executive network states?

3. *Neurodiversity drives invention:* How were the children behaving? Did teachers meet children where they were and move with them from that place?

4. *Teaching creativity:* How was creativity present in the curriculum? How was it taught, if at all? How was the day split between direct *instruction* and *constructivism*?

5. *Creativity exists outside of the classroom:* What did creativity look like in libraries? What did librarians do, and how did children react?

6. *Creativity supports equity and diversity:* What kind of racial and ethnic diversity existed in the setting? Was it acknowledged? How did that change learning experiences?

7. *Creativity helps address trauma:* Were there any signs of stress or challenges from home that might have affected the children? How were they addressed by educators?

What follows are careful and thorough descriptions of our visits, each surprisingly different from one another. They are written to emphasize the details of what we saw and heard without assessing significance or value. We then invite readers to take the ideas discussed in the book and see which ones fit the descriptions. We end by sharing our reflections, but please consider your own thoughts before you read ours. Part of the benefit of reading our reflections is to note what is similar to or different from your own ideas. We offer this approach as a model for furthering your own learning about creativity. You begin with careful observation, captured with as much detail as you can remember or record. Then, and only then, do you reflect on what your experience tells you about creativity. Our reflections are not any sort of "right answer." They are just our thoughts about what we had learned of creativity and what we had observed.

Observation 1: Van Meter Four-Year-Old Preschool Program, Van Meter Community School District

Background and Mission Statements

Van Meter Preschool mission: To provide a "safe, nurturing, child-centered learning environment which is enticing, creative, and stimulating. It is our goal to prepare students to be life-long learners. This will be accomplished by recognizing the value of each individual and promoting academic and personal growth in a challenging and caring environment" (Van Meter Community School District 2023, 4).

Van Meter Preschool is part of the Iowa Statewide Voluntary Preschool Program for Four-Year-Old Children. It is state funded and is obligated to follow a set of standards to ensure high quality. Van Meter follows the Iowa Quality Preschool Program Standards. Related to creativity, the standards require programs to implement a curriculum that does the following:

- Per Standard 2.5: "incorporate[s] content, concepts, and activities that . . . integrate key areas of content including literacy, mathematics, science, technology, **creative expression and the arts**, health and safety, and social studies."

- Per Standard 2.6: provides "children learning opportunities, experiences, and projects that extend over the course of several days and incorporates **time for . . . creative expression**."

- Per Standard 2.26: provide[s] "many and varied open-ended opportunities and materials to **express themselves creatively through music, drama, dance and two- and three-dimensional art**." (Iowa Department of Education 2017, 3, 4, 7; emphasis added)

Our Time at Van Meter Preschool

Tom visited Van Meter preschool during its parent STEM open house from 4:00 to 5:30 on Friday, March 31, 2023. The open house was an opportunity for families to visit the Van Meter preschool classroom, see the artifacts from its recent Project Approach study of clothes, and watch and participate in hands-on STEM activities. The Project Approach (Helm et al. 2023) is a project-based inquiry learning model where students explore as a class a real-world subject of their choosing in depth.

The lead teacher is Rebecca Wilson, who is also a coauthor on the latest edition of Judy Harris Helm and Lilian G. Katz's book about the Project Approach. Rebecca is a colleague of Tom's, and both have served on the play committee of the Iowa Association for the Education of Young Children. When Tom arrived, the classroom was full of children and their families. Rebecca acknowledged Tom's presence from afar with a nod and a smile but returned her attention to the many families who were in attendance.

Tom observed the many STEM-related centers around the packed classroom. Parents/guardians and their children engaged in activities at the crowded centers. Some of the children were students in Rebecca's morning or afternoon preschool class, while others were older or younger siblings of the students.

Tom visited the activity areas in succession, taking pictures. At the water table, children poured water in and out of pitchers and filled up vessels and squeeze bottles, sometimes with a plastic water pump. Adjacent were tables with sponges, eyedroppers, clear plastic tumblers, small cylindrical pill bottles, and clear cubic containers. And next to that was a table with clear Plexiglas panels supported upright by wooden holders. Children were using spray bottles to wet down the panels, then observing the falling droplets and wiping them away with sponges, only to do it all over again.

Next was a ramp wall, an upright whiteboard with movable magnetized supports. The supports held PVC pipes that had been cut in half lengthwise, ideal for observing a rolling ball. Manipulating the supports would produce various pathways down the wall. Children could add blocks to stop the rolling or make the ball ricochet onto another ramp. One girl and her father set up a system where the ball ran the entire length of the wall and landed in a cup. When a ball landed, the girl celebrated with a hurrah, clapping her hands and jumping up and down. Other users had failed to place a cup at the end of the lowest ramp and were forever chasing balls around the classroom.

In a distant corner was a light table. Users could place on the table translucent plastic shapes of various colors, including plastic tumblers, translucent button-shaped objects, and magnetized translucent squares that could be constructed into cubes. The colors from all these objects glowed from below as children added and subtracted objects. Some children saw these as fancy blocks and constructed a gleaming tower.

Last was a water wall, clearly the most popular area. It consisted of a white pegboard supported upright in a PVC pipe frame with plastic tubs underneath. The pegboard allowed for metal cupholders to be fastened at any place on the board; the cups available for placement had holes in their bottoms or sides. When a person poured water in a cup at the top, it flowed down in a stream into lower cups until it finally reached the tubs beneath. Tom watched one girl, perhaps three years old, play with this wall for a full ten minutes. But with many activity options, the children varied greatly in their engagement level, some moving quickly from thing to thing and others engaging deeply with the materials.

Artifacts from the class's months-long clothes project were also on display for parents and visitors. Documenting the exploration and sharing that documentation is an essential part of the Project Approach. The project began with a topic word web developed by the class, with every conceivable idea or word children could imagine when they thought of the word *clothes*. Those words were displayed on flip chart paper on the wall, one that was completed at the start of the project and another at the end. Also on display were different objects associated with clothes-making, like buttons, pins, thread, and shears. Drawings of clothes filled a large mural taped to the wall. The class had collected a list of new vocabulary words, and every student picked a word and then drew a picture. Each class had created a three-dimensional sewing machine model out of cardboard. The children had visited the high school Family and Consumer Sciences class to see what they knew about clothes. Their fancy sewing machines had digital screens, and so the children included one in their model.

Pause and Reflect

Take a moment to pause and reflect on this case study from Van Meter Preschool. Write down at least three connections to the topics discussed throughout this book.

Connection 1:_____

Connection 2:_____

Connection 3:_____

We authors made the following connections to the topics in this book.

Authors' Connection 1: The extended open-ended play opportunity provided by the open house illustrated the endless positive and creative work that can emerge from children when constraints are removed. Giving children freedom to select where to focus their attention demonstrated Big Idea 2 about neural connections, engaging both default and executive networks.

Authors' Connection 2: The entire time Tom was there, the room was abuzz with activity. Big Idea 1 was prominently on display as energy was released and new things emerged from the materials as they underwent constant change.

Authors' Connection 3: Connecting to Big Idea 4 (domain-general and domain-specific), the clothes project was a domain-specific example in which the accumulation of knowledge led to more exploration and creative endeavor. For example, after their field trip to the high school taught them about computer-operated sewing machines, the children added a display screen to their sewing machine model.

Observation 2: Story Time at Newton Public Library

Background and Mission Statements

The Newton Public Library is the public library for a community of more than fifteen thousand residents. The library offers a full array of services, focusing on four areas:

1. Supporting lifelong learning by satisfying curiosity

2. Being a comfortable place to visit through its physical and virtual spaces

3. Creating young readers by supporting early childhood literacy

4. Being a community resource by knowing and serving the community well

(Newton Public Library Board of Trustees 2019)

Our Time at Newton Public Library

We were greeted by children's librarian Phyllis Peter. She took us on a tour of the children's department, a dynamic area that includes materials, a space for programming, and computers featuring applications that support early learning. She talked about the library's partnerships with local child care centers. She explained how story time includes a variety of activities that stimulate engagement, learning, and socialization. A handout for parents and caregivers discussed what to expect from story time. It noted that some children are shy at first and may not want to participate but that is normal, and that children get something out of the time even if they are not actively involved. After the tour and conversation, we headed to the program space for story time.

We attended a story time advertised for three-year-olds; that morning it welcomed families with children ranging from infants to three years old. The space includes a large carpet for families to sit on as well as built-in benches. The materials gathered for this program included books, egg-shaped shakers, a CD player, scarves, and a bubble machine.

Activities emphasized a multisensory experience. At the start of the program, families were encouraged to participate in the song "Teddy Bear, Teddy Bear, Turn Around." We observed a child in the arms of a parent, a child playing with a puppet from the library, and an adult making close eye contact with their child to mimic the moves from the song.

Another activity was a shaker song. The song taught color recognition with the lyrics "If you're wearing [color] today, stand on up." Children shook their eggs, and some stood up when their color was called. Some just stood and shook their eggs. One specific family engaged by raising the shaker in the air, mimicking facial expressions, and cradling the child as they swung back and forth.

Story time concluded with a bubble activity. Giggling children popped bubbles as music played in the background. Then the children and families played with playdough. Families were given a rolling pin and worked together to roll out the dough. Children also played with the dough by touching, stretching, and kneading.

Pause and Reflect

Pause and reflect on this case study from Newton Public Library. Write down at least three connections to the topics discussed throughout this book.

Connection 1:_____

Connection 2:_____

Connection 3:_____

The authors made the following connections to the topics in this book.

Authors' Connection 1: This public library story time took place in an informal learning space, which is central to Big Idea 5. Newton Library made conscious efforts to connect to early learning development and objectives. The families attending had the freedom to decide how much or little to participate in the program.

Authors' Connection 2: The playdough activity is an example of "creative instruction," as we discussed in chapter 7 (Big Idea 4). Even in this informal setting, the librarian planned in advance to introduce a rolling pin into the playdough activity to provide children a new way to manipulate the playdough. Creative instruction includes intentionally adding novel experiences to promote creative thinking. The librarian also provided creative opportunities in story time through multisensory experiences (bubble play and working with playdough) that might appeal to children who rate high on "openness to experience" (Big Idea 4), a personality characteristic associated with creativity. At the same time, advising parents/guardians with shy children who might be "slower to warm" how to participate (or not) made it feel safer for them to engage more fully.

Authors' Connection 3: The story time in Newton was full of multisensory experiences. The music and the egg shakers, the physical movement of the teddy bear dance, the popping bubbles (which were perfumed), and noticing the colors on their clothes and the book engaged four of the five senses. By exposing children to all their senses, the librarian was encouraging multiple neural connections (Big Idea 2).

Observation 3: MATURA Head Start, Winterset

Background and Mission Statements

Winterset Head Start is operated by MATURA Action Corporation of Creston, Iowa. Winterset is a rural town in Madison County with a population of 5,353.
The following are the MATURA Head Start belief statements:

- We believe children are unique individuals with thoughts, feelings, and ideas, which should be respected by others.

- We believe children grow best in a non-threatening environment where values of respect, self-worth, honesty, concern of others, and trust are modeled.

- We believe play is an essential ingredient in a child's learning by using hands[-on] experiences, imaginations, and choosing activities at their developmental level.

- We believe children's basic needs must be met for healthy social, emotional, cognitive, and physical development. (MATURA Head Start 2022, 7)

MATURA Head Start Philosophy: "We believe that children should be provided with a safe, secure learning environment. This environment will provide a variety of successful experiences that help children make good choices, become independent learners [and] problem solvers, and learn to the best of their abilities" (MATURA Head Start 2022, 7).

Our Time at Winterset Head Start

Tom visited the Winterset Head Start class on a sunny Wednesday morning, April 26, 2023. Tom met lead teacher Daina McKeever and her two assistant teachers. The class included three-, four-, and five-year-olds, many of whom would start kindergarten in the fall.

Tom arrived as the children were finishing breakfast. Next was an hour-long center time, during which children were free to go to any area of the room for the activity or toys there. Tom wandered around. One table featured plastic dinosaur figures that were brought to life by the children with roars and animated attacks. Another area had Lego-like building blocks. Two boys were working together to assemble a backhoe following printed directions. The kitchen area, with a play stove and refrigerator, was the stage for some house play. Children moved plates of plastic food in and out of ovens and served them at a table. In one area of the kitchen was a small crib and stroller, each occupied by a baby doll the children would "feed" by holding toy food or a bottle to their mouths.

After center time was a short small-group time during which children gathered around tables. Children were given a sheet to write down something they had learned in the past year. They wrote things like "throw a ball," "write words," "color," and "play," each with a drawing and invented spelling, some with invented alphabet characters. One girl pulled Tom over to explain her drawing of a person at a desk. In the middle of the desk was a tiny piece of paper with marks on it. She had learned to write words.

The children excitedly left the classroom when outdoor time was announced. For thirty minutes they played outside, riding tricycles, digging in an elevated sandbox, climbing on equipment, and popping in and out of the windows of a small playhouse. Some children played tag. At another point, a boy using trowels from the sandbox began to dig in the dirt next to the gutter downspout. He may have brought some sand over too. Another boy followed suit.

Ms. McKeever brought out a plastic ball the size of a softball. She set up a throwing clinic, showing proper form for throwing an overhand pitch. As they all went after the ball, Ms. McKeever suggested they get into a line so each could practice throwing on their own. The children imitated her movement. One girl even practiced a few times without the ball as she waited her turn. With more throws, a crowd gathered and other children took turns throwing the ball.

Retrieving the thrown ball was as exciting as throwing it, sometimes involving a number of excited retrievers.

One little boy, despite Ms. McKeever's modeling, kept throwing underhand. Eventually, after four tries, he succeeded. But after the clinic was over, he went back to throwing it underhand. This time, playing by himself, he threw the ball straight up in the air, losing it for a second and then finding it as it landed.

Back inside, the class came together for circle time with a read-aloud and show-and-tell. A girl showed the class a doll she brought from home. As the children were excused one at a time to wash hands for lunch, they were invited to meet one-on-one with the doll under the careful supervision of its owner. Boys and girls alike stopped, stroked its hair, held it, and hugged it.

After washing hands, the class sat down at tables for a family-style lunch, serving themselves from larger dishes and passing food around. As lunch began, Tom left. The strongest impression this visit made on Tom was how everything progressed through the schedule. While organized and managed, never once did it feel confining or restrictive.

Pause and Reflect

Pause and reflect on this case study from Winterset Head Start. Write down at least three connections to the topics discussed throughout this book.

Connection 1:_____

Connection 2:_____

Connection 3:_____

The authors made the following connections to the topics in this book.

Authors' Connection 1: The energy exhibited during the outdoor time was considerable, like it was a real release. It was not wild, or at least not entirely so. The hallmark of the *élan vital*, as we discussed in Big Idea 1, is that it is relentless, implacable, and strong but not necessarily wild. It is, instead, purposeful, moving toward greater expanse and intent. That is possible only if there is freedom to act. That running around was complemented with moments of curiosity and exploration—throwing a ball, digging dirt by the downspout. The children, uninhibited, found an equilibrium: run then stop, take a deep breath and pause, then move on. One may not have seen it if there was not freedom to act. Coupled with that freedom was also direct instruction on the overhand throw. Then it was open season as each child threw and ran after the ball or repeated an underhand throw, shooting the ball high in the sky and watching it fall. There was a rhythm to the flow of energy. Understanding the change in energy flow is essential to working cooperatively with children's energy, coconstructing the moment when a child can be fully engaged and active.

Authors' Connection 2: In accord with our recommendations around Big Idea 4, constructivist time outnumbered instructive time in the schedules, as planned and as executed. The planning and the consistent routine helped children learn to function independently but also cooperatively.

Authors' Connection 3: During center and outdoor time in Winterset, the children had choices. Indoors it could be dinosaurs, a backhoe made of bricks, or the kitchen. Outdoors, a sandbox, a game of tag, or throwing a ball. Giving children choices increases their initiative and their openness to explore something new, as we discussed with Big Idea 4: creative tendencies are the product of openness and intellect.

Observation 4: Kids World Daycare and Preschool

Background

Kids World Daycare and Preschool is a licensed child care and preschool center, earning four stars on the Iowa Quality Rating System. It includes a state-funded four-year-old preschool classroom. The center is in Centerville, Iowa, which has a population of 5,412 residents. The center opened its doors in 1991 and serves children from the ages of six weeks to twelve years of age. It implements the state-supported Pyramid Model for social-emotional development.

Our Time at Kids World Daycare and Preschool

When we arrived on the morning of May 2, 2023, we were welcomed by the center director, Dawn Johnson. Immediately we noticed the topic word webs and photo displays in the hallway. One photo collage depicted children and families participating in Pint-Size Picassos, a family night event during which families painted portraits. The child and the parent/guardian sat across from each other at tables and drew "what they saw." We were full of questions that Dawn graciously answered. Then we were ushered into the four-year-old classroom, where lots of smiles from children greeted us.

The class was singing as they transitioned to center time. At the conclusion of the song, children quickly separated out to activity centers. Dawn walked us through the activity centers, including an arts and craft center, a music and theatrical center, a rice and objects center, a reading center, a kitchen center, and a building block center. She mentioned that children were making hats for Mother's Day. Then Tom and Zach spent time observing and, at times, participating in activities with children. These are some of the key observations:

- **Music and theatrical center:** Children were offered a suitcase with musical instruments and songbooks. We observed them trying out each instrument and making up their own songs. Some children demonstrated how each instrument worked. Zach opened a songbook and began singing to the children. The children smiled and laughed, and some joined him.

- **Kitchen center:** We both spent the most time in this center. We were offered food, anything we wanted, and then were obliged to wait through the preparation and the serving. Two girls in particular were engaged for quite a while, moving plastic vegetables and other items—like a few random blocks from other baskets of manipulatives—out of mixing bowls to the toy stove pots to plates and back again. These short-order chefs were busy attending to us and a few dolls. The dolls required more time as they had to be hand-fed and have their clothes changed. Tom was offered a plastic bottle of faux hot sauce, and he spiced up his serving with a generous amount. The children expressed concern that it would be too hot for him.

- **Building center:** In this center, children explored different shapes and sizes of blocks. We saw two children working together to build a tower. They used a variety of shapes and sizes of blocks each time. They built a small foundation together and then took turns putting one block on the top of the others until their towers tumbled to the ground. The children never got upset at themselves or at each other. They laughed a few times and then tried it again. The fall was part of the build.

- **Art center:** This center had markers of every imaginable color, rulers, scissors, and four different colors of masking tape. The common canvas for these art projects was discarded computer paper with sprocket holes and telltale green-and-white striping. Most of the supplies in the art center were recycled. We saw children drawing, painting, and creating. Some students would work meditatively—slowly and deliberately—as they cut paper, taped pieces together, and added lines and drawings with colored markers. The children wanted to make us things. A popular subject this morning was Christmas trees (yes, it was May). Tom received a completely unsolicited product from the art center while he was sitting elsewhere, a heart-shaped drawing. He asked the artist, "Did you give this to me because you like me?" She nodded. Tom replied, "I like you too."

- **Playdough:** This creative resource was available at the art center table, where some children mashed different colors of dough together. We saw one girl making a snowman-like figure that she embellished with plastic feet and a cowboy hat, accessories from a Mr. Potato Head.

- **Lego area:** This table was equipped with two kinds of Lego bricks. Two boys worked together almost the entire time. We watched them on and off as they built a parking garage, worked through a few design disagreements, took the entire thing apart, and then rebuilt it. Tom asked about a pulley system they had installed. This was to raise and lower cars to the desired level. There were no cars. They were still, apparently, in the design phase.

- **Hat painting:** Next to the art center was a painting area dedicated exclusively to painting Mother's Day hats. Large pieces of paper were placed on children's heads, and a piece of masking tape defined a brim. The hats were then ready for painting, either purple or pink or both. One girl, in a meditative state, occasionally distracted by the considerable ambient noise, painstakingly covered the entire surface area of the hat with purple paint.

Dawn's center is famous across Iowa, and maybe even across the country, for its Project Approach work (the Project Approach book *Young Investigators* by Judy Harris Helm, Lilian Katz, and Rebecca Wilson features a food truck project from the center). She hosts a Facebook group called Southeast Iowa Project Group, where she posts photos of the three to six projects they do every year.

When we were there, Dawn talked about their current project on art and artists. This was built on a very successful project done the previous year, "Young at Art." They began their project study by inviting local artists in their community to come to their center, talk about what they did as artists, and then do some art projects with the children. They also studied more famous artists like Claude Monet, Pablo Picasso, Piet Mondrian, Vincent van Gogh, and Andy Warhol. Using examples from these artists, the children did their own version, experiencing and experimenting with each artist's unique approach. The results were fascinating, offbeat, and remarkably beautiful. They were so beautiful that the center sponsored a gala at a gallery space in downtown Centerville, where the work was open to the public. (See examples on page 176)

Typical of the Project Approach, they first made an art- and artist-themed word web when they started in January and then another one four months later. Looking at the before and after webs makes this a class-wide "assessment" tool (see photos below). By comparing the two pictures, we can see what concepts were learned over a three-month period. For example, "watercolors" was added as an art medium.

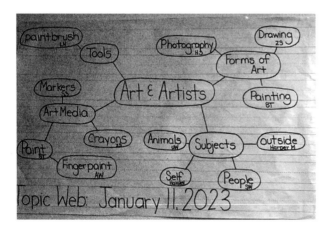
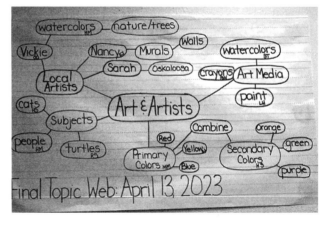

We concluded our two-hour visit with a debrief with Dawn. After our visit, she posted on her Facebook group a picture of Zach and Tom, adding, "This morning, Tom Rendon and Zach Stier visited our . . . classroom. . . . They came to observe the children demonstrating their creativity in the classroom. . . . We are so proud of our preschool programming!" We think they should be.

Pause and Reflect

Pause and reflect on this case study from Kids World Daycare and Preschool. Write down at least three connections to the topics discussed throughout this book.

Connection 1:_____

Connection 2:_____

Connection 3:_____

We authors made the following connections to the topics in this book:

Authors' Connection 1: The arts and crafts activity center draws a connection to the default network, which is part of Big Idea 2. Children are provided choice in materials, and daydreaming is encouraged. In our observation, we saw some children who were not quick to draw or construct something; rather, they were wondering, processing, and socializing with their peers. One girl who worked meditatively on painting her hat seemed to be in a "flow" state or something related to the default network, discussed in Big Idea 2 (chapter 5).

Authors' Connection 2: When the children developed their final word web, among their associations with the words *art* and *artists* was *local artists*, whom they included by name. They could do that because they enjoyed visits from local artists as they were exploring their project on art and artists. This is precisely what we mean when we discuss, as we do with Big Idea 5, how the community itself is a resource for learning and nurturing creativity by introducing new ideas.

Authors' Connection 3: During the Pint-Size Picasso project, the child and their family members drew portraits of one another. This reminds us of the bioecological model by highlighting the relationships among the child and their caregivers as part of the mesosystem. The bioecological model describes the context for creativity but also suggests ways we can modify and enhance that context to support and nurture creativity. In this case, the model suggests we look at who is connecting in the mesosystem. It could be the child and the parent/family member, child and teacher, or child and other caregiver. As we mentioned in chapter 3, the bioecological model informs many of the big ideas, especially Big Ideas 4, 5, 6, and 7.

Observation 5: Moore Elementary School, Kindergarten

Background and Mission Statement

Moore Elementary School is one of thirty-eight elementary schools in the Des Moines Public School District. Moore is an International Baccalaureate (IB) world school, accepted by the International Baccalaureate Organization. At the elementary school level, IB schools are designed to build educational foundations and prepare students for educational success at an IB standard through high school graduation. IB's Primary Years Program helps learners "use their initiative to take responsibility and ownership of their learning. By learning through inquiry and reflecting on their own learning, PYP students develop knowledge, conceptual understandings, skills and the attributes of the IB Learner profile to make a difference in their own lives, their communities, and beyond" (International Baccalaureate 2024).

Moore Elementary mission statement: "Our Moore community will empower learners to take action and become knowledgeable, internationally minded, compassionate leaders who will promote a more peaceful world" (Moore Elementary School 2024).

Our Time at Moore Elementary

Our visit began on a Tuesday morning, May 23, 2023. The principal is Mary Minard, who started her career as an elementary school teacher in the Des Moines district. We talked for about fifteen minutes in her office about her time at Moore and the International Baccalaureate recognition. Mary was finishing up her first year as principal, having moved from another Des Moines elementary school. Moore's IB status had been at the initiative of past leadership. She was proud to continue the effort with its high standards as well as infusing her own values of care and compassion for individual students. Three pillars—the learner, learning and teaching, and the learning community—frame the IB's approach to education.

Mary then took us on a tour while the kindergarten class we were planning to visit was taking recess outside on a sunny spring day. Flags from many countries lined the hallway, and children's artwork and project artifacts were everywhere to be seen. As we made our way to the kindergarten classroom, we took a detour to the art room and met the art teacher, Sydney Williams. Her reflections about teaching at Moore, where she has been for five years, revealed a keen appreciation for the racial and ethnic diversity of the children who attend the school. They represent, from their respective families of origin, dozens of different countries. Des Moines is a majority-minority district, with 34.7 percent of students identifying as white (Des Moines Public Schools 2022).

Sydney described her approach to art education as focusing on the experience of creativity for each student as they worked on art projects. Though examples of their art products were all over the room, she emphasized that helping children think and process creatively was most important.

It turns out that creativity is a central value to IB. It believes that "every person has the ability, and the right, to be creative" (International Baccalaureate 2023). This was not lost on Sydney.

We walked to the kindergarten room and waited until the children came in from recess. There was a remnant attached to the wall from an earlier brainstorming session about ways to express creativity. The children's ideas were put on sticky notes and placed on a large sheet of paper under the heading "Creativity." Mostly written by children in emerging penmanship and spelling, the ideas included:

- Bake something.

- Play outside.

- (a drawing of a teacher)

A similar exercise was also documented, but this time the prompt was "I wonder . . . " A few of the contributions include the following questions:

- How long have alligators been around?

- How long has the earth been around?

- How long have humans been around?

- How long has Moore been here?

- What do ants eat?

- How long does it take to go from Des Moines to Las Vegas?

- What's the oldest dino?

- How long have Komodo dragons been around?

- Why do turtles move slow?

- How does the moon float in space?

- Do all living things have blood?

- Why does ice fall from clouds?

- Why are oranges so juicy?

- How long does it take to learn to read?

- How long is a giraffe's neck?

We also noticed a learning aid taped to a window that read: "Line of Inquiry: Connections between creativity and our ideas." Clearly, they thought a lot about creativity.

We were not finished looking around the room when Jennifer Sloma brought her kindergartners in from recess. She had them sit around the room to engage in a variety of activities: playing games, reading books, and talking with the teacher. Tom sat down on the carpet next to a boy and girl who were playing a matching game involving the letters at the beginning of words. Zach watched children work on a puzzle that, when constructed, created words.

Other commitments cut our time short. With many salutations directed at us from nearly every individual child, we left.

Pause and Reflect

Pause and reflect on this case study from Moore Elementary School. Write down at least three connections to the topics discussed throughout this book.

Connection 1:_____

Connection 2:_____

Connection 3:_____

We authors made the following connections to the topics in this book.

Authors' Connection 1: The IB priorities and emphasis provide a concrete way to implement Big Idea 4 from chapter 7, namely, that creativity is how you learn everything. IB calls for a focus on asking questions and thinking critically.

The kindergarten class's "I wonder" board showed a promising start. Their questions became a creative approach to learning by constraining and directing exploration.

Authors' Connection 2: Moore's student body is racially, ethnically, and culturally diverse, and that fact is acknowledged and celebrated in the hallways and among the staff. As we wrote with Big Idea 6, access to creativity is a vital equity practice.

Authors' Connection 3: We wrote in chapter 4 about Henri Bergson's "creative evolution" and Big Idea 1 regarding *élan vital*. His ideas resurfaced in our minds when we talked with Sydney Williams about art ideas and the focus on the experience of children making art. She is not interested in making art. She is interested in making artists. That impulse is about tapping into creativity in its purest form, moving a child forward in their own way, and exploring how the creative energy is moving around, coming out, and expressing itself. That seems to us to be the essence of art education.

Observation 6: Story Time at Pella Public Library

Background and Mission Statement

Pella Public Library serves the Pella community, a town of more than ten thousand people in south-central Iowa.

Mission statement: "The Pella Public Library enriches our community by welcoming, creating, and nurturing curious minds and supporting lifelong learners" (Pella Public Library 2024).

Our Time at Pella Public Library

We drove to Pella on May 26, 2023, and were greeted with a smile from children's librarian Katie Dreyer. This was a special story time because May is a transition month between their spring programming and the summer reading program. Katie led us to the story time space, a single elongated room with a high ceiling and high windows. Katie showed us her story time plan, which included a variety of songs and stories about ice cream. She explained that she allows for several options because story times have a tendency to change course. She had an array of books she *could* read and songs or fingerplays she *could* do.

Katie started with an opening song to get children and parents/guardians prepared for the program. Following this, she read *Should I Share My Ice Cream?* by Mo Willems. She used dialogic reading strategies throughout, asking participants, "Do you think elephants eat ice cream?" "Who here enjoys eating ice cream?" and "What kind of ice cream is your favorite?" She used facial expressions throughout her reading to enhance the experience for each child and parent/caregiver. She also read *Groovy Joe: Ice Cream and Dinosaurs* by Eric Litwin.

Following the readings, families sang songs related to the theme. One of the songs was "Take Me Out for Some Ice Cream." Families recognized the tune from "Take Me Out to the Ball Game" and joined in with, "Take me out for some ice cream." The second song was "Dinosaur, Dinosaur, Turn Around." Children used fine- and gross-motor skills, including stomping, turning around, touching their nose, and touching their toes. A lengthy rendition of "Wheels on the Bus" included original and off-the-wall verses like "The unicorn on the bus sprinkles kindness." Throughout the program, children and families laughed and interacted, highlighting the social experience the story time provides. Story time concluded with children popping bubbles from a bubble machine.

Pause and Reflect

Pause and reflect on this case study from Pella Public Library. Write down at least three connections to the topics discussed throughout this book.

Connection 1:_____

Connection 2:_____

Connection 3:_____

The authors made the following connections to the topics in this book.

Authors' Connection 1: During this story time, we recognized the importance of informal learning to a child's creative development. Pella Public Library has a dedicated room for story time, demonstrating the value they place on growth and development of the children in the community. Designing and providing a creative space is an idea we discussed in chapter 8 (Big Idea 5).

Authors' Connection 2: The children were full of excitement from the start of story time to the end, showing how important it is for adults to follow children's energy. The way the story time moved forward was based on, and maybe driven by, the participation of the children. Katie was prepared to go in different directions, and while there was a plan there was also a lot of flexibility. Having options allows her to move in response to the children, using their energy instead of fighting or deflecting it. These are strategies related to Big Idea 1 (chapter 4). We also talked about the teaching paradox of being planful and improvisational in chapter 7 (Big Idea 4). It is as vital a strategy for children's librarians as it is for teachers.

Authors' Connection 3: We observed Katie using dialogic reading strategies, asking questions and encouraging children to ask questions, and using facial expressions and an animated voice as they discussed their experiences eating ice cream. This was enhanced and repeated as they took various approaches to exploring the theme of ice cream: reading two books about ice cream and singing a few songs about it. Big Idea 4 encourages the asking of questions (see the teaching behaviors recommended in figure 4 in chapter 7). When Katie asked, "Do you think elephants eat ice cream?" that is precisely the kind of unexpected question that provokes creative responses. Questions are also useful in helping children with ADHD focus (see Big Idea 3).

Conclusion

Actions may speak louder than words, but they are also a lot harder to control. They come out messier. So some of our more beautiful and artistic ideas may come off as a little flat or forced when applied to real-life circumstances. What it all points to for us is that nurturing creativity must begin with learning how to watch children in a new way, to see what was always there but we never noticed.

We found it impossible to know whether our Big Ideas around neurodiversity and trauma were being played out in any way. It felt too intrusive to ask specifically about any individual child. If children were differently abled or experiencing debilitating stress, it was not immediately noticeable. In general we saw no behavior that educators could not manage quickly and with aplomb. It helped that we were visiting at the end of the school year, after a solid eight months of guidance and socialization had had a chance to shape the children's social comportment.

We hope that our initial reflections are only the beginning of an ongoing dialogue about how creativity shows up in classrooms, early education programs, and informal educational settings. And further, we hope that these case studies encourage you to engage in your own action research around creativity, how it shows up, what encourages it to show up, and what you can use or reject from our many ideas.

Think about It

- Review the case studies again and see what connections you can make with the seven Big Ideas.

- Visit an early childhood setting or a story time at a library or a children's museum, and use our approach to analyze how the Big Ideas show up in these situations.

Chapter Twelve **Creativity Now!**

Restarting your creative life

Given our belief that each of us is creative and that our creativity makes it possible for us to uniquely express and present our individual selves, then it makes sense that we end this book on a personal note and a call to action. If we are right in these two statements, then the best thing we can offer the reader is our encouragement to center creativity in their lives and the lives of the children they love and care for. In the end, creativity is about a way of seeing and then living life. Every day we are alive, we are creating our life. Every choice we make, everything we say, and all our thoughts and feelings are creations, and they make up who we are and what our life is all about. So, to be succinct: creativity now!

We want to end our book on a personal and inspirational note. We drop the editorial "we" and move to first-person singular, telling the stories of our own creativity biographies. These narratives talk about the role creativity plays in our lives. We then talk about what stands out as especially significant to us in the book. Your reading of this book mirrors our own three-year journey to explore and understand what creativity means and why it is important. We learned a lot, and we hope you did too, in reading this book.

Zach and Creativity

Reflecting on this book, I realize that my understanding of creativity came from the roadblocks I faced with my learning disability. A true struggle for me was advocating for a course of action and the tools I needed to be successful. I realized that creativity has always helped me through those periods when I was struggling. My successes in school came when I had the freedom to use creative skills such as art, theater, and storytelling. A few examples: when I learned the parts of an atom and built a model out of candy; when I developed a script and acted out the story of *King Arthur and the Knights of the Round Table*; when I produced a story using an animated studio program. But when I struggled to complete an assignment, such as math, and I was not allowed to use my creative skills, I failed.

I started working in public libraries when I was fifteen years old and went on to develop my skills academically and professionally. In 2011 I accepted my current position as a children's librarian in Boone, Iowa, where I develop programs to support infants through fifth graders and their families. Even before I cowrote this book, creativity was at the center of the programs I developed. Some examples of creativity in my programs include the following:

- **Story time:** Creativity is foundational for a story time program. At the start of story time, I often bring out a puppet or two. Children are offered the chance to pet, kiss, or hug the puppet. I use dialogic questioning to engage with children: "What sound does our friend make?" or "Where might our friend live?" or "What food does our friend enjoy?" Toward the end of story time, I let children play with the puppet friend or any of the library's other puppets in the puppet theater. It is always a delight to see children creating and acting out a story with adults enjoying the show.

- **Free space to play:** The children's department has a large space for free play filled with toys, books, audio materials, and DVDs. Children play with trains, puzzles, puppets, wall toys, and activities from a STEM cart. At times I offer free play after a story time ends, bringing out puppets, art and craft supplies, puzzles, and toys for as long as families care to stick around.

- **Special program offerings:** Throughout the year, we offer special programming, such as guest readers, artists, musicians, and performers. In our program Stories Alive, we rent storybook character costumes to bring them to life at the library. This program includes a story time, an activity that connects to the story, and a meet and greet with the character. We engage children's creativity, asking them to put on their imagination caps so the character can come to life. We also include creativity in each of the extension activities.

In 2020 Tom and I took the plunge and began a research journey to learn about creativity in greater detail, resulting in this book. Throughout our writing, I had several transformative moments based on the research we collected, processed, and analyzed on the topic of creativity.

The first pivotal moment occurred early on in our writing as we considered the process of infinite creativity. I reflected the most on the intended vision and the incubation parts of the process. When we provide space to be creative, a clearer vision will evolve to aid us throughout the process. Furthermore, this space gives us permission to rest, to be aware and present throughout the creative process. It became clearer to me that nurturing the creative process is not the responsibility of only a parent, guardian, caregiver, teacher, or librarian; rather, it is the responsibility of all who are part of an ecological system.

The second pivotal moment was learning about the bioecological system. I was already aware of the ecological system and the important role an environment has on development. However, discovering that Bronfenbrenner evolved the theory to the bioecological system was transformative for me, and I began framing our discussion around a bidirectional relationship. I no longer could contain creativity within a silo where each party works independently. Additionally, focusing on the bidirectional relationship highlighted children's role, emphasizing that we must pause and listen to them so they can help us identify what they need to support their growth and development.

My third pivotal moment was my realization that daydreaming is in fact a necessity, and allowing children to daydream, creating space and time for it, is a central way to support children's creativity. I've always valued daydreaming, and learning about the default network reaffirmed to me that providing children the space as well as time to daydream is critical. I connected the dots to see how daydreaming enhances exploration, improves critical thinking, and sparks opportunities for children to learn more about themselves as individuals and as learners. Thus, daydreaming must be nurtured inside and outside the learning environment.

It was a fourth pivotal moment for me to write about the "power of place" and the importance of public libraries in a child's creative development. As a practicing children's librarian, it was a delight to write about how, as an informal learning space, public libraries offer children an expansive collection of books and materials alongside programs that allow free space for children to create and to interact with their family and other children to develop their social skills.

Finally, my fifth pivotal moment came in unpacking the relationship between creativity and trauma. I experienced trauma unrelated to my learning disability early on in my life, and the chapter opened up locked doors that I had kept shut for a long time. I was already aware of the impact trauma has on development; however, I was not aware of its generational connection. Specifically, I read about how traumatic events like the Holocaust and the attacks of September 11, 2001, had an impact on those who experienced them, but also on the generations that followed. I also learned about the healing power of creativity to work through traumatic experiences. That's why it is important to allow space for children to express themselves creatively. You may not know how you are benefiting them.

Tom and Creativity

My earliest memory of being creative was when I was three or four, playing in my backyard. I was living on the island of Guam, in the middle of the Pacific Ocean, digging in the dirt. I discovered something unexpected. I thought it might have been a bullet cartridge because people there at the time were forever digging up munitions left over from World War II. After all, this was only seventeen years after the end of the war on an island that was the site of intense combat.

I waved it around proudly like I had discovered gold, only to have my brothers dismiss it as a CO_2 cartridge, something they found all the time. What I most remember about this discovery was my disappointment that it had not been a more exciting find. It was only a CO_2 cartridge, and they were used for a lot of purposes, not all military. Yet my imagination had taken over, driven by my need to be special and important. As the youngest of four children, that need often felt desperate.

I was precocious as a child, not the least because my mother, a kindergarten teacher, took me to her classroom every day beginning at age two. The joke was that I had three years of kindergarten. When we returned to the mainland, my age told the educational system that I belonged in kindergarten, and so I started my fourth year at that level. Schoolwork came easily, and the secrets of pleasing teachers were plain to me, though I was later told it had mainly to do with my soft brown eyes. That stopped working in fourth grade when I got glasses. What could I do now to be special, noticed, and admired? Be super creative?

During a vacation to my grandmother's house in Buffalo, New York, we kids had discovered a book my mother had written. Her fine penmanship could pass for typesetting, and there were simple ink-drawn illustrations. It struck me at the time as an amazing achievement, which was even more shocking when I learned she had written it when she was twelve. This was like learning that Mozart composed music at age three, a fact I still marvel at. These geniuses were all around me. Why wasn't I one?

At some point, maybe in elementary school, maybe in junior high, I discovered parody. Suddenly everything was open to me for mimicry and mockery. I remember finding a book at the library called *1000 Insults for All Occasions*. I loved it. Along with it came a healthier appreciation for humor in general. I had always loved jokes and riddles. I could waste whole afternoons reading a treasury of *Peanuts* cartoons; after hours of being so immersed in that reality, when I was called to dinner I felt like I was coming home from Charlie Brown's house. In junior high school and high school, I discovered Laurel and Hardy, Charlie

Chaplin, and Buster Keaton. The Marx Brothers were revelations. Their cleverness and sharp wit were awe-inspiring.

My parents had a subscription to *Horizon Magazine*, a magazine about the arts. And for a while, it featured a series by a film critic, Stanley Kauffmann, that described in shot-by-shot detail great films and explained why they were great. I was deeply absorbed. Yes, a flow moment. I remember him writing about great European movies like Federico Fellini's *8½*, Michelangelo Antonioni's *L'Avventura*, and Ingmar Bergman's *Persona*. It would be years later before I actually saw any of these films. I just saw *Persona* two years ago, and I still have never seen *8½* all the way through. But Kauffmann's praise of these works inspired me. While I was still in high school, the Greenwich (Connecticut) Public Library offered a film series through which I saw Fellini's *Juliet of the Spirits*. The stunningly beautiful film opened up my world. I wanted to be a filmmaker.

My obsession with films and filmmaking was therapeutic as well. High school was a cold and unfriendly place for me. My few friends and I stuck steadfastly to one another. They shared my interest in movies, and so we formed a film club and started to make our own. My friend and I wrote a feature-length screenplay about the perfidy of high school relationships called *Graduation*. The last scene was the two high school outsiders driving across the country to Los Angeles as if they had just escaped prison. We were explicitly turning our emotional pain into art.

Many days I came home from high school emotionally bruised, so I played piano and sang music, mostly from Broadway musicals. It was exactly as Mr. Rogers told us. Sometimes feelings can be scary and powerful, and sometimes it can help to express them in ways that don't hurt us or others. One of his favorite ways was playing the piano. And it became true for me.

I went off to college at Northwestern University with my filmmaking ambitions. Through many twists and turns, suffice it to say that I never became a great writer or filmmaker. Instead, I became a freelance writer for a while, and then a public television publicist and outreach coordinator. That introduced me to children's television and then led me to the early childhood field, where I have been ever since, finally retiring from a position as the Head Start State Collaboration Office coordinator. More and more, I have no regrets and great appreciation for the life I led, and not for the life I once wished I had.

Telling my creativity biography brings to light exactly what we have been writing throughout this book. The accidental nature of life is pulled together into coherence by creativity. We make meaning of what is truly random. And the resources around us—the books and subscriptions my parents brought into our house, the public library, and school—all give us the knowledge and inspiration, the skills and experiences, the tools and encouragement to create that meaning and express it, and to help us see life as worth living. Writing this book was a discovery or rediscovery of the creativity that has helped me through difficult times in life, moving me forward to a life and a career I could be proud of and that meant something.

It was Zach's idea to write a book about creativity. He had written about creativity for his dissertation. During the COVID-19 shutdown, we collaborated on a conference presentation about creativity in early childhood for the Iowa Association for the Education of Young Children (IAAEYC) fall conference. Zach's interest and passion in the topic was infectious (pun intended). What followed was a tireless three years of research and conversations, as well as two presentations at national conferences. Early enthusiasm from Redleaf Press helped us know we had an end point. We just had to get there.

My first pivotal moment in writing this book was stumbling onto the idea of the *élan vital*. I had never even heard of Henri Bergson before. The only reason I became curious about him was because his book had the word *creative* in the title. This opened my mind to the depth and power of creativity. As a religious person, the idea that creativity is an energy force connected to the divine added a dimension to my spiritual life. Yes, I believed in God, but now I believed in, as the Nicene Creed puts it in its very first words, the maker of heaven and earth. A creator God is not something I have to believe in. It is something I want to believe in.

A second pivotal moment was in our second Big Idea about neurological connections, not neurological destinations. This made such intuitive sense to me because I knew that what made life survivable was my connections to others. As Brené Brown (2012, 8) writes, "We are hardwired to connect with others, it's what gives purpose and meaning to our lives, and without it there is suffering." Let's celebrate the connection and the flow.

When these two ideas came early in our research, I knew we were onto something and that maybe, just maybe, we had a book. But it was the chapter on trauma that opened up new memories and my third pivotal moment. I talked about how film and piano playing got me through my hard years of high school. But there was another time when creativity came to my rescue. My wife and I were living in Fargo, North Dakota. The long winters don't just change your mood, they change your personality. And I was struggling. My mother had died suddenly, my marriage was in trouble, and my second daughter was soon to come. I felt trapped and depressed. Sometime during all of this, I was introduced to Julia Cameron's

The Artist's Way (1992). Her two simple tasks—morning pages and the artist's date—helped me survive that dark time. Morning pages are simply fifteen minutes of writing you do first thing every morning, unloading whatever is on your mind. It is unedited, random, whatever comes out. Sometimes I would write, "I don't know what to write" over and over again. I filled a lot of notebooks. The artist's date is a weekly date you have with yourself where you go someplace you want to spend time and just enjoy yourself for an hour. For me, it was a walk in the woods or browsing a bookstore or eating a nice meal by myself. One time spending an hour in a hardware store was revelatory. Again, creativity came to the rescue.

Creativity is healing, but not in a way the body heals by scabbing over, protecting the wound from infection and giving the antibodies a chance to win their battle. Though we use the word *heal* in chapter 10, we are not sure it is exactly right. You don't heal from trauma. You just learn to weaken its symptoms so they don't control your life. Creativity can help. It helps you face your pain and make it part of you.

One of my favorite authors, Richard Rohr, says that only two things really change you: great love and great pain. So I had to ask myself, what was the pain telling me I needed to change? And, ultimately, I am not sure you actually can change yourself very much. I am still that little boy waving around a CO_2 cartridge, wishing it was a bullet. More than anything, I find if I stop fighting what is happening to me and surrender to the inevitable, that is when creativity can help me think in a new way about my circumstances and my life. What we wrote in chapter 10, especially about leading with care and compassion, helped me see that surrender is not losing but winning. What is lost is regained tenfold. That is what religion was trying to teach me all along. And creativity became, for me, as the psalmist writes about "God's Word," a lamp unto my feet and a light unto my path. It helps us know and trust the path forward.

Calls to Action

Our own stories show how our early experiences of creativity gave us something to trust when life dealt us the inevitable misfortunes that befall us all. To help you be that positive influence for others, we offer some calls to action, some things to do as suggestions and inspirations. They are things to do *now*!

We divide them into two sections: one for nurturing your own creativity and the other for nurturing the creativity of the young children in your life, be they your own children, family members, grandchildren, children in your care, or students.

Nurturing Your Own Creativity

Truly the best way to nurture creativity in young children is to nurture creativity in yourself. If that seems like too much of a stretch, think about it as nurturing the creativity of your inner child. Remember your early moments of wonder, curiosity, and exploration. You can rekindle that delight anytime by remembering or reexperiencing those moments. Then you can make them more real by intentionally planning creative activities and creative experiences in your day.

Call to Action #1: Write your own creativity biography. Think about your earliest memory and describe it. What was creative about it? How else has creativity been your companion and served you well—throughout your early years, your schooling, your professional life, your personal life? What worked for you in the past will work for you now. You just need to remember what it was.

Call to Action #2: Get a copy of *The Artist's Way* and commit to following its twelve-week program. When Tom started this journal thirty years ago, it led him to a new career, a new field, and a new home. Be careful. It will change your life.

Call to Action #3: Even though we have stressed that creativity is so much more than the arts, the arts are still a useful and important doorway into creativity. That's why drawing, painting, building, writing, acting, and dancing are so important for everyone to do. It is not about how good you are. It is about your own journey of discovery to find your own creativity. If it is true that each of us is creative and that as we express that creativity we express our unique selves, then it must also be true that you are creative and unique. Exploring any art form is your journey of discovering how you are creative and how creativity lives in you, throughout you, and out of you. So pick something and do it. Now.

Nurturing the Creativity of Young Children

Call to Action #1: Our first call to action is to let children be children. They are daydreamers and curious little humans. They need adults to provide them a supportive space to be creative.

Call to Action #2: Children have an active role in their creative development. In the end, it is children's creative energy and their movement and their discoveries that matter. All you can be is a help on the side. But families and educators play an oversized role, especially when they inspire us, believe in our creative impulses, and provide an inspiring example of creativity. (Remember Tom's mother's book.) Be open to evolving your teaching practices to support the needs of all learners. Express to children that they have the freedom to advocate for what they need to be successful.

Call to Action #3: Take your children to the library at least once a week. Take them to a museum or a park at least once a month. Engage with children in the activities they are interested in. Just the way that many early childhood experts recommend you read to children each day, plan specific things you can do with them each day that are creative.

◁ ◁ ▷ ▷

When we interviewed Scott Barry Kaufman, host of *The Psychology Podcast*, we asked him, as Ezra Klein does at the end of his podcast, *The Ezra Klein Show*, to suggest three books for us to read. One of them was Rollo May's (1975) *The Courage to Create*. We read this early in our research, and it influenced a lot of what we wrote. For example, May writes:

> Imagination, broadly defined, seems to me to be a principle in human life under-lying even reason, for the rational functions, according to our definitions, can lead to understanding—can participate in the constitution of reality—only as they are creative. Creativity is thus involved in our every experience as we try to make meaning of our self-world relationship. (134)

The ideas here are present in virtually every chapter of this book. It explains the central paradox of creativity, which is the wild, the out of control, and the spontaneous contrasting with the meaning-making, the purposeful, and the helpful. It is central in our definition of creativity: originality plus utility.

May's title says it all: it takes courage to create. And if there seems to be a lack of creativity in our world, among our friends, and in our schools and com-munities, perhaps it is a paucity of courage. May writes about three kinds of creativity—moral creativity, physical creativity, and social creativity—and argues that each must have its own courage: moral courage, physical courage, and social courage. Courage comes, we would argue, from assessing the risks of a particular course of action and judging it to be worth it. Rather than trying to muster up courage, one way to increase courage is to deem the outcome worth any risk or negative outcome from failure. Do we care about something, do we think it is so important to us that we are willing to risk everything to attain it? That is where courage comes from, when we can reweight the cost-benefit equation so it tilts in the direction of action.

We have argued as persuasively and compellingly as we can that creativity is of immense importance to humans, especially when they are very young. We hope that tilts the balance toward creativity and gives you the courage to create and the courage to nurture the creativity of young children.

References

AAP (American Academy of Pediatrics). 2016. "Media and Young Minds." *Pediatrics* 138 (5): e20162591. https://doi.org/10.1542/peds.2016-2591.

———. 2023. "ASD–What Is Autism Spectrum Disorder?" *Pediatric Patient Education.* March 13. https://doi.org/10.1542/ppe_document143.

Adams, Margaret L., and Jie-Qi Chen. 2012. "Understanding Young Children's Kinds of Creating." In *Contemporary Perspectives on Research in Creativity in Early Childhood Education,* edited by Olivia N. Saracho, 343–54. Charlotte, NC: Information Age Publishing.

ALA (American Library Association). 2019. "Library Bill of Rights." ALA. Updated January 29, 2019. www.ala.org/advocacy/intfreedom/librarybill.

Allport, Gordon W., and Henry S. Odbert. 1936. "Trait-Names: A Psycho-Lexical Study." *Psychological Monographs* 47 (1): i–171.

AMS (American Montessori Society). 2023. "Fast Facts: Public Montessori Schools." AMS (website). Accessed October 4. https://amshq.org/About-AMS/Press-kit/Public-Schools#by-the-numbers.

Andreasen, Nancy. 2015. "Dr. Nancy Andreasen on the Brain and Creativity, Part 1." Rappler. Recorded live at the ASPAC Conference, April 27. YouTube video. www.youtube.com/watch?v=QnkXWc0oGnw.

APA (American Psychiatric Association). 2013. *Diagnostic and Statistical Manual of Mental Disorders* (DSM-5), 5th ed. Washington, DC: American Psychiatric Publishing.

Aspiranti, Kathleen B. 2011. "Preoperational Stage (Piaget)." In *Encyclopedia of Child Behavior and Development,* edited by Sam Goldstein and Jack A. Naglieri, 1155–56. Boston, MA: Springer. https://doi.org/10.1007/978-0-387-79061-9_2228.

Ayman-Nolley, Saba. 1992. "Vygotsky's Perspective on the Development of Imagination and Creativity." *Creativity Research Journal* 5 (1): 77–85.

———. 1999. "A Piagetian Perspective on the Dialectic Process of Creativity." *Creativity Research Journal* 12 (4): 267–75.

Baron-Cohen, Simon. 2020. *The Pattern Seekers: How Autism Drives Human Invention.* New York: Basic Books.

———. 2022. "How Autism Drives Human Invention with Simon Baron-Cohen." Science and Cocktails. February 19. YouTube video. www.youtube.com/watch?v=kHmvZBQjB0g.

Baumer, Nicole, and Julia Frueh. 2021. "What Is Neurodiversity?" *Harvard Health Publishing* (blog), Harvard Medical School. November 23, 2021. www.health .harvard.edu/blog/what-is-neurodiversity-202111232645.

Beaty, Roger E. 2020. "The Creative Brain." *Cerebrum: The Dana Forum on Brain Science* 2020 (January–February). www.ncbi.nlm.nih.gov/pmc/articles/PMC7075500.

Beaty, Roger E., Paul Seli, and Daniel L. Schacter. 2019. "Network Neuroscience of Creative Cognition: Mapping Cognitive Mechanisms and Individual Differences in the Creative Brain." *Current Opinion in Behavioral Sciences* 27 (June): 22–30.

Beghetto Ronald A., James C. Kaufman, and John Baer. 2015. *Teaching for Creativity in the Common Core Classroom.* New York: Teachers College Press.

Behr, Gregg, and Ryan Rydzewski. 2021. *When You Wonder, You're Learning: Mister Rogers' Enduring Lessons for Raising Creative, Curious, Caring Kids.* New York: Hachette Books.

Benedek, Mathias, Martin Karstendiek, Simon M. Ceh, Roland H. Grabner, Georg Krammer, Izabela Lebuda, and Paul J. Silvia, et al. 2021. "Creativity Myths: Prevalence and Correlates of Misconceptions on Creativity." *Personality and Individual Differences* 182 (November). https://doi.org/10.1016/j.paid.2021.111068.

Beneke, Sallee, Michaelene M. Ostrosky, and Lilian G. Katz. 2018. *The Project Approach for All Learners: A Hands-On Guide for Inclusive Early Childhood Classrooms.* Baltimore, MD: Brookes Publishing.

Benson, Herbert. 1975. *The Relaxation Response.* New York: William Morrow.

Bergson, Henri. 1911. *Creative Evolution.* Translated by Arthur Mitchell. London: Macmillan.

Blake, Sally, and Duane M. Giannangelo. 2012. "Creativity and Young Children: Review of Literature and Connections to Thinking Processes." In *Contemporary Perspectives on Research in Creativity in Early Childhood Education*, edited by Olivia N. Saracho, 293–318. Charlotte, NC: Information Age Publishing.

Blake, William. 1950. "Auguries of Innocence." *Poets of the English Language.* New York: Viking Press. Published online by the Poetry Foundation. www.poetry foundation.org/poems/43650/auguries-of-innocence.

Bodrova, Elena, and Deborah Leong. 2007. *Tools of the Mind: The Vygotskian Approach to Early Childhood Education.* 2nd ed. Upper Saddle River, NJ: Pearson-Prentice Hall.

Bremner, J. Douglas. 2006. "Traumatic Stress: Effects on the Brain." *Dialogues in Critical Neuroscience* 8 (4): 445–61. https://doi.org/10.31887/DCNS.2006.8.4/jbremner.

Bronfenbrenner, Urie. 1979. *The Ecology of Human Development: Experiments by Nature and Design.* Cambridge, MA: Harvard University Press.

Bronfenbrenner, Urie, and Stephen J. Ceci. 1994. "Nature-Nurture Reconceptualized in Developmental Perspective: A Bioecological Model." *Psychological Review* 101 (4): 568–86. https://doi.org/10.1037/0033-295X.101.4.568.

Brown, Brené. 2012. *Daring Greatly: How the Courage to Be Vulnerable Transforms the Way We Live, Love, Parent, and Lead.* New York: Avery Publishing.

Cabello, Marcella, and Stuart M. Butler. 2022. "How Public Libraries Help Build Healthy Communities." Brookings Institute. March 9. www.brookings.edu /articles/how-public-libraries-help-build-healthy-communities.

Cameron, Julia. 1992. *The Artist's Way*. New York: Tarcher Books.

CAST. 2024. "About Universal Design for Learning." CAST (website). Accessed October 20. https://udlguidelines.cast.org.

Cattell, Raymond B. 1978. *The Scientific Use of Factor Analysis in Behavioral and Life Sciences*. New York: Plenum.

CDC (Centers for Disease Control and Prevention). 2024a. "About Child Abuse and Neglect: Quick Facts and Stats." Child Abuse and Neglect Prevention. May 16. www.cdc.gov/child-abuse-neglect/about/index.html.

———. 2024b. "About Youth Violence." Youth Violence Prevention. February 15. www.cdc.gov/youth-violence/about/index.html.

———. 2024c. "Epigenetics, Health, and Disease." Genomics and Your Health. May 15. www.cdc.gov/genomics-and-health/about/epigenetic-impacts-on-health.html.

Center on the Developing Child. 2011. *Building the Brain's "Air Traffic Control" System: How Early Experiences Shape the Development of Executive Function: Working Paper No. 11*. Harvard University. http://developingchild.harvard.edu/wp-content /uploads/2011/05/How-Early-Experiences-Shape-the-Development-of-Executive -Function.pdf.

———. 2015. "Brain Architecture." Harvard University. March 18, 2015. https:// developingchild.harvard.edu/science/key-concepts/brain-architecture.

———. 2024. "A Guide to Toxic Stress." Harvard University. https://developingchild .harvard.edu/guide/a-guide-to-toxic-stress.

Chen, Quinlin, Roger E. Beaty, and Jiang Qiu. 2020. "Mapping the Artistic Brain: Common and Distinct Neural Activations Associated with Musical, Drawing, and Literary Creativity." *Human Brain Mapping* 41 (12): 3403–19. https://doi .org/10.1002/hbm.25025.

Children's Equity Center/Bipartisan Policy Center. 2020. *Start with Equity: From the Early Years to the Early Grades*. Mesa, AZ/Washington, DC: Children's Equity Center/Bipartisan Policy Center.

Chopra, Deepak. 2017. "The Secret to Infinite Creativity—Deepak Chopra, MD." Jiyo4life. YouTube video. www.youtube.com/watch?v=A6Jw-exAuBo.

Cook, Alexandra, Margaret Blaustein, Joseph Spinazzola, and Bessel van der Kolk, eds. 2003. *Complex Trauma in Children and Adolescents: White Paper from the National Child Traumatic Stress Network Complex Trauma Task Force*. Los Angeles, CA, and Durham, NC: National Child Traumatic Stress Network. www.nctsn.org /sites/default/files/resources/complex_trauma_in_children_and_adolescents.pdf.

Coombs, Philip H., and Manzoor Ahmed. 1974. *Attacking Rural Poverty: How Non-Formal Education Can Help*. New York: Johns Hopkins University Press.

Coon, Dennis. 2006. *Psychology: A Modular Approach to Mind and Behavior*. 10th ed. Belmont, CA: Thomson Wadsworth.

CPB (Corporation for Public Broadcasting). 2011. *Findings from Ready to Learn: 2005–2010.* Washington, DC: CPB. https://rockman.com/docs/downloads /FindingsFromReadyToLearn2005-2010.pdf.

Cremin, Teresa, Pamela Burnard, and Anna Craft. 2006. "Pedagogy and Possibility Thinking in the Early Years." *Thinking Skills and Creativity* 1 (2): 108–19. https:// doi.org/10.1016/j.tsc.2006.07.001.

Cropley, Arthur. 2006. "In Praise of Convergent Thinking." *Creativity Research Journal* 18 (3): 391–404. https://doi.org/10.1207/s15326934crj1803_13.

Csikszentmihalyi, Mihaly. 1990. *Flow: The Psychology of Optimal Experience.* New York: Harper & Row.

———. 1996. *Creativity: Flow and the Psychology of Discovery and Invention.* New York: Harper Collins.

Daly, Lisa. 2022. *Transforming Your Outdoor Early Learning Environment.* St. Paul, MN: Redleaf Press.

de Saint-Exupéry, Antoine. (1943) 2000. *The Little Prince.* Translated by Richard Howard. San Diego, CA: Harcourt.

De Stefano, Cristina. 2022. *The Child Is the Teacher: A Life of Maria Montessori.* Translated by Gregory Conti. New York: Other Press.

DEC/NAEYC (Division of Early Childhood, Council of Exceptional Children /National Association for the Education of Young Children). 2009. *Early Childhood Inclusion.* Joint position statement. Chapel Hill, NC: The University of North Carolina, FPG Child Development Institute. www.naeyc.org/sites/default/files /globally-shared/downloads/PDFs/resources/position-statements/ps_inclusion _dec_naeyc_ec.pdf.

Demangeon, Alison, Stéphanie Claudel-Valentin, Alexandre Aubry, and Youssef Tazouti. 2023. "A Meta-Analysis of the Effects of Montessori Education on Five Fields of Development and Learning in Preschool and School-Age Children." *Contemporary Educational Psychology* 73 (April). https://doi.org/10.1016/j .cedpsych.2023.102182.

Des Moines Public Schools. 2022. *Des Moines Public Schools: 2021–22 Information Brief: 20-Year Student Demographic Trends.* Report. January 4. https://data .dmschools.org/uploads/1/3/3/6/13361550/dmps_20_year_student_demographics _2021-22.pdf.

Dewey, John. 1998. "Part V: The Aims of Education." In *The Essential Dewey, Vol. 1: Pragmatism, Education, Democracy,* edited by Larry A. Hickman and Thomas M. Alexander, 250–56. Bloomington: Indiana University Press.

DeYoung, Colin G. 2015. "Openness/Intellect: A Dimension of Personality Reflecting Cognitive Exploration." In *APA Handbook of Personality and Social Psychology, Vol. 4. Personality Processes and Individual Differences,* edited by Mario Mikulincer, Phillip R. Shaver, Lynne M. Cooper, and Randy J. Larsen, 369–99. Washington, DC: American Psychological Association. https://doi.org/10.1037/14343-017.

Dombro, Amy Laura, Judy Jablon, and Charlotte Stetson. 2011. *Powerful Interactions: How to Connect with Children to Extend Their Learning.* Washington, DC: NAEYC.

Dornfeld, Ann. 2019. "White Kids Usually Get the Most Recess in Seattle. Black Kids, the Least." KUOW NPR Network. August 26. www.kuow.org/stories/white-students -tend-to-get-the-most-recess-in-seattle-black-students-the-least.

Dowling, Shannon. 2020. "The Modern Learner: Formal and Informal Learning Environments." *Ideas* (blog). Ayers Saint Gross. February 20, 2020. https://ayers saintgross.com/ideas/read/the-modern-learner-formal-and-informal-learning -environments.

Duckworth, Eleanor. 1964. "Piaget Rediscovered." *The Arithmetic Teacher* 11 (7): 496–99.

Dweck, Carol. 2008. *Mindset: The New Psychology of Success*. New York: Ballantine Books.

Early Childhood Iowa. 2019. *The Iowa Early Learning Standards*. 3rd ed. Des Moines, IA: Early Childhood Iowa. https://earlychildhood.iowa.gov/sites/default/files /documents/2020-11/final_iels_12.5.2018_full_verison_0.pdf.

Eby, Judy W., Adrienne L. Herrell, and Michael Jordan. 2009. *Teaching in the Elementary School: A Reflective Action Approach*. 5th ed. New York: Prentice Hall.

Ellamil, Melissa, Charles Dobson, Mark Beeman, and Kalina Christoff. 2012. "Evaluative and Generative Modes of Thought During the Creative Process." *Neuroimage* 59 (2): 1783–94.

Erikson, Erik. 1950. 1963. *Childhood and Society*. New York: W. W. Norton.

Feldman, David Henry. 1974. "Universal to Unique." In *Essays in Creativity*, edited by Stanley Rosner and Lawrence Edwin Abt, 45–85. Croton-on-Hudson, NY: North River Press.

Finkelhor, David, Heather Turner, Richard Ormrod, Sherry Hamby, and Kristen Kracke. 2009. "Children's Exposure to Violence: A Comprehensive National Survey." *Juvenile Justice Bulletin*. Rockville, MD: Office of Juvenile Justice and Delinquency Prevention, US Department of Justice. www.ojp.gov/pdffiles1 /ojjdp/227744.pdf.

Fiske, Donald W. 1949. "Consistency of the Factorial Structures of Personality Ratings from Different Sources." *The Journal of Abnormal and Social Psychology* 44 (3): 329–44. https://doi.org/10.1037/h0057198.

Fogarty, Laurel, Nicole Creanza, and Marcus W. Feldman. 2015. "Cultural Evolutionary Perspectives on Creativity and Human Innovation." *Trends in Ecology & Evolution* 30 (12): 736–54. https://doi.org/10.1016/j.tree.2015.10.004.

Froebel, Friedrich. 1885. *The Education of Man*. New York: A. Lovell & Co.

Galinsky, Ellen. 2010. *Mind in the Making: The Seven Essential Life Skills Every Child Needs*. New York: HarperCollins.

Garooei, Bita, and Hamid Saghapour. 2015. "The Role of Environmental Effects on Developing Creating in Children." *International Research Journal of Engineering and Technology* 2 (5): 373–77. www.irjet.net/archives/V2/i5/IRJET-V2I567.pdf.

Gharib, Malaka. 2020. "Feeling Artsy? Here's How Making Art Helps Your Brain." *Shots* (blog). NPR. January 11. www.npr.org/sections/health-shots/2020/01/11 /795010044/feeling-artsy-heres-how-making-art-helps-your-brain.

Gilkerson, Linda, Mimi Graham, Deborah Harris, Cindy Oser, Jane Clarke, Tody C. Hairson-Fuller, and Jessica Lertora. 2013. "Trauma-Informed Part C Early Intervention: A Vision, A Challenge, A New Reality." *Zero to Three* 34 (2): 34–45.

Gilliam, Walter S., Angela N. Maupin, Chin R. Reyes, Maria Accavitti, and Frederick Shic. 2016. *Do Early Educators' Implicit Biases Regarding Sex and Race Relate to Behavior Expectations and Recommendations of Preschool Expulsions and Suspensions?* Research study brief. New Haven, CT: Yale University Child Study Center. https://files-profile.medicine.yale.edu/documents/75afe6d2-e556-4794-bf8c-3cf105113b7c.

Glăveanu, Vlad P., and Ronald A. Beghetto. 2021. "Creative Experience: A Nonstandard Definition of Creativity." *Creativity Research Journal* 33 (2): 75–80. https://doi.org/10.1080/10400419.2020.1827606.

Goulding, Anne. 2009. "Engaging with Community Engagement: Public Libraries and Citizen Involvement." *New Library World* 110 (1/2): 37–51. https://doi.org/10.1108/03074800910928577.

Gruber, Howard E., and J. Jacques Vonéche, eds. 1995. *The Essential Piaget: An Interpretive Reference and Guide.* Northvale, NJ: Jason Aronson.

Guilford, J. P. 1967. "Creativity: Yesterday, Today and Tomorrow." *Journal of Creative Behavior* 1 (1): 3–14.

Guy-Evans, Olivia. 2023a. "Thalamus Anatomy, Function, and Disorders." Simply Psychology (website). July 12. www.simplypsychology.org/thalamus.html.

———. 2023b. "What Is the Limbic System? Definition, Parts, and Functions." Simply Psychology (website). July 19. www.simplypsychology.org/limbic-system.html.

Hahn, Nic. 2020. "Celebrating Creativity with Peter H. Reynolds and Paul Reynolds (Episode 148)." *Everyday Art Room* (podcast). The Art of Education University. July 2. https://theartofeducation.edu/podcasts/celebrating-creativity-with-peter-reynolds-and-paul-reynolds-ep-148.

Hallaert, Jenelle M. 2019. "Flow, Creativity, and Suicide Risk in College Art Majors." *Creativity Research Journal* 31 (3): 335–41.

Hallman, Ralph J. 1964a. "Can Creativity Be Taught?" *Educational Theory* 14 (1): 15–23. https://doi.org/10.1111/j.1741-5446.1964.tb00151.x.

———. 1964b. "The Concept of Creativity in Dewey's Educational Philosophy." *Educational Theory* 14 (4): 270–85. https://doi.org/10.1111/j.1741-5446.1964.tb00184.x.

Hallowell, Edward M., and John J. Ratey. 2011. *Driven to Distraction: Recognizing and Coping with Attention Deficit Disorder from Childhood through Adulthood.* Rev. ed. New York: Anchor Books.

Harris, Sam. 2020. "A Good Life: A Conversation with Scott Barry Kaufman." *Making Sense* (podcast), episode 209. July 3. www.samharris.org/podcasts/making-sense-episodes/209-a-good-life.

Harvard Medical School. 2017. "A Strengths-Based Approach to Autism." *Harvard Health* (blog). Harvard Medical School. April 20. www.health.harvard.edu/blog/a-strength-focused-approach-to-autism-2017042011607.

Head Start Early Childhood Learning and Knowledge Center. 2020. *A National Overview of Grantee CLASS® Scores in 2020*. Washington, DC: Office of Head Start. https://eclkc.ohs.acf.hhs.gov/data-ongoing-monitoring/article/national-overview-grantee-class-scores-2020.

———. 2024. "Learn More about the CLASS." Updated May 2. Washington, DC: Office of Head Start. https://eclkc.ohs.acf.hhs.gov/teaching-practices/article/learn-more-about-class.

Helm, Judy Harris, Lilian G. Katz, and Rebecca Wilson. 2023. *Young Investigators: The Project Approach in the Early Years*. 4th ed. New York: Teachers College Press.

Hershfeld, Lawrence A., and Susan A. Gelman. 1994. *Mapping the Mind: Domain Specificity in Cognition and Culture*. New York: Cambridge University Press.

Humphreys, Kathryn L., Joelle LeMoult, John G. Wear, Hannah A. Piersiak, Aaron Lee, and Ian H. Gotlib. 2020. "Child Maltreatment and Depression: A Meta-Analysis of Studies Using the Childhood Trauma Questionnaire." *Child Abuse and Neglect* 201 (April): 1–9. https://doi.org/10.1016/j.chiabu.2020.104361.

Inside Amazon. 2018. "Diverse Perspectives at Amazon." YouTube video. September 6. www.youtube.com/watch?v=6zdmitPQg8k.

International Baccalaureate. 2024. "Primary Years Programme." Accessed October 20 www.ibo.org/programmes/primary-years-programme.

———. 2023. "Creativity in IB Programmes." June 6. www.ibo.org/programmes/teach-more-than-one-ib-programme/creativity-in-ib-programmes.

Iowa Department of Education. 2017. *Iowa Quality Preschool Program Standards*. Des Moines: Iowa Department of Education. https://educate.iowa.gov/media/7266/download?inline.

Jacobs, Tom. 2018. "How Artists Can Turn Childhood Pain into Creativity." *Greater Good Magazine*. May 8. https://greatergood.berkeley.edu/article/item/how_artists_can_turn_childhood_pain_into_creativity.

Johnson, Martin, and Dominika Majewska. 2022. *Formal, Non-formal, and Informal Learning: What Are They, and How Can We Research Them?* Research report. Cambridge University Press and Assessment Research. https://files.eric.ed.gov/fulltext/ED626005.pdf.

Jordan, Ijumaa. 2022. "Both/And: Early Childhood Education Needs Both Play and Equity." *Young Children* 77 (2): 51–52. www.naeyc.org/resources/pubs/yc/summer2022/play-equity.

Kaufman, James C. 2016. *Creativity 101*. 2nd ed. New York: Springer Publishing.

Kaufman, Scott Barry. 2020. *Transcend: The New Science of Self-Actualization*. New York: TarcherPerigee.

———. 2021. "Simon Baron-Cohen: How Autism Drives Human Invention." *The Psychology Podcast* (podcast), February 18. https://scottbarrykaufman.com/podcast/simon-baron-cohen-how-autism-drives-human-invention.

———. 2023. "What Is Creativity? The Human Potential Lab." *The Psychology Podcast* (podcast), April 27. https://scottbarrykaufman.com/podcast/what-is-creativity-the-human-potential-lab.

Kenny, Anthony J. P., and Anselm H. Amadio. 2024. "Philosophy of Mind of Aristotle." *Encyclopedia Britannica* (online). Updated May 25. www.britannica.com/biography/Aristotle/Philosophy-of-mind.

Kinsner, Kathy. 2019. "Rocking and Rolling. Fresh Air, Fun, and Exploration: Why Outdoor Play Is Essential for Healthy Development." *Young Children* 74 (2). www.naeyc.org/resources/pubs/yc/may2019/outdoor-play-is-essential.

Knop, Brian. 2020. "Children in Poverty Less Likely to Participate in Sports, Gifted Programs." Washington, DC: US Census Bureau. www.census.gov/library/stories/2020/09/children-in-poverty-less-likely-to-participate-in-sports-gifted-programs.html.

Koestler, Arthur. 1968. *Drinkers of Infinity: Essays 1955–1967*. New York: One 70 Press.

Kozol, Jonathan. 2005. "Still Separate, Still Unequal: America's Educational Apartheid." *Harpers* 311(1864): 41–54.

Lahad, Mooli, Moshe Farchi, Dmitry Leykin, and Nira Kaplansky. 2010. "Preliminary Study of a New Integrative Approach in Treating Post-Traumatic Stress Disorder: SEE FAR CBT." *The Arts in Psychotherapy* 37 (5): 391–99. https://doi.org/10.1016/j.aip.2010.07.003.

Lane, Mary Rockwood. 2005. "Creativity and Spirituality in Nursing: Implementing Art in Healing." *Holistic Nursing Practice* 19 (3): 122–25.

Lee, Virginia S., David B. Greene, Janice Odom, Ephraim Schechter, and Richard W. Slatta. 2004. "What Is Inquiry-Guided Learning?" In *Teaching and Learning through Inquiry: A Guidebook for Institutions and Instructors*, edited by Virginia S. Lee, 3–16. Sterling, VA: Stylus Publishing.

Leopold, Aldo. 1986. *A Sand County Almanac: And Sketches Here and There*. New York: Ballantine Books.

Limb, Charles J., and Allen R. Braun. 2008. "Neural Substrates of Spontaneous Musical Performance: An fMRI Study of Jazz Improvisation." *PLoS ONE* 3 (2): e1679. https://journals.plos.org/plosone/article?id=10.1371/journal.pone.0001679.

Linstead, Stephen. 2002. "Organization as Reply: Henri Bergson and Casual Organization Theory." *Organization* 9 (1): 95–111. www.researchgate.net/profile/Stephen-Linstead/publication/254315499_Organization_as_Reply_Henri_Bergson_and_Casual_Organization_Theory/links/548733bf0cf289302e2ed622/Organization-as-Reply-Henri-Bergson-and-Casual-Organization-Theory.pdf.

Liu, Sijuan, Ho Ming Chow, Yosheng Xu, Michael G. Erkkinen, Katherine E. Swett, Michael W. Eagle, Daniel A. Rizik-Baer, and Allen R. Braun. 2012. "Neural Correlates of Lyrical Improvisation: An fMRI Study of Freestyle Rap." *Scientific Reports* 2 (1). https://doi.org/10.1038/srep00834.

Lohmann, Marla J. 2023. *Creating Young Expert Learners: Universal Design for Learning in Preschool and Kindergarten*. St. Paul, MN: Redleaf Press.

Malchiodi, Cathy A. 2015. "Neurobiology, Creative Interventions, and Childhood Trauma. In *Creative Interventions with Traumatized Children*, 2nd ed., edited by Malchiodi, 3–23. New York: Guilford Press.

Marchese, David. 2022. "A Genius Cartoonist Believes Child's Play Is Anything but Frivolous. *New York Times Magazine*. September 2. www.nytimes.com/interactive /2022/09/05/magazine/lynda-barry-interview.html.

MATURA Head Start. 2022. *Winterset Head Start Family Handbook 2022–2023*. www.maturacommunityaction.com/_files/ugd/e753a2_47f41e2a349c463792df 5b1a78d90ffe.pdf.

May, Rollo. 1975. *The Courage to Create*. New York: Norton.

Miller Edward, and Joan Almon. 2009. *Crisis in the Kindergarten: Why Children Need to Play in School*. College Park, MD: Alliance for Childhood.

Montessori, Maria. (1912) 1964. *The Montessori Method*. New York: Schocken Books.

———. (1949) 1967. *The Absorbent Mind*. Cutchogue, NY: Buccaneer Books.

Moore Elementary School. 2024. "Moore Mission Statement." Website. Accessed July 22. https://moore.dmschools.org/ibpyp/moore-mission-statement.

Moseley, Brandon. 2023. "Kay Ivey Fires Early Childhood Education Secretary Barbara Cooper." *Alabama Today*. April 24. https://altoday.com/archives/51098-kay -ivey-fires-early-childhood-education-secretary-barbara-cooper.

Mottron, Laurent. 2017. "Should We Change Targets and Methods of Early Intervention in Autism, in Favor of a Strengths-Based Education?" *European Child and Adolescent Psychiatry* 26 (7): 815–25. www.doi.org/10.1007/s00787-017-0955-5.

Mudde, Cas. 2023. "What Is behind Ron DeSantis's Stop-Woke Act?" *The Guardian*. February 6. www.theguardian.com/commentisfree/2023/feb/06/what-is-behind -ron-desantis-stop-woke-act.

Muñiz, Jenny. 2020. *Culturally Responsive Teaching: A Reflection Guide*. Policy paper. Washington, DC: New America. www.newamerica.org/education-policy/policy -papers/culturally-responsive-teaching-competencies.

Murray, Charles, and Richard J. Herrnstein. 1994. *The Bell Curve: Intelligence and Class Structure in American Life*. New York: Free Press.

NAEYC (National Association for the Education of Young Children). 2019. *Advancing Equity in Early Childhood Education*. Position statement. Washington, DC: NAEYC. www.naeyc.org/sites/default/files/globally-shared/downloads/PDFs /resources/position-statements/advancingequitypositionstatement.pdf.

———. 2022. *Developmentally Appropriate Practices in Early Childhood Programs Serving Children from Birth through Age 8*. Washington, DC: NAEYC.

Nancekivell, Shaylene E., Priti Shah, and Susan A. Gelman. 2020. "Maybe They're Born with It, or Maybe It's Experience: Toward a Deeper Understanding of the Learning Style Myth." *Journal of Educational Psychology* 112 (2): 221–35. http:// dx.doi.org/10.1037/edu0000366.

NASEM (National Academies of Sciences, Engineering, and Medicine). 2015. *Transforming the Workforce for Children Birth through Age 8: A Unifying Foundation*. Washington, DC: The National Academies Press. https://doi.org/10.17226/19401.

———. 2016. *Parenting Matters: Supporting Parents of Children Ages 0–8*. Washington, DC: The National Academies Press. https://doi.org/10.17226/21868.

———. 2017. *Promoting the Educational Success of Children and Youth Learning English: Promising Futures.* Washington, DC: The National Academies Press. https://doi .org/10.17226/24677.

———. 2018. *How People Learn II: Learners, Contexts, and Cultures.* Washington, DC: The National Academies Press. https://doi.org/10.17226/24783.

NCTSN (National Child Traumatic Stress Network). 2024. "Creating Trauma-Informed Systems." Accessed October 20. www.nctsn.org/trauma-informed-care /creating-trauma-informed-systems.

New York Times. 1994. "Erik Erikson, 91, Psychoanalyst Who Reshaped Views of Human Growth, Dies." *New York Times* (obituary). May 13. https://archive .nytimes.com/www.nytimes.com/books/99/08/22/specials/erikson-obit.html.

Newton Public Library Board of Trustees. 2019. *Newton Public Library Strategic Plan: January 2019–January 2024.* January 24. www.newtongov.org/DocumentCenter /View/4617/Strategic-Plan-2019.

NPDC (National Professional Development Center on ASD). 2015. "Peer-Mediated Instruction and Intervention (PMII)." AFIRM (Autism Focused Intervention and Resource Modules). https://afirm.fpg.unc.edu/sites/afirm.fpg.unc.edu/files/imce /resources/PMII%20Evidence-base.pdf.

Odom, Samuel L., and Phillip S. Strain. 1984. "Peer-Mediated Approaches to Promoting Children's Social Interaction: A Review." *American Journal of Orthopsychiatry* 54 (4): 544–57. https://doi.org/10.1111/j.1939-0025.1984.tb01525.x.

Office of Head Start. 2018. *Head Start Early Learning Outcomes Framework: Ages Birth to Five.* Washington, DC: Administration for Children and Families. https://eclkc .ohs.acf.hhs.gov/sites/default/files/pdf/elof-ohs-framework.pdf.

Ohio Department of Education and Ohio Department of Job and Family Services. 2022. *Early Learning and Development Standards.* Columbus, OH: Ohio Department of Education, and Ohio Department of Job and Family Services. https://education .ohio.gov/getattachment/Topics/Early-Learning/Early-Learning-Content-Standards /Early-Learning-and-Development-Standards.pdf.

Oleynick, Victoria C., Colin G. DeYoung, Elizabeth Hyde, Scott Barry Kaufman, Roger E. Beaty, and Paul J. Silvia. 2017. "Openness/Intellect: The Core of the Creative Personality." In *The Cambridge Handbook of Creativity and Personality Research*, edited by Gregory J. Feist, Roni Reiter-Palmon, and James C. Kaufman, 9–27. Cambridge University Press. https://doi.org/10.1017/9781316228036.002.

Online Etymology Dictionary. 2024. "Evolve (v.)." Online Etymology Dictionary (website). Accessed October 20. www.etymonline.com/search?q=evolve.

Park, Sun-Hyung, Kwang Ki Kim, and Jarang Hahm. 2016. "Neuro-Scientific Studies of Creativity." *Dementia and Neurocognitive Disorders* 15 (4):110–14. www.doi.org /10.12779/dnd.2016.15.4.110.

PBS (Public Broadcasting Service). 2005. *The Ready to Learn Service. A Historical Perspective: 1991–2005.* Alexandria, VA: PBS.

Peiffer, Emily. 2019. "Segregated from the Start: Comparing Segregation in Early Childhood and K–12 Education." October 1. Washington, DC: Urban Institute. www.urban.org/features/segregated-start.

Pella Public Library. 2024. "About the Library." Accessed October 20. www.cityofpella .com/315/About-the-Library.

Perry, Bruce D., and Maia Szalavitz. 2007. *The Boy Who Was Raised as a Dog: And Other Stories from a Child Psychiatrist's Notebook*. New York: Basic Books.

Phares, E. Jerry. 1986. *Introduction to Personality*. 2nd ed. Glenview, IL: Scott, Foresman & Co.

Piaget, Jean. (1945) 1962. *Play, Dreams and Imitation in Childhood*. New York: Norton.

Rathus, Spencer A. 2008. *Childhood and Adolescence: Voyages in Development*. 3rd ed. Belmont, CA: Thomson Higher Education.

Reneau, Annie. 2017. "7 Simple Ways to Nurture Your Children's Creativity at Home." *Scary Mommy* (blog). May 9, updated February 11, 2021. www.scary mommy.com/nurture-childrens-creativity-home.

Rhodes, Mel. 1961. "An Analysis of Creativity." *Phi Delta Kappan* 42 (7): 305–10.

Robb, Michael B., and Alexis R. Lauricella. 2015. "Connecting Child Development and Technology: What We Know and What It Means." In *Technology and Digital Media in the Early Years: Tools for Teaching and Learning*, edited by Chip Donohue, 70–85. New York: Routledge/Washington, DC: NAEYC.

Robinson, Ken. 2006. "Do Schools Kill Creativity?" TED video. www.ted.com/talks /sir_ken_robinson_do_schools_kill_creativity.

———. 2010. "Changing Education Paradigms." Animated by RSA Animate. TED video. www.ted.com/talks/sir_ken_robinson_changing_education_paradigms.

Rogers, Fred. 1979. "Did You Know?" The Neighborhood Archive. www.neighborhood archive.com/music/songs/did_you_know.html.

———. 1994. *You Are Special: Neighborly Words of Wisdom from Mister Rogers*. Pittsburgh, PA: Family Communications.

Rogers, Fred, and Barry Head. 1983. *Mister Rogers Talks with Parents*. Pittsburgh, PA: Family Communications.

Rogoff, Barbara. 2003. *The Cultural Nature of Human Development*. New York: Oxford University Press.

Rosenblatt, Alan I., and Paul S. Carbone. 2019. *Autism Spectrum Disorder: What Every Parent Needs to Know*. Itasca, IL: American Academy of Pediatrics.

Rovelli, Carlo. 2014. *Seven Brief Lessons on Physics*. New York: Riverhead Books.

Rubinstein, Dori, and Mooli Lahad. 2023. "Fantastic Reality: The Role of Imagination, Playfulness, and Creativity in Healing Trauma." *Traumatology* 29 (2): 102–11. https://doi.org/10.1037/trm0000376.

Runco, Mark A. 2007. *Creativity: Theories and Themes: Research, Development, and Practice*. Burlington, MA: Elsevier Academic Press.

Runco, Mark A., and Garrett J. Jaeger. 2012. "The Standard Definition of Creativity." *Creativity Research Journal* 24 (1): 92–96. https://doi.org/10.1080/10400419.2012.650092.

Russ, Sandra W. 2006. "Pretend Play, Affect, and Creativity." In *New Directions in Aesthetics, Creativity and the Arts: Foundations and Frontiers in Aesthetics*, edited by Paul Locher, Colin Martindale, and Leonid Dorfman, 239–50. New York: Routledge.

Russ, Sandra W., and Astrida Seja Kaugars. 2001. "Emotion in Children's Play and Creative Problem Solving." *Creativity Research Journal* 13 (2): 211–19. https://doi.org/10.1207/S15326934CRJ1302_8.

Ryan, Alan. 1994. "Apocalypse Now?" *The New York Review* 41. www.nybooks.com/articles/1994/11/17/apocalypse-now.

SAMHSA (Substance Abuse and Mental Health Services Administration (SAMHSA). 2024. "Trauma and Violence." Accessed October 20. www.samhsa.gov/trauma-violence.

SAMHSA's Trauma and Justice Strategic Initiative. 2014. *SAMHSA's Concept of Trauma and Guidance for a Trauma-Informed Approach*. US Department of Health and Human Services, Substance Abuse and Mental Health Services Administration. https://ncsacw.acf.hhs.gov/userfiles/files/SAMHSA_Trauma.pdf.

Santrock, John W. 2009. *Educational Psychology*. 4th ed. New York: McGraw-Hill.

Sawyer, R. Keith. 2003. "Emergence in Creativity and Development." In *Creativity and Development*, edited by R. Keith Sawyer, Vera John-Steiner, Seana Moran, Robert J. Sternberg, David Henry Feldman, Jeanne Nakamura, and Mihaly Csikszentmihalyi, 12–60. New York: Oxford University Press.

———, ed. 2011. *Structure and Improvisation in Creative Teaching*. New York: Cambridge University Press.

———. 2015. "A Call to Action: The Challenges of Creative Teaching and Learning." *Teachers College Record* 117 (10): 1–34. https://doi.org/10.1177/016146811511701001.

———. 2019. *The Creative Classroom: Innovative Teaching for 21st-Century Learners*. New York: Teachers College Press.

Seale, Colin. 2022. *Tangible Equity: A Guide for Leveraging Student Identity, Culture and Power to Unlock Excellence in and beyond the Classroom*. New York: Routledge.

Siviy, Stephen M. 2016. "A Brain Motivated to Play: Insights into the Neurobiology of Playfulness." *Behaviour* 153 (6–7): 819–44.

Smolucha, Larry, and Francine Smolucha. 2012. "Vygotsky's Theory of Creativity: Figurative Thinking Allied with Literal Thinking." In *Contemporary Perspectives on Research in Creativity in Early Childhood*, edited by Olivia Saracho, 63–87. Charlotte, NC: Information Age Publishing.

Sobel, David. 2020. *The Sky Above and the Mud Below: Lessons from Nature Preschools and Forest Kindergartens*. St. Paul, MN: Redleaf Press.

Souto-Manning, Mariana. 2017. "Is Play a Privilege or a Right? And What's Our Responsibility? On the Role of Play for Equity in Early Childhood Education." *Early Child Development and Care* 187 (5–6): 785–87. https://doi.org/10.1080/03004430.2016.1266588.

Sporns, Olaf. 2013. "Structure and Function of Complex Brain Networks." *Dialogues in Clinical Neuroscience* 3:247–62. www.doi.org/10.31887/DCNS.2013.15.3/osporns.

Stockstill, Casey. 2023. *False Starts: The Segregated Lives of Preschoolers.* New York: New York University Press.

Stoltz, Tania, Fernanda Hellen Ribeiro Piske, Maria de Fátima Quintal de Freitas, Marlene Schüssler, and Járci Maria Machado. 2015. "Creativity in Gifted Education: Contributions from Vygotsky and Piaget." *Creative Education* 6 (1): 64–70. http://dx.doi.org/10.4236/ce.2015.61005.

Stop WOKE Act. 2022. FL CS/HB 7: Individual Freedom, Chapter 2022-72. www.flsenate.gov/Session/Bill/2022/7/BillText/er/PDF.

Sullivan, Debra Ren-Etta. 2016. *Cultivating the Genius of Black Children: Strategies to Close the Achievement Gap in the Early Years.* St. Paul, MN: Redleaf Press.

Swedo, Elizabeth A., Maria V. Aslam, Linda L. Dahlberg, Phyllis Holditch Niolon, Angie S. Guinn, Thomas R. Simon, and James A. Mercy. 2023. "Prevalence of Adverse Childhood Experiences among U.S. Adults—Behavioral Risk Factor Surveillance System, 2011–2020." *Morbidity and Mortality Weekly Report* 72 (26): 707–15. http://dx.doi.org/10.15585/mmwr.mm7226a2.

Thomas, Alexander, Stella Chess, and Herbert G. Birch. 1970. "The Origin of Personality." *Scientific American* 223 (2): 102–9. https://doi.org/10.1038/scientificamerican0870-102.

Thomson, Paula. 2018. "Trauma, Attachment, and Creativity." *Play and Creativity in Psychotherapy*, edited by Terry Mark-Tarlow, Marion Solomon, and Daniel J. Siegel, 167–90. New York: W. W. Norton.

Thomson, Paula, and S. Victoria Jaque. 2018. "Childhood Adversity and the Creative Experience in Adult Professional Performing Artists." *Frontiers in Psychology* 9. https://doi.org/10.3389/fpsyg.2018.00111.

Torrance, Ellis Paul. 1962. *Torrance Tests of Creative Thinking.* Bensonville, IL: Scholastic Testing Service.

———. 1965. *Rewarding Creative Behavior: Experiments in Classroom Creativity.* Englewood Cliffs, NJ: Prentice Hall.

———. 1971. "Are the Torrance Tests of Creative Thinking Biased against or in Favor of 'Disadvantaged' Groups?' *Gifted Child Quarterly* 15 (2): 75–80.

———. 1988. "The Nature of Creativity as Manifest in Its Testing." In *The Nature of Creativity: Contemporary Psychological Perspectives*, edited by R. J. Sternberg, 43–75. Cambridge, England: Cambridge University Press.

———. 1998. *The Torrance Tests of Creative Thinking Norms—Technical Manual Figural (Streamlined) Forms A & B.* Bensenville, IL: Scholastic Testing Service.

Travers, Mark. 2021. "New Research Highlights 15 Myths about Creativity." *Forbes.* June 30, 2021. www.forbes.com/sites/traversmark/2021/06/30/new-research-highlights-15-myths-about-creativity.

Urban Libraries Council. 2007. "Making Cities Stronger: Public Library Contributions to Local Economic Development."

Van Meter Community School District. 2023. *Van Meter 4-Year-Old Preschool Program Parent Handbook*. Updated June 19, 2023. https://core-docs.s3.amazonaws.com /documents/asset/uploaded_file/2362/vanmeteria/3343047/Van_Meter_CSD _Preschool_Handbook_2023-24.pdf.

Vaughan, Michael. 2007. "Introduction: Henri Bergson's *Creative Evolution*." *Sub-Stance* 36 (3): 7–24. www.jstor.org/stable/25195137.

Vinney, Cynthia. 2018. "Understanding the Big Five Personality Traits." ThoughtCo (website). September 27. www.thoughtco.com/big-five-personality-traits -4176097.

Vygotsky, Lev. 2004. "Imagination and Creativity in Childhood." *Journal of Russian and East European Psychology* 42 (1): 7–97.

Wallas, Graham. 1926. *The Art of Thought*. Kent, England: Solis Press.

Wei, Ju-Hui, Hsueh-Hua Chuang, and Thomas J. Smith. 2022. "The Relationship between a School Culture's Openness to Creative Solutions and Inquiry Based Teaching Practices." *The Journal of Creative Behavior* 56 (3): 382–95.

Wiebe, Eric N., Malinda Faber, Jeni Corn, Tracey Louise Collins, Alana Unfried, and LaTricia Townsend. 2013. "A Large-Scale Survey of K-12 Students about STEM: Implications for Engineering Curriculum Development and Outreach Efforts (Research to Practice)." Paper presented at 2013 ASEE Annual Conference and Exposition, Atlanta, GA, June 23. www.doi.org/10.18260\1-2—19073.

Wolraich, Mark L., and Joseph F. Hagan. 2019. *ADHD: What Every Parent Needs to Know*. 3rd ed. Itasca, IL: American Academy of Pediatrics.

Yates, Tuppett M., and Ana K. Marcelo. 2014. "Through Race-Colored Glasses: Preschoolers' Pretend Play and Teachers' Ratings of Preschooler Adjustment." *Early Childhood Research Quarterly* 29 (1): 1–11. https://doi.org/10.1016/j.ecresq .2013.09.003.

Zablotsky, Benjamin, Amanda E. Ng, Lindsey I. Black, and Stephen J. Blumberg. 2023. "Diagnosed Developmental Disabilities in Children Aged 3–17 Years: United States, 2019–2021." *NCHS Data Brief,* no. 473. Atlanta, GA: Centers for Disease Control and Prevention, National Center for Health Statistics. www.cdc.gov/nchs /data/databriefs/db473.pdf.

Zaleski, Annie. 2013. "Interview: Brian Molko of Placebo on New Record 'Loud Like Love,' the Band's Evolution, and the Most Vulnerable Moment of His Career." *Vanyaland*. October 18. https://vanyaland.com/2013/10/18/interview-brian-molko -placebo-new-record-loud-like-love-bands-evolution-since-90s-vulnerable -moment-career.

Index

accommodation of schemas, 33, 34, 35

active learners, 29

Adams, Margaret, 110, 111–112

ADHD
  characteristics of, 84–85, 86
  creativity and, 85–87
  defining, 84
  genetics and, 85
  medication and, 85
  reflecting on children displaying tendencies of, 94
  screening for, 92–93

Advancing Equity in Early Childhood Education (NAEYC), 133, 135, 137, 139

adverse childhood experiences (ACEs), 149
  See also trauma

Ahmed, Manzoor, 120

Allport, Gordon, 73

American Academy of Pediatrics (AAP), 80

American Library Association (ALA), 121

Approaches to Learning domain, 98–99

appropriateness, in formula for creativity, 9

Aristotle, 54, 63

The Artist's Way (Cameron), 191

Art of Experience (Dewey), 29

The Art of Thought (Wallas), 16

assimilation of schemas
  accommodation of schemas and, 35
  building on prior knowledge when teaching and, 34
  described, 33
  equilibration-disequilibration-equilibration cycle and, 61
  life-force and, 55

attachment and advancing through life stages, 39

autism spectrum disorder (ASD)
  creativity and, 82, 83–84
  describing, 80, 82–83
  genetics and, 82

IF-AND-THEN patterns and, 81–82
  medication and, 85
  reflecting on children on the spectrum, 94
  screening, 92–93
  STEM fields and, 82
  treating children with, 83–84

autonomy
  importance of, for children, 117
  informal learning and, 120
  as initiative, 40
  materials allowing, 117, 118
  versus shame and doubt as psychosocial dilemma (1–3 years old), 40
  spaces allowing, 117

Baer, John, 9

Bandura, Albert, 118

Baron-Cohen, Simon, 81–82, 86

Baumer, Nicole, 79

Beghetto, Ronald, 9, 18, 19

behaviors
  associated with openness, 74
  autonomy/initiative as purposeful, 40
  as child's expression of identity, 41, 73
  creativity-supporting, 101–102
  of educators to encourage creativity, 102
  examples of creative, 104
  executive function and, 71
  finding creative, in children daily routines, 15–16
  of neurodivergent children, 80, 83, 84–85, 87, 92, 94
  Piaget's schemas and, 33
  trauma and, 151, 152

Behr, Gregg, 68–69

The Bell Curve (Murray and Herrnstein), 145

Benedek, Mathias, 12

Beneke, Sallee, 76

Bergson, Henri, 54, 55–56, 58, 61, 62–63, 190

Berry, Lynda, 154
Big Five model of personality, 73–76
bioecological model, 5, 45–47
bioecological model/PPCT Model, 49
Birch, Hector, 20
Blake, Sally, 111
Blake, William, 9
Bodrova, Elena, 38
boredom, 68
Bounds, Tania San-Miguel, 134
The Boy Who Was Raised as a Dog (Perry and Szalavitz), 149
brain
    activation of areas during play, 67
    creativity
        as about connections in, 66–67
        neural activations during activities involving, 97, 155
    curiosity as priming, for learning, 68
    default network of, 67–70, 71, 72
    executive network of, 70–72
    IF-AND-THEN patterns and, 81
    multisensory stimulation and, 119
    response to trauma, 151–152, 155
brainstorming, 14
Bronfenbrenner, Urie, 44–47
Brown, Brené, 190
Bruan, Allen, 71–72
Bruner, Jerome, 118

Cameron, Julia, 190–191
"Can Creativity Be Taught?" (Hallman), 28–29
Casa dei Bambini, 30
Cattell, Raymond, 73
Ceci, Stephen, 45–47
Chen, Jie-Qi, 110, 111–112
Chen, Qunlin, 97
Chess, Stella, 20
child development
    in children on autism spectrum, 83
    core principles of, 24, 25–26
    Erikson and stages of, 23
    goal of field of, 24
    inappropriate, and ADHD, 84–85
    influences on, 44–45
        creativity as driver of, 24, 25–26
        culture and, 139–140
        as driven by life-force, 61
        epigenetics and, 153
        negative experiences and, 149
        PTI and delays in, 93
        role of language in, 36
    Piaget and creativity in, 35

reflecting on, 42
Childhood and Society (Erikson), 38–41
children
    characteristics of creativity in, 56
    "commonality" of creativity in all, 27
    creativity as energy of life and, 56, 59
    default network of brain in, 68
    as first and foremost creative beings, 7
    importance of autonomy for, 117
    inner forces driving growth of, 56–57
    percent of
        diagnosed with ADHD, 84
        diagnosed with autism, 80
        diagnosed with disabilities, 79
Chopra, Deepak, 17–18
chronosystem, 45
Chuang, Hsueh-Hua, 76–77
CLASS (Classroom Assessment Scoring System), 108–109
cognitive development
    nurturing creativity in children and, 8
    personality trait openness/intellect, 74
    pretend play and, 111
    stages of, 33
collaboration
    idea generation and, 14
    learning and, 31, 105, 109
"commonality" of creativity in all children, 27
constraints, as expander of creativity, 110
constructivist education, 28, 36, 194
context characteristics in PPCT Model, 46
convergent thinking, 72–73
conversation, learning during, 36
Coombs, Philip H., 120
Cooper, Barbara, 131–132
cortisol toxicity, 152
courage, 193–194
The Courage to Create (May), 193
Creanza, Nicole, 8
Creative Arts standards in Iowa Early Learning Standards, 98–99
The Creative Classroom (Sawyer), 96, 106
Creative Development domain, 99–100
Creative Evolution (Bergson), 54, 55–56, 61
creative imagination, 37
creative instruction
    "creative learning paradox" and, 106–107
    elements of, 113
    improvisation in, 107
    reflecting on, 113
    teaching strategies, 108–112
"creative learning paradox," 106–107

creative-person myths about creativity,
13–14
creative-process myths about creativity, 13
creative-stimulation myths about creativity, 14
creativity
    ADHD and, 85–87
    autism and, 82, 83–84
    bioecological model/PPCT Model and, 49
    as central to human experience, 18–19,
        20, 59–60
    characteristics of, in children, 56
    cognitive processes occurring during, 15
    "commonality" of, in all children, 27
    constraints as expander of, 110
    courage and, 193
    creation of knowledge and, 103–105
    culture and, 140–142
    as cumulative and consummatory, 3
    curiosity and, 1
    default network of brain and, 68–69, 70,
        71, 72
    defining, 8–9, 12–13, 19, 21
    Dewey and, 2829
    diversity and, 134–135, 142
    as divine attribute, 20, 23, 190
    as driver of child development, 24,
        25–26
    as energy of life, 56, 59
    equity and, 135–137, 142
    as evolution, 55–56
    as form of human experience, 29
    formula for, 9
    hands-on learning and, 3
    imagination and, 8, 74–75
    inclusion and, 138–139, 142
    inspiration and, 12, 13, 17
    intelligence and, 8, 9, 74–75
    as kind of intelligence, 146
    learning standards and, 98–101
    life-force as propelling, 57
    myths about, 12–15
    neurodiversity and, 79–80, 92
    neuroscience of, 66–67, 70–72
    nurturing
        calls to action for, 192–193
        characteristics of spaces, 115–119
        cognitive and social-emotional learning and, 8
        importance of, x
        open-ended statements, 118
        public spaces, 116, 117, 121–123
        relationships and, 138–139
        resources for, 77, 193
        suggestions for, 59–60, 72
    openness to experience and, 3, 73–74
    play as stage for performance of, 41
    precursors/habits significant to, 19
    as predictor of resilience, 156
    process to access infinite, 17–18, 186–187
    race and, 144
    reflecting on
        role, of in learning, 64
        teaching, 113
        ways to support, 148
    structural barriers to
        dismantling, 146–147
        income inequality and, 142–144
        standardized tests, 145
        teacher bias, 144
    teaching
        aids for, 101–102
        in domain-general approach, 96, 97,
            99–100
        in domain-specific approach, 96–97,
            98–99
        ideas for, 104–106
        learning standards and, 98–101, 103
    thinking as, 15, 29, 35
    time for, as necessary, 19
    trauma and, 150, 154–158, 191
    TTCT for measuring, 145
    uniqueness of each individual's, 115
    as way to make sense of world, 37
    as work of Muses, 11–12
cronosystem, 47, 49
Csikszentmihalyi, Mihaly, 86, 137
Cultivating the Genius of Black Children
        (Sullivan), 141
The Cultural Nature of Human Development
        (Rogoff), 139–140
"cultural processes," 140
culture, 139–142
curiosity
    as driver of creativity, 1
    force characteristics in PPCT Model
        and, 46
    as priming brain for learning, 68
    zone of proximal development and, 36
curriculum
    creativity in standards and, 100–101
    rigidity of mandated, 142–143
    UDL and, 146–147
curriculum paradox, 106

daydreaming
    default network of brain during, 67, 68,
        69

ideas for encouraging, 69
as necessary, 187
"default mode network," 18–19
default network of brain, 67–70, 71, 72
definition myths about creativity, 12–13
demand characteristics and PPCT Model,
    45
De Stefano, Cristina, 30
development, etymological stems of,
    24
Developmentally Appropriate Practices
    (NAEYC 2022), 25, 61, 131–132
Developmental Trauma Disorder (DTD),
    152
Dewey, John, 3, 28–29, 120–121
digital technology, 127
disability/disabilities
    ADHD, 84–87, 92–93, 94
    autism, 80–84, 92–93, 94
    defining, 79
    IEPs, 89, 90, 93
    IFSPs, 93
    inclusion of children with, 138
    percent of children diagnosed with, 7
    PTI and, 93
    "special education" programs, 88–91
divergent thinking, 72–73
diversity
    creativity and, 134–135, 142
    defining, 133
    as foundational NAEYC value, 134
    response to, as choice, 133
    as WOKE issue, 132–133
domain-general approach
    creativity as object of learning, 97
    defining, 96
    reflecting on, 113
    teaching creativity in, 96, 97, 99–100
domains of mind, 97
domain-specific approach
    defining, 96
    reflecting on, 113
    teaching creativity in, 96–97, 98–99
Dombro, Amy Laura, 109
doubt: autonomy versus, as psychosocial
    dilemma (1–3 years old), 40
Dowling, Shannon, 120
Dreyer, Katie, 181–182
Driven to Distraction (Hallowell and Ratey),
    84
DSM-5 (*Diagnostic and Statistical Manual of
    Mental Disorders,* 5th edition), 152
Duckworth, Eleanor, 35
Dweck, Carol, 99

"Eclipsed Time" (Lin), ix
ecological systems theory, 44
The Ecology of Human Development (Bron-
    fenbrenner), 44
education
    defining, 10
    goals of, 28, 35
    holistic nature of, 28, 29
    peer-mediated, 36
    scaffolding to support creativity, 20
    WOKEness and, 131–132, 144
    See also learning
The Education of Man (Froebel), 56–57
educators
    bias of, 144
    creativity and
        behaviors to encourage, 102
        nurturing, in self, 192
        teaching, 101–106
    Florida's WOKE Act and, 131
    "framing" by, 111–112
    guiding and collaborating role of, 57,
        59–60, 62
    mandated instruction, 142–143
    partnerships with
        museums, 125
        public librarians/libraries, 123, 129
        public television, 127–128
    role of observation, 111
effectiveness in formula for creativity, 9
"Eight Stages of Man" (Erikson), 38
élan vital. *See* life-force
Ellamil, Melissa, 71
environment
    activities centers at Kids World Daycare
        and Preschool, 174–175
    activities centers at Winterset Head
        Start, 171
    characteristics of spaces nurturing cre-
        ativity, 115–119
    directed and spontaneous learning and,
        48
    factors in evaluating child's, 47–48
    multicultural spaces, 119
    reflecting on creative spaces, 129
    relationship with individual of, 44–45
    as Rhodes's place domain, 16–17
    STEM activities areas at Van Meter
        Preschool, 166–167
epigenetics, 152–153, 187
equilibration–disequilibration–
    equilibration cycle, 33, 61
equity
    creativity and, 135–137, 142

defining, 135
inclusion and central issues of, 138
income inequality and, 144
as WOKE issue, 132–133
Erikson, Erik
on child development, 23
developmental dilemmas of each stage,
39–40
life-span development theory of, 38–41
on play, 40–41
Esquire, ix
The Essential Piaget (Gruber and Vonéche),
54
Everything Everywhere All at Once (film),
128
evolution, 55–56, 58, 61, 62–63
executive network of brain, 70–72
exosystem, 44–45, 49
experience(s)
child development and negative, 149
creativity as form of human, 29
imagination and, 29
inclusive, 137
learning as built on previous, 121
multisensory, 119
openness to, 3, 19–20, 99, 117
public television as launching, 126
role of, in learning, 28, 29
social engagement and, 118–119
spaces providing opportunities for new,
117
time as temporal-bound, in PPCT
Model, 47
See also trauma
exploration and default network of brain,
68
"expressive therapies," 155–156

fairness. *See* equity
*False Start: The Segregated Lives of Pre-
schoolers* (Stockstill), 143–144
Feldman, Marcus, 8
figurative thinking, 38
Fiske, Donald, 73
Fogarty, Laurel, 8
force characteristics and PPCT Model, 45
formative assessments, 105
four Ps of creativity
people domain, 15–16
place domain, 16–17
process domain, 16
products domain, 16, 118, 137
"framing," 111–112
freedom of expression, 31

Froebel, Friedrich, 56–57, 59
From Neurons to Neighborhoods, 51
Frueh, Julia, 79

Galinsky, Ellen, 71
Gardner, Howard, 97
Garooei, Bita, 47–48
Gelman, Susan, 97
"generative inventions," 81
Giannangelo, Duane, 111
giftedness, 91–92, 136
Glăveanu, Vlad, 18, 19
Goswami, Neha, 135
Grandin, Temple, 84
Greenfield, Susan, 11
Gronlund, Gaye, 98
"growth mindset," 99
Gruber, Howard, 54
Guardian, 131
Guilford, J. P., 72
guilt: initiative versus, as psychosocial
dilemma (3–5 years old), 40

Hagan, Joseph, 84, 85
Hahm, Jarang, 66
Hallman, Ralph, 28–29
Hallowell, Edward, 84, 86–87
hands-on learning, creativity as require-
ment for, 3
*Head Start Early Learning Outcomes Frame-
work*, 100
helpers, importance of, 43
Herrnstein, Richard, 145
Hershfeld, Lawrence, 97

identity
behaviors as child's expression of, 41, 73
culture and, 139–140
play and formation of, 41
IF-AND-THEN patterns, 81–82
imagination
creativity and, 8, 74–75
experience and, 29
opposites brought together in, 29
personality trait of openness/intellect
and, 74
implementation, as necessary to access
creativity, 17
improvisation
in creative instruction, 107
"Yes, and" rule in, 108, 109
impulsiveness, 86, 87
incarnation, as necessary to access creativity, 18

inclusion
    central issues of equity and, 138
    of children with disabilities, 138
    creativity and, 138–139, 142
    defining, 137
    as WOKE issue, 132–133
income inequality and barriers to creativ-
        ity, 142–144
incubation, as necessary to access creativ-
        ity, 17
Individual Family Services Plans (IFSPs),
        93, 94
Individualized Education Programs
        (IEPs), 89, 90, 93, 94
Individuals with Disability in Education
        Act (IDEA, 1975), 79
infinite creativity, process to access, 17–18,
        186–187
informal learning
    defining, 119–120
    importance to creativity of, 120–121
    institutions offering
        museums, 116, 121, 124–125
        public libraries, 116, 117, 121–123
        public television, 116, 121, 126–127
    in parks and playgrounds, 128
    reflecting on, 129
information: gathering and analyzing, as
        necessary to access creativity, 17
initiative: versus guilt as psychosocial
        dilemma (3-5 years old), 40
inquiry-based learning
    importance in STEM of, 111
    Project Approach, 165, 167, 175–176
    reflecting on, 69, 75–76, 78
    resources for, 77
    school culture and, 76–77
insight, 17, 18
inspiration
    insight compared to, 18
    as requirement for creativity, 12, 13, 17
Instructional Support domain, 108–109
integration, as necessary to access creativ-
        ity, 18
intelligence(s)
    creativity and, 8, 9, 74–75
    race and, 145
    types of, 97
intuitive thought, 34
inventions, as result of creativity, 21
Iowa Early Learning Standards, 98–99, 103
Iowa Quality Preschool Program Stan-
        dards, 165
Ivey, Kay, 131–132

Jablon, Judy, 109
Jaeger, Garrett, 9
Jaque, S. Victoria, 154
Johnson, Dawn, 173, 175
Johnson, Martin, 120
Jordan, Ijumaa, 143
journaling, 191
Junod, Tom, ix

Katz, Lilian G., 76
Kaufman, James, 9, 11, 72, 110, 145
Kaufman, Scott Barry
    creativity as intelligence and imagina-
        tion, 74–75
    creativity defined by, 8
    importance of exploration, 69
    precursors significant to creativity, 19
    The Psychology Podcast, 80–81
    resources for nurturing creativity, 193
Kaufmann, Stanley, 189
Kids World Daycare and Preschool case
        study, 173–178, 184
Kim, Kwang Ki, 66
knowledge, creativity and creation of,
        103–105
Koestler, Arthur, 8, 48
Kozol, Jonathan, 142–143

Lahad, Mooli, 155, 156
Lane, Mary Rockwood, 155
language, 34, 36
learning
    active, 29
    as built on previous experience(s),
        121
    child-directed, 31
    collaborative, 31, 105, 109
    during conversation, 36
    creativity as object of, in domain-
        general approach, 97
    curiosity as priming brain for, 68
    curriculum and improvisational, 106
    defining, 10
    environment and, 48
    hands-on, 3
    importance of outdoor, 62
    lifelong, 120
    making it one's own, 105–106
    No Child Left Behind guidelines, 98
    play and standards-based approach to,
        98
    reflecting on creative process in, 64
    rote, 143
    as social, 36–37, 38

teacher and pupil as same individual and, 48
See also informal learning; inquiry-based learning
learning disabilities, 88–91, 185–186
learning paradox, 106
learning standards
  creativity and, 98–101
  Iowa Early, 98–99, 103
  Iowa Quality, 165
  Ohio Early, 99–100
Leong, Deborah, 38
Leopold, Aldo, 57
libraries. *See* public libraries
Library Bill of Rights (1939, ALA), 121
life-force
  Bergson and, 61
  describing, 53, 55
  as driver of child development, 57, 61
  evolution and, 55–56, 61, 62–63
  Piaget and, 54–55
  as propelling creativity, 57
  reflecting on, 64
  religion and, 59, 190
Limb, Charles, 71–72
Lin, Maya, ix
Linstead, Stephen, 56
The Little Prince (Saint-Exupéry), 54
Locke, John, 28

macrosystem, 45, 49
Majewska, Dominika, 120
make-believe, 27
Malchiodi, Cathy, 151–152, 155
Marcelo, Ana, 144
Marin, Mario, 135
materials
  allowing children autonomy in engagement, 117, 118
  multifunctional nature of, 31
  multisensory nature of, 31
  openness in, 16
MATURA Head Start at Winterset case study, 170–173
May, Rollo, 193
McKeever, Daina, 171
medication and neurodivergent children, 85
memory, as mother of creativity, 11–12
mesosystem, 44, 45, 49
microsystem, 44, 45, 49
Minard, Mary, 178
Mister Rogers' Neighborhood, 27, 43
Molko, Brian, 161

Montessori, Maria, 30–32
The Montessori Method (Montessori), 31–32
Moore Elementary School, kindergarten case study, 178–181, 184
morning pages, 191
Mottron, Laurent, 83–84
Mudde, Cas, 131
multicultural spaces, 119
Murray, Charles, 145
Muses, 11–12, 97
museums
  informal learning and, 116, 121, 124–125
  as multicultural spaces, 119
  partnerships with educators, 125
myths about creativity
  creative-person, 13–14
  creative-process, 13
  creative-stimulation, 14
  definition, 12–13
  Muses, 11–12

National Association for the Education of Young Children (NAEYC)
  Advancing Equity in Early Childhood Education, 133, 135, 137, 139
  ages of young children defined by, 24
  core principles of child development, 25–26
  Developmentally Appropriate Practices, 25, 61, 131–132
  diversity as foundational value of, 134
National Child Traumatic Stress Network, 151
Nature and Experience (Dewey), 29
neurodiversity/neurodivergent children
  ADHD, 84–87, 92–93, 94
  autism, 80–84, 92–93, 94
  challenges of, 82–83
  creativity and, 79–80
  defining, 79
  giftedness behind, 91–92
  medication and, 85
  reflecting on, 94
  supporting creativity in, 92
Newton Public Library case study reflections, 169
The New York Times, ix
The New York Times Magazine, 154
No Child Left Behind Act (2001), 98

object substitution, 37–38
observation, role of, 111
Ohio Early Learning and Development Standards, 99–100

open-ended statements, 118
openness
    to experiences, 19–20, 99, 117
    in materials, 16
    as personality trait, 73–74, 75–76
    in questions, 16
    as receptivity and surrender, 29
originality, 9, 10
Ostrosky, Michaelene M., 76
outdoor learning, 62

Parent Training and Information Centers
        (PTI), 93
Park, Sun-Hyung, 66
parks and playgrounds, 128
PBS Kids, 126, 128
Pella Public Library case study, 181–183
people domain of creativity, 15–16
Perry, Bruce, 149
person: characteristics of, in PPCT Model,
        46
personality, 73–76
Peter, Phyllis, 168
philosophy and science, 63
Piaget, Jean
    basic facts about, 32, 54
    creativity in child development, 35
    equilibration-disequilibration-
        equilibration cycle and, 61
    learning as constructing understanding
        of world, 10, 33
    life-force and, 54–55
    schemas, 32–35, 55
place domain of creativity, 16–17
    See also environment
Plato, 10
play
    adult's versus child's, 41
    brain activation during, 67
    creativity and, 41
    formation of identity and, 41
    as function of cgo, 41
    as problem solving, 40–41
    race and restrictions on, 144
    as stage for performance of creativity, 41
    standards-based approach to learning
        and, 98
    as work of child, 34
    See also pretend play
post-traumatic stress disorder (PTSD)
        symptoms, 152, 155
power, as father of creativity, 11–12
Powerful Interactions (Dombro, Jablon, and
        Stetson), 109

PPCT Model, 45–47
preoperational stage of cognitive develop-
        ment, 33–34
press domain of creativity, 16–17
    See also environment
pretend play
    cognitive and affective processes associ-
        ated with, 111
    language development during, 34
    object substitution in, 37
    safety of, 41
problem solving
    brainstorming, 14
    creative processing involved in, 111
    play as, 40–41
    ways of, 72–73
process domain of creativity, steps in, 16
process in PPCT Model, 45–46
products domain of creativity, 16, 118, 137
The Project Approach for All Learners
        (Beneke, Ostrosky, and Katz), 76
Project Approach inquiry-based learning
        model, 165, 167, 175–176
The Project Approach in the Early Years
        (Helm, Katz, and Wilson), 76
The Psychology Podcast, 80–81, 193
public libraries
    creativity in programs at, 186
    educators' partnerships with, 123, 129
    informal learning and, 116, 117, 121–123
    Newton Public Library case study,
        168–170
    Pella Public Library case study, 181–183
    products from "kids' activities" in, 118
    reflecting on resources of, 129, 159
    social interaction in, 118
public television
    informal learning and, 116, 121, 126–127
    offerings described, 125–126
    partnerships with educators, 127–128
    reflecting on, 129
Pyramid Model for social-emotional devel-
        opment, 173–178

race and barriers to creativity, 144
race and intelligence, 145
"radical finalism," 55
radical mechanism, 55
Ratey, John, 84, 86–87
Rathus, Spencer A., 24
reflections
    on behaviors of neurodivergent chil-
        dren, 94
    on bioecological model/PPCT Model, 49

on child development, 42
on creative instruction, 113
on creative process in learning, 64
on creative spaces, 129
on creativity in own life, 22
on domain-specific and domain-general
    approaches, 113
on IEPs and IFSPs, 94
on implementing trauma focus in
    instruction, 159
on informal learning, 129
on inquiry-based learning, 69, 75–76, 78
Kids World Daycare and Preschool case
    study, 177, 184
on life-force, 64
on MATURA Head Start at Winterset
    case study, 172, 184
on Moore Elementary School, kinder-
    garten case study, 180, 184
on neurodivergent children, 94
Newton Public Library case study, 169
on Pella Public Library case study, 182
on public television, 0
on resources of public libraries, 129, 159
on teaching creativity, 113
on Van Meter Preschool case study, 167
on ways to support creativity, 148
relationships
    ability to form, and advancing through
        life stages, 39
    creativity and, 138–139
    mesosystem and, 44
    microsystem and, 44, 45
    power of, 149
    reflecting on improving, 49
    unidirectional, between adult and child,
        44
religion
    creativity as divine attribute, 20, 23, 190
    life-force and, 59
Rendon, Tom, 98
Reneau, Annie, 8
resilience, creativity as predictor of, 156
resource characteristics and PPCT Model,
    45
resources
    for nurturing creativity, 77, 193
    for supporting those with mental health
        concerns, 158
Reynolds, Peter, 115
Rhodes, James Melvin, 15–17
Robinson, Ken, 14, 142
Rogers, Fred, ix, 27, 43, 54, 68, 138
Rogoff, Barbara, 139–140, 147–148

Rohr, Richard, 191
rote learning, 143
routines, creativity in, 15–16
Rovelli, Carlo, 57–58
Rubinstein, Dori, 155, 156
Runco, Mark, 9
Rydzewski, Russell, x
Rydzewski, Ryan, ix–xi, 68–69

Saghapour, Hamid, 47–48
A Sand County Almanac (Leopold), 57
Saving Play (Rendon and Gronlund), 98
Sawyer, Keith, 96–97, 102, 106–108
scaffolding
    individualizing, to support creativity, 20
    in learning paradox, 106
    Vygotsky and, 36, 37
scarymommy.com, 21, 77
schemas
    accommodation of, 33, 34, 35
    describing, 32
    organization of schemas, 33
    as way of making sense of world, 33
    See also assimilation of schemas
school culture, 76–77
science and philosophy, 63
Seale, Colin, 137
SEE FAR CBT treatment, 156
sensorimotor stage of cognitive develop-
    ment, 33
shame: autonomy versus, as psychosocial
    dilemma (1–3 years old), 40
Sharapan, Hedda, 128
Siviy, Stephen, 67
Smith, Thomas J., 76–77
Smolucha, Francine, 37, 38
Smolucha, Larry, 37, 38
social-emotional learning, 8, 173–178
social interaction, 118–119, 120
solutions, as result of creativity, 21
Souto-Manning, Mariana, 144
standardized tests, 145
STEM subjects, 82, 111, 166–167
Stetson, Charlotte, 109
Stockstill, Casey, 143–144
Stoltz, Tania, 35, 37
Stop Wrongs to Our Kids and Employees
    (WOKE) Act (Florida), 131
Strang, Christianne, 154
stress and cortisol toxicity, 152
Structure and Improvisation in Creative
    Teaching (Sawyer), 106
Substance Abuse and Mental Health Ser-
    vices Administration (SAMHSA), 151

Sullivan, Debra, 141
symbolic function, 34
"systemizing mechanism" brain circuitry,
    81–82
Szalavitz, Maia, 149

talented and gifted (TAG) programming,
    136
"Tangible Equity," 137
teacher paradox, 106
temperaments of children, 20
thinking
    constructive, 34, 35
    convergent, 72–73
    as creative, 15, 29, 35
    divergent, 72–73
    figurative, and creative imagination, 38
    flexibility in, 70
    outside the box, 96
    paradoxes and, 107
thinking problems, 34, 35
Thomas, Alexander, 20
Thomson, Paula, 154–155
time characteristics in PPCT Model, 47, 49
time for creativity, cordoning off, 19
Tools of the Mind (Bodrova and Leong), 38
Torrance, E. Paul, 9, 145
Torrance Tests for Creativity Thinking
    (TTCT), 145
trauma
    basic facts about, 150
    behaviors and, 151, 152
    brain response to, 151–152
    child development and, 149
    creativity and, 150, 154–158, 191
    defining, 151
    learning environments responding to
        impact of, 153–154
    PTSD symptoms, 152, 155
    reflecting on implementing focus on, in
        instruction, 159
    resources, 158
    statistics, 149–150
    transmission of, over generations,
        152–153, 187

trauma-informed care, 153–154, 156–158
trust: versus mistrust as first stage's psy-
    chosocial dilemma, 39–40

uniqueness, of each individual, 10
Universal Design for Learning (UDL),
    146–147
Urban Libraries Council, 122
utility, 9, 11

Van Meter Preschool case study,
    165–168
Vaughan, Michael, 63
vision, as necessary to access creativity,
    17
"visual isomorphisms," 38
Vonéche, J. Jacques, 54
Vygotsky, Lev
    basic facts about, 36
    creativity defined by, 8
    importance of social interaction, 118
    learning as social, 36–37
    role of creative imagination, 37
    scaffolding, 36, 37
    ZPD and, 36, 37

Wallas, Graham, 16
Wei, Ju-Hui, 76–77
When You Wonder, You're Learning (Behr
    and Rydzewski), 68–69
"the whole child approach," 63
Wiebe, Eric, 120
Williams, Sydney, 179
Wilson, Rebecca, 166
Winterset Head Start case study, 170–173
WOKEness and education, 131–132, 144
Wolraich, Mark, 84, 85
world, 10, 33

Yates, Tuppett, 144
"Yes, and" rule, 108, 109
Yoffe, Eli, 134

zone of proximal development (ZPD),
    36, 37